THE NARCISSISTIC CONDITION

Psychotherapy Series

SELF-IN-PROCESS SERIES
VOLUME I

THE NARCISSISTIC CONDITION

A Fact of Our Lives and Times

Edited by
Marie Coleman Nelson

With a Foreword by
Benjamin Nelson

HUMAN SCIENCES PRESS
Formerly **BEHAVIORAL PUBLICATIONS INC.**
72 FIFTH AVENUE, NEW YORK, N.Y. 10011 (212) 243-6000

Library of Congress Catalog Number 76-20724

ISBN: 0-87705

Copyright © 1977 by Human Sciences Press 72 Fifth Avenue, New York, New York 10011

Printed in the United States of America
789   987654321

Library of Congress Cataloging in Publication Data
Main entry under title:
    The Narcissistic condition.

    (Self-in-process series; v.1)
    Bibliography: p.
    Includes index.
    1. Narcissism. I. Nelson, Marie Coleman.
BF575.N35N37 155.2'32 76-20724

For Margaret Fries, Joost
Meerloo and Hyman Spotnitz—
their influence endures.

CONTENTS

11

FOREWORD

Benjamin Nelson

The Self-in-Process Series begins its life with the present interdisciplinary volume on narcissism for two main reasons:

One reason is the fact that narcissism is now evidently the focal point of concentration of the major disputes, contradictions and paradoxes engaging the various schools of psychoanalysis and psychotherapy. This awareness has grown steadily keener over the last three decades with the emergence of ego psychology as a central clinical and theoretical emphasis in psychoanalysis proper.

A second reason is that the issue of narcissism presents problems as well as opportunities both for the self as agent and for the scientific study of the self at every critical interface of biosocial, sociocultural, and historical contexts: men as biological organisms; men as face-to-face participants in so-called primary groups; men knotted together in patterned interactions, whether voluntary or directed, in their institutional milieus and wider worlds.

In brief, in the entire matrix of men's everyday activities few issues are and will remain as fateful as the ascendancies and qualities of narcissism in continuing but historically differentiated shapings of selves in the process of social and cultural change.

The papers in the present work have been arranged with a view to encouraging a systematic asking of questions against the myriad backgrounds of human action.

It is no accident, therefore, that we begin our symposium with a chapter from a life lived in the midst of maelstrom. Writing out of deep personal experience and commitment, Ann Braden Johnson calls upon us to see the links in the multiple appearances of narcissism over the last two decades—the collective narcissisms of alienated youth, the official public narcissisms of governments and bureaucracies, the apocalyptic narcissisms born of great expectations, the gloomy narcissisms bred of frustration, the despairing narcissisms that find their way to heroin, the narcissisms of ecstatic flights into ultimate experiences, the narcissisms of No-Mind and protean polymorphism.

A most powerful element in this essay is the evidence that the narcissisms of 1967, both of apocalyptic collective self-assertion and millenial hope, were soon enough—by 1974—to express themselves in narcissisms marked by the pursuit of self-discovery and self-enhancement through stringent regimes of self-effacement.

Once wholly committed to the counter-culture groups, Ms. Johnson now wonders how, in the remarkably short span of seven years, very many were able to move "from the love feasts of 1967 and the radical fury of 1969 to the Jesus-freaks and the Hare Krishnas of 1974." She is perplexed that "from sexual freedom and wanton aggressive acts we have come to rigid, authoritarian cults dedicated to the spreading of obscure and ascetic religious practices."

Her present view is that "the self-same kids who were hip or radical and have now turned to religion" were from first to last narcissistic. "There is," she explains, "a common thread of desperation and self-preoccupation running through all these movements, leading to a total rejection of the adult world and the effort to find a permanent substitute for it or avoid it altogether by a regressive narcissistic retreat from the world."

Joel Emanuel tells of his experiences in the classroom over a seven-year period during which, as he relates, a shift occurred in the student composition from 50 percent middle-class students to over 90 percent lower socioeconomic status students.

The blends of narcissism exhibited by disaffected minority students and their teachers, as described by Mr. Emanuel, illustrate an often neglected facet of our theme. Surely the narcissistic expressions of the students arise in part from the shared rage born of the dictates to act reasonably in a world marked by the "omnipresence of the grotesque." We are not looking here at a single clinical entity.

Mr. Emanuel's students can't see why they should care for anyone else or, for that matter, for any*thing*—either their own or anyone else's. Mr. Emanuel believes that such disregard for the feelings of another or for their very existence is a natural consequence of the exaggerated praise of self-assertion in our time. His account ends with a report of the psychological damage and dehumanization experienced by the teacher. There is hardly a teacher who escapes paying a heavy price in the form of crippling negative transference.

The author makes an interesting effort here to develop the concept of a cycle of narcissism and transference. He also suggests that teachers expecting assignment in the public school system might be wise to undertake personal therapy.

Dr. Samuel Rubin reports on research done by himself and a collaborator on "some of the larger issues involving loss of self-esteem from a psychoanalytic point of view." He

takes exception to a number of Mr. Emanuel's interpretations of the evidence, stressing particularly the extent to
which historical and social conditions have roots which go
deep in the history of our country.

Part II comprises three papers illustrating variant approaches to the theories and therapies of narcissism.

Dr. Spotnitz has never been put off by the apparent
hopelessness of the narcissistic condition, as we were reminded by both Mr. Emanuel and Dr. Rubin. Indeed, this
noted clinician's main stress is on the treatability of so-
called narcissistic disorders by techniques that go beyond
the strictly classical repertoire of therapeutic procedures.
Disputing the prevalent belief that narcissism represents
love withdrawn or withheld from disappointing objects and
invested in the self, Dr. Spotnitz holds that narcissism pre-
serves the object and turns hatred—often murderous—
upon the self. The primary problem to be worked through
in these cases, Dr. Spotnitz contends, is "internalized aggression." By way of illustrating his approach, the author
adopts a most engaging literary device: he undertakes to
treat *Narcissus Redivivus,* a latter-day recreation of the
famed rendering by Ovid.

Since Narcissus is a mythological figure and Dr. Spotnitz's prime interest is clinical, he makes no special effort
here to see today's narcissi in the multifarious settings of
their experiences in historical, social, and cultural reality.
Readers wishing to have wider access to the theories underlying his ten-step treatment plan, including his recommen-
dations for the "object-oriented question," will need to
look into Dr. Spotnitz's recent and forthcoming publications.

Dr. Ben Bursten emphatically opposes all energy theories of libido and rejects the widely accepted view that
narcissism represents a developmental arrest at the oral
stage. "A purely oral character," he counters, "doesn't exist." There are, indeed, four types of narcissistic person-

ality: craving, paranoid, manipulative, and phallic narcissists.

A particularly helpful feature of Dr. Bursten's essay is
his correlation of his views with those of two of the foremost clinical students of narcissistic phenomena in our
time. They are Heinz Kohut, author of *Analysis of the Self*,
and Otto Kernberg, whose outstanding monographs on the
subject are widely acclaimed. Kohut describes two lines of
development of narcissistic libido proceeding from the
cathexis of an undifferentiated self-object (primary narcissism). Kernberg also sees narcissistic libido as a type of
instinctual energy. By contrast, Dr. Bursten writes:

> Having set aside the concept of energy, I can no longer
> define narcissism in terms of the nature of the instinctual
> charge (Kohut, 1971, p. 26) or even in terms of the cathexis
> of the self (Hartmann, 1950) and "self-objects." Instead, I
> shall define it simply as an interest in (or focus on) the self.
> Narcissistic personalities have a very intense interest in their
> selves—so much so that they often can see others only as
> extensions of themselves, or existing for the purpose of
> serving themselves. With this definition in mind, we can
> rephrase the question of the narcissistic course. We can ask,
> "Why do these people need to have so high an interest in
> themselves?" Perhaps the answer is that they cannot take
> themselves (their selves) for granted; they constantly need
> to confirm their selves.

What shall we say of the often claimed advantages of
existential and ontoanalytic approaches in the diagnosis
and therapy of schizoid and narcissistic personalities?

Dr. Frank Johnson makes an unusually searching effort
to go below the level of cliché and prejudice in discussing
this theme. Drawing largely upon literary and philosophical
characterizations of the so-called Alienated Man—a subject
which has fascinated major novelists and philosophers of
our time, such as Sartre, Camus, Heidegger and Eugene
Minkowski—Dr. Johnson ventures an exceptionally hard-

headed discussion of the declared benefits and the recurring costs of the antipsychoanalytic theories and procedures. According to him,

> in preferring a less objectified and interpretive interpreta-
> tion thrust, existential procedures may unintentionally reify
> the patient's convictions about his inherent "badness"
> through averting more conventional psychoanalytic tech-
> niques which focus on the historical separation of the past
> from the present. . . . [Still] phenomenology has succeeded
> in refocusing attention onto the immediate nature of lived
> experience in an effort to comprehend otherwise elusive
> dimensions of personal and social reality. In many ways,
> such a focus acts as an antidote against the patient's notion
> of his own isolation and idiosyncrasy.

Existentialistic and ontoanalytic techniques may be
beneficial in so far as they focus on contemporaneous experience. Similarly, the emphasis on an existential communion between analyst and patient and the importance of an
articulated empathy are seen as providing the therapist
with an intellectual and emotional bridge to his severely
estranged patient. On the other hand, concludes Dr. Johnson, existentialistic-ontoanalytic procedures with their
"bracketing of the world" and ambiguity in subject-object
distinctions may unintentially collaborate to solidify pseu-
do-identification and other forms of compartmentalization
of human experience.

Part III comprises four papers which throw light on the
bearings of narcissisms of philosophy; the constitutions of
world-view, notably the experience of time and history; the
development of mathematics and mathematicians; and the
formation of ego-ideals in the light of social evolution.

Professor John Hanson offers a strikingly ingenious
reconstruction of the dreams of Descartes, dreams that
have proved fascinating to more than a few scholars in our
time. It was Descartes' dreams, Hanson contends, that lie

at the very center of the so-called dreams of reason. Hanson writes:

> One might say that the adult Descartes made a virtue of his childhood condition of abandonment by creating a philosophy of solitude. In drawing a set of rigid boundaries around the *cogito*, in withdrawing the ego from the world and the body, his sustained philosophical rejection of interaction avoided what he felt was a cosmic rage.

Dr. Hanson's essay constitutes a strong restatement of a theme which has played a large part in twentieth-century thought. Descartes has again and again been identified— for example, by A. N. Whitehead, Edmund Husserl, Jacques Maritain—as an evil genius, the progenitor of equally unwanted polar oppositions of egoistic rationalism and mechanical materialism. Within a century of his death the dualism of *res cogitans* and *res extensa* he had sponsored was broken down, to yield the materialism of De la Mettrie's *l'homme machine* (1747) and the rationalism of the Enlightenment *philosophes*.

In Hanson's view the dreams Freud dreamed were the undoing of Descartes' "dream of reason." Hanson writes:

> The repudiation of Descartes found its most forceful expression in another man's "*Olympica,*" Sigmund Freud's *The Interpretation of Dreams*. With Freud's work the science of mental life was redreamed and Descartes' thought became yet another dream of reason laid to rest.

Dr. Mark Stern offers us an ambitious and imaginative study of the constitution of the phenomenological world, especially of the temporal and spatial orientations of both narcissist and schizophrenic. In this connection he writes:

> Narcissists are often persons whose character defenses just about ward off a complete regression into schizophrenia. What differentiates schizophrenics from narcissists is not so

much their tendency to deny time, but rather the ways in
which each appeals to the "forces" of submergence. For the
narcissist this submergence takes the form of play-acting
time-defying roles. For the schizophrenic denial of time occurs through an over-investment in primary process.

The chief actor of Dr. Stern's drama is Shakespeare's
Hamlet. Dr. Stern's essay also includes an extremely interesting case history of "Andrew," a homosexual engineer.

The two closing essays in Part III stress a point that
nearly gets lost in the welter of current writings on narcissistic pathologies: There is normal and productive, as well
as self-defeating narcissism.

Drs. Reuben and Benjamin Fine, father and son, both
mathematicians, organize convincing evidence on the side
of normal and productive narcissism as it is manifested in
mathematicians, and Dr. Esther Menaker carries this aspect
of narcissism further in her thoughtfully conceived essay
"The Ego Ideal: An Aspect of Narcissism." In it she identifies narcissism as a component of human growth and self-
realization. Without an access of narcissistic energy to the
self, she proposes, there is little hope that an adequate ego
ideal can be developed.

Dr. Menaker's positive evaluation of the role of narcissism with respect to the ego-ideal may remind psychoanalytic scholars of a related position taken over a
half-century ago by a devoted student and friend of Freud,
Lou Andreas-Salomé. Her sense seems to have been that
Freud's commitment to the economic theory of the libido
required him to see all self-references as narcissistic. Was
this not to miss the fact that every human being is fated to
be a self or self-structure of some sort?

The present writer may be permitted to add a few
words about some apparently paradoxical findings of his
own in respect to wider implications of contemporary views
and appearances of narcissism. Can it be that Freud himself

may have provided a strategic opening for the narcissistic constructions placed upon his aims and work by many who put themselves forward as Freud's "true" heirs? Quite clearly, Herbert Marcuse and Norman O. Brown and their many peers and followers do not feel restrained by the fact that Freud talked of his work as the third blow against human narcissism. Indeed, Marcuse credits Freud's very way of describing primary narcissism as the spur to his own new beginning, the celebration of Narcissus as the anti-Promethean hero who reveals the way to the liberation of man from the domination of the repressive "performance principle," the perversion of the true nature of reality.

If truth be told, we would have to say that narcissism has been a great deal more than a clinical condition over the last decade and a half; it has been a popular cult and a ruling fashion. Clearly a fourth blow remains to be struck, one needing to be directed against the constructions—or misconstructions—placed upon Freud's *third* blow. The next blow will have to affirm the critical importance of a truly sociocultural as well as psychosocial *social* reality principle.

The central task of this series will be to understand the stirrings and faces of self-in-process. Among these faces are the particular faces of Narcissus explored herein, as well as other faces that remain to be explored in later volumes. It remains to venture some hints on ways of averting the pitfalls which regularly await investigators in these domains.

The familiar fashion of regarding selves regularly locate selves almost entirely in two allegedly primary backgrounds: the biological substratum of the individual organism or the socialization experiences of the growing child in the very first years of life in the bosom of the family. These perspectives may lead to a large mass of carefully designed and well-reported empirical studies which in the end do not necessarily add up to a greatly expanded understanding of our selves-in-process, including our generational selves and group selves in our differential histories across times and spaces.

The heavy overconcentrations on the facets of selves that come into prominence in the specialized environments of the laboratory and the psychiatric clinic may easily lead us astray; we can forget the threads which tie the individual biography to social histories and group structures. The same effect results when, out of a taste for melodrama, we fix our attention unduly on the spectacular surfaces of narcissistic phenomena. To be sure, narcissisms in the restricted clinical sense occur everywhere in the growing up of children during their early years. This may tell us little, however, of the workings of narcissisms at different levels of human function and organization. To understand the latter we need to understand the relative intensity and influence of narcissistic orientations in the different spheres of social and personal development. Nor can we omit the importance here of the institutional and cultural structures of great civilizational and societal complexes. It would clearly be a mistake to suppose that all lands across the world produce the same kinds and the same amounts of narcissism. Different societies have very different extents and structures of individuation and individualism.

Societies are not destroyed or even greatly disarranged by an individual narcissist who appears in treatment. But the malignant potential of narcissism is vastly magnified whenever anyone with pronounced narcissistic psychopathology comes to play a large part in political affairs.

To relate to the full range of phenomena known to be linked to narcissism, we need to be prepared to move beyond Freud's mapping of narcissism to other perspectives which attend more closely than did Freud to social and cultural processes and patterns. Among these perspectives are those of Erikson, Durkheim, Marx, Weber, Piaget, and a number of others who continue to be active on the frontiers of theory and research.

We hope that this volume will constitute a step in the needed new directions.

Part I

NARCISSISM IN OUR TIMES

Chapter 1

A TEMPLE OF LAST RESORTS: YOUTH AND SHARED NARCISSISMS

Ann Braden Johnson

As far as Jan could tell, they were of all ages from five to fifteen, yet they all moved with the same speed, precision, and complete indifference to their surroundings.

Then Jan saw their faces. He swallowed hard, and forced himself not to turn away. They were emptier than the faces of the dead, for even a corpse has some record carved by time's chisel upon its features, to speak when the lips themselves are dumb. There was no more emotion or feeling here than in the face of a snake or an insect. The Overlords themselves were more human than this.

"You are searching for something that is no longer there," said Karellen. "Remember—they have no more identity than the cells in your own body. But linked together, they are something much greater than you."

Arthur C. Clarke, *Childhood's End*

This is a chapter about troubled, unhappy people lost to the real world but found by obscure, strange, and exclusive cults that are emphatic in their rejection of the larger culture. While the numbers of these people are not overwhelming, they are considerable, and the cults themselves are fast becoming ubiquitous. Residents of our major cities have grown accustomed to the sight of young men and women dancing on street corners, dressed in saffron robes and sneakers. Most people must have seen or read something about the lavish proceedings at the Houston Astrodome in November, 1973, in honor of a 16-year-old Indian guru who is reputed to be God incarnate. A large number of fundamentalist Christian sects have come to light as a result of Ted Patrick's highly publicized efforts to kidnap their members and "deprogram" them. The fact is that there are currently sizable numbers of American youths who practice one or another brand of religion which is foreign, by and large, to our culture.

I have been intrigued by this phenomenon for some time, mostly because I was a student throughout the sixties and have vivid memories of the hip culture and the political movement; and I have found it puzzling, to say the least, that the age-old phenomenon of a religious revival should have sprung, fullblown, from such free-and-easy beginnings. Actually, the similarities between the love-feasts of 1967, the pitched battles of 1969, and the sidewalk chantings of 1974 far outweigh the differences. There is a common thread of desperation and self-preoccupation running through all these movements, leading ultimately to a total rejection of the adult world and the effort to find a permanent substitute for it, or avoid it altogether by a regressive, narcissistic retreat from the world. The element of narcissism was present from the beginning and characterized the stoned flower-children and the radical bomb-throwers as well as the pacified religious devotees. Witness:

> The total self-absorption of both drug use and meditation

> The grandiosity implicit in the belief that by bombing a branch bank in California one can halt a war in Asia waged by the largest government on earth

The belief that by arcane measures like the practice of astrology and witchcraft one can be so powerful as to predict the future or control the forces of nature

The childish effort to aggrandize the self through an unrealistic choice of one's supposed previous incarnations

Last but hardly least, the shared narcissism of a retreat into a new world of one's own making, occupied only by the chosen of one's peers.

The astute reader will note at once that the thread quickly turns into a spider's web of influences, causes, and component parts, and he will further note a paucity of conclusions. The reason for the first is that the religious movement, like all cultural movements where individual psychopathology coexists with social change, is a complicated problem with many facets and interwoven elements. The reason for the second is that I don't know where the movement is headed; either this is a temporary situation which will change in five years or it isn't—I can only recognize its existence and try to ferret out its meaning for today.

One final warning: from all that I have read and heard and seen, the people attracted to the new religious cults are really quite disturbed and certainly very troubled. I think it entirely likely that at least some will turn for help to clinics, hospitals, or social agencies sometime in the future, and I think it essential that we be aware of what they are coming from. I once heard an eminent psychiatrist dismiss yoga-based dietary beliefs held by a patient as "delusional"; this bothers me more than I can say, because, if he was right, many thousands of people share that delusion and believe in it as fervently as a Roman Catholic believes in transubstantiation. These are not beliefs to be challenged lightly.

I

Everything not forbidden is compulsory

T. H. White, *The Once and Future King*

A variety of cults devoted to the practice of Eastern religion exist and claim sizable memberships in the United States today. They share certain beliefs in common but recognize different gods; practice meditation almost universally but require different degrees of devotion, ranging from daily periods of reading and meditation to 24-hour-a-day communal life. One thing which is typical of all groups is a sense that religious practice is a constant pursuit, hardly something to be shunted to a corner of one's life in the form, say, of attendance at a weekly service; one is, rather, religious all the time or one is not. Thus even the mildest of routines prescribed by a relatively lenient cult will include two 20-minute meditations per day.

The reason for this all-or-nothing kind of devotion is said by one writer to derive from the fact that

> a certain quality of everyday life is necessary if the awakening of direct religious experience is not to plunge one into further illusion. Drawn largely by the wish for intensity of experience, the followers of the new religions discover a motive for accepting the need for a better quality of everyday life. There is then a *reason* for mortality instead of the authoritarian commands of popular religious forms—a reason which relates to the deepest wishes of the individual himself. (Needleman, 1970, p.229)

This constant daily immersion in one's faith is a crucial component of the Eastern faiths and its importance cannot be minimized, nor should its unusualness in view of the standard organized religions of the West—as practiced by most people, that is—go unnoticed.

With this all-important fact in mind, then, we can take a look at a sample of the cults now in existence.

Baba-lovers

The followers of Meher Baba are a loosely organized group who have been around for some years, beginning sometime in the 1920s in India. Baba himself was a "Perfect Master," a rank of spiritual enlightenment assigned to a few gurus (teachers) by other Perfect Masters by a process which is obscure and probably entirely intuitive. At some time in his life, Baba decided he was the Avatar, or earthly representative of God, as were Jesus, Buddha, Mohammed, et al. He is especially remarkable for having decided in 1927 never to speak again, a decision that nonetheless permitted him to set down his teachings in a great many books, including a three-volume set of *Discourses,* in which he sets out the rules and guidelines for the spiritual life, as well as a number of books with titles like *Spiritual Jingoism, Evil as a Relic,* and *The Calculus of Opposites.*

Although Baba was himself schooled in traditional Hinduism, he seems to have founded his own Way (as in "way of life"), which can be summed up in one word: *love.* Baba is the loving god, who loves everyone and everything, and his followers in turn love Baba, each other, and everyone else, without exception. A friend of mine who is a Baba lover told me, "Yes, even Nixon—you see how far we have to go!" On a more theoretical level this concept is explained by two followers who state that Baba "is seen as the personification of the latent identity of all persons. . . . His immanence universalizes and thus legitimates loving relationships not only among Baba Lovers but among everyone" (Robbins and Anthony, 1972, p. 122).

Although the members often choose to live together this cult does not require communal living, and besides one's daily meditation and other spiritual exercises such as fasting, group practice is limited to regular meetings and discussions of Baba's theological writings. Pilgrimages to the cult's ashram/retreat at Myrtle Beach, South Carolina, or India are optional but encouraged.

Zen Buddhism

Like Yoga, Zen is an old discipline and hardly new to Americans; the Beats of the 1950s were very much involved in Zen. Zen is a very demanding, highly ritualized discipline involving regular and intensive meditation periods under the supervision of a *roshi* (master). Meditation is held in a temple, ideally, in company with other devotees and always at ungodly times like five in the morning, often for hours at a stretch. The adept meditates on the *koan* (Zen riddle —for example, "What is the sound of one hand clapping?" or "What did your parents look like before you were born?") which is assigned to him by the master, with whom he meets regularly until the master is satisfied that the *koan* has been understood and/or answered by the disciple, who then moves on to another, more difficult *koan*.

The long hours of intense concentration while sitting immobile in physically exacting positions make Zen practice among the most difficult of religious disciplines, as does the fact that disciples who fall asleep during meditation are hit on their backs. The quality of Zen practice is very hard to grasp; one author does as well as anyone (and better than most) in the following:

> Meditation is an exercise aimed at detachment, at loosening one's ties. . . . To sit still is a way of creating distance, of isolating oneself, of breaking away not only from what happens around us but also from what happens within, in the mind itself. . . . One tries to become one with the *koan*, to close the distance between oneself and the *koan*, to lose oneself in the *koan*, until everything drops or breaks away and nothing is left but the *koan* which fills the universe. And

if that point is reached, enlightenment, the revelation follows. (Wetering, 1974, p. 15)

Divine Light Mission

I find it hard to disguise my bias against this group, which has received perhaps the most publicity of all the cults, thanks to its superb public relations staff. This organization is devoted to the nineteen-year-old Guru Maharaj Ji. The guru is an Indian boy whose father was a genuine Hindu master—of whom there are hundreds in India—who allegedly selected his youngest son to carry on his practice after he dropped the body (Indian mystics never die; they just shed their earthly form). The guru was eight at the time but rose to the occasion and has vastly overachieved his father's aims. He is hailed and acclaimed as God himself by his followers, a practice he does nothing to discourage, although he avoids validating it.

The DLM, as it is known, is a large and multifaceted organization which runs restaurants, clinics, ashrams, and the like; it also puts out a very slick magazine called *And It Is Divine,* of which the "Supreme Editor-in-Chief" is, of course, the guru himself. The outfit also maintains a computer with all followers' special talents and interests on call should they be needed for special projects. What is so astonishing about the DLM is its openly materialistic policy as regards the guru and his family, who now own several luxury cars, jet planes, and large houses all around the world, a condition somewhat at odds with the traditionally abstemious life of self-sacrifice maintained by Hindu masters for many centuries. A. C. Bhaktivedanta Swami Prabhupada, leader of the Hare Krishna sect, calls Maharaj Ji a "cheap cheat" (*Newsweek,* April 1, 1974).

The DLM claims six million members, whose entire financial assets, turned over upon joining up, support the organization, along with contributions and donations. The guru's actual theology is inscrutable at best; perhaps typical of his style is his answer to the question "Is there a life after death?" [*Answer:*] "Die and See" (Cameron, 1973, p. 94). The real meat of the sect's religious practice is The Knowledge, a four-part technique for meditation taught by disciples of high rank called Mahatmas, techniques which are supposedly highly esoteric but easily mastered, *if* taught by a real live Mahatma. Meditation using the four techniques —and, obscurely, carried on under a sheet—plus at least two months of lectures ("satsang"), gets one to the point where, according to one premie (devotee), "I don't have to think; I *know*; I have Guru Maharaji Ji's Knowledge" (1974, television documentary).

The advantages of following the guru are apparently not to be articulated, for they are never spelled out; rather, premies divulge their lurid pasts as dopers, crooks, mental patients, and swear that the guru made the difference. The proselytizing done by the group appeals to the experiential (you'll *see,* he'll *prove*).

Hare Krishna or Krishna Consciousness Society

I have chosen to explore this sect in greater detail below in order to examine the inner workings of these religious organizations in general and to isolate the qualities that appeal to the members, so a quick sketch should suffice here.

The sect is especially interesting in two ways: one, it is probably the strictest, requiring 24-hour-a-day group participation; and two, it is dramatically at odds with the larger culture, dressing its members in saffron robes and renaming them in Hindi. The group was founded by A. C. Bhaktivedanta Swami Prabhupada, a businessman turned Hindu mystic and Vedantic scholar, who opened a storefront mission in New York's East Village in 1967. Despite its very strict rules the KCS boasts 65 centers around the world (30 in the United States) and maintains its own school in Texas for devotees' children.

The sect worships the god Krishna, a blue gentleman with many arms and 16,000 wives, who is but one of the Hindu gods and whose pre-eminence is questioned by other scholars of the Vedas, the basic Hindu texts. The Hare Krishna devotees spend their time proselytizing, selling incense and literature on the streets of major cities, and memorizing Prabhupada's "official" translation of the *Bhagavad-Gita.* They also learn Sanskrit, debate theology, and work at one task or another for most of the day. This is no lightweight religious life—the official temple day begins at 3:30 A.M., ends at 9:45 P.M., and every minute in between is tightly scheduled. Every area of human life has its special rules; there are rules for marital sex, for the preparation and ingestion of food, for thinking, for eliminating bodily wastes.

Others

There are countless sects, some well-known, others not. Among the more curious is Scientology, originally called Dianetics and developed as a new form of psychotherapy involving scientific measures of interior residues of trauma, thanks to the "E-meter," a useful gadget for measuring the galvanic skin response, much lauded by Scientology therapists ("auditors") as infallible in determining mental status. Scientology was founded in the early 1950s by one L. Ron Hubbard, then an obscure officer in the U.S. Navy. Hubbard published his theories in a science fiction magazine, gained a serious following, and parlayed this into a multi-million dollar business in England. Scientology has been attacked by most of the more traditional psychological institutions and seems to be viewed as something of a swindle by the British authorities, who deported Hubbard in 1968, since which time he has lived on a yacht anchored beyond the three-mile limit. Perhaps to protect itself from further legal action, Scientology has transformed itself into a full-blown religion replete with choirs, sermons, and creed (Evans, 1974, p. 132).

The countless "Jesus freak" organizations are well known thanks to "deprogrammer" Ted Patrick and his activities on behalf of parents of "brainwashed" children. Examples include New Testament Missionary Fellowship (New York), the Tony and Susan Alamo Foundation (California), the Children of God (who took Comet Kohoutek as a sign to leave the country and presumably have done so). These are very authoritarian, ultrafundamentalist Christian religions whose members proselytize endlessly and live in rigidly structured groups, one of whose cardinal rules seems to be never to give out information.

A unique group called the Brotherhood of the Spirit was founded by an ex-Hell's Angel in Massachusetts and now maintains four separate campuses for its members' communal, agrarian living. The most interesting part of their spiritual practice is the fact that the members have dropped their contemporary identities in favor of their previous incarnations—self-determined and including such luminaries as Queen Elizabeth I and St. Peter (Houriet, 1971, pp. 346ff). It is remarkable that no one ever claims to have been an obscure Bulgarian peasant.

Perhaps the most frightening of the lot are the Satanic cults, including the Process Church of the Final Judgment. This group worships the total God, both Good and Evil forces, as represented by the three Great Gods of the Universe, Jehovah, Satan, and Lucifer. One has the right to choose one's side—Black or White, Evil or Good—on which to play the game of life. Interestingly, the leader of the Process is a gentleman who greatly resembles Jesus and goes by the name of Robert de Grimstone, who was once a Scientologist (Evans, 1974, p. 118). Also interesting in its hideous way is the fact that Charles Manson's horrible cult was inspired to some degree by the Process Church—especially by the cult's attention to evil and the forces of Satan (see Sanders, 1971).

The groups in which these religions are practiced have a number of aspects in common, regardless of whether they are highly or loosely organized. Probably the single most important requirement for any religious group that wants to remain a going concern is that it have a very strong leader—and they all do. Generally the leadership is hierarchical, with levels of authority which are clearly delineated; but invariably one person is firmly in command. Even in these liberated times, the hierarchy is for men only, women being subjugated fairly efficiently in classic helpmeet fashion. There are exceptions, of course—notably Guru Maharaj Ji's mother and Robert de Grimstone's wife, both formidable ladies—but even these are invariably in partnership with men. The hierarchy of the average Hare Krishna temple, for instance, has Krishna at the top and Prabhupada his delegate, and the temple president, Prabhupada's.

The leader's authority is generally absolute. He makes all decisions and expects complete surrender of the underlings. The Hare Krishna people have carried autocracy to a high art; the temple president's decision-making powers include devotees' work duties, mate selection, and access to the telephone. Prabhupada has decreed that members will be vegetarian, remain celibate unless married, forgo outside associations or friendships, wear nonleather shoes, bathe three or four times a day, forgo the use of toilet paper, wear Indian clothes, send any offspring to year-round boarding school at age five (Levine, 1974, pp. 42–43)—in short, no area of life is left uncovered or open to individual choice.

The preferred lifestyle for religious devotees is communal; even in those groups which do not require it, members often choose to form communes among themselves. The advantages of such close association among members to those in charge are obvious; it is much easier to set rules, policies, and see them carried out. The advantages to the members are also obvious; they always have friends around who speak the same language, as it were. The brotherhood concept so important to the religious groups is carried to its furthest extreme in the teachings of Baba (1971), who posits socalled "group-souls"—one soul shared by several bodies. Even more, he says that "there is only one cosmic soul which gathers experience through all the different forms [that is, bodies], sometimes appearing to separate itself into group-souls and at other times into souls which come under the body-soul equation [one body: one soul]" (pp. 56–57). Tasks are assigned and carried out in efficient order, thanks to the powerful authority of the leadership; the work of daily living gets done by the close aggregate of fellow souls.

Nothing is more foreign to the Western mind than some of the Eastern ideas about food and sex, ideas which are central to the practice of all these mystical religions. Some of the notions about food peculiar to macrobiotics form part of the various groups' theories and rules for eating, the most important of which is that eating and food are central to the practice of religion. Vegetarianism is the rule, usually because the groups aim at complete harmony with nature—a harmony they feel would be violated by eating animals. Grains, fruits, and vegetables are the staples, and almost all groups bar the use of any stimulants; coffee and tea are forbidden, as are tobacco and alcohol. The basic text of macrobiotics observes that "food should be the primary concern of even the most spiritual of mankind. Without food, no Buddha or Christ. Eating is being" (Nyoiti, 1965, p. 63).

All too frequently, however, members approach nonbeing through poor and inadequate nutrition—the stories of macrobiotic devotees who have died of malnutrition are legion—but it is important to stress the fact that, misguided or not, these dietary habits amount to religious beliefs and as such really deserve respect, however lunatic they may sound. It does seem crazy to believe, say, that a diet of brown rice, green tea, and soy sauce will cure paranoia and schizophrenia (Nyoiti, 1965, pp. 126–127), but large numbers of people do believe it. For the Hare Krishnas, food is actually incorporated every day into their religious ceremonies, and the food placed on Krishna's altar is literally prayed to.

The role of food in these sects can hardly be minimized, then, and clinicians hearing wild claims for the curative properties of the radish would do well to bear the religious enormity of many such ideas in mind.

Some of the religious groups have interesting ideas about sexual activity, the most famous, of course, being the extreme abstinence practiced by the Hare Krishnas. Virtually every group flatly prohibits extramarital sex—I cannot think of one that permits it, although I wouldn't bet on satanic cults like the Process. The Hare Krishnas, however, have taken this moral stance one step further and have established regulations for all sexual practice—between marital partners only, of course. Sexual intercourse is to take place on the fifth day after the wife's menstrual period only, if the couple has done the obligatory six hours of chanting beforehand. At the age of thirty, the woman is considered to be past childbearing age and sexual activity from then on is forbidden, since procreation is believed to be the only purpose of sex in the first place. Far from minding this puritanical attitude, devotees accept it willingly: " 'You can give up sex,' a young, pretty wife said. . . . 'It's certainly not worth giving up Krishna for' " (Levine, 1974, p. 111).

A remarkable benefit of belonging to one of these groups is that one no longer has to take the responsibility for his own behavior. A concept crucial to the unusual system of accountability held by these religions is *karma*, which itself presupposes a belief in reincarnation, subscribed to by all the cults with Eastern roots. Karma assumes that a sum of all one's actions in a lifetime will be taken and will determine one's fate in the next. A murderer in one life might well be a victim in the next, although it is vastly more complicated than that and involves an infinitely extended process of divine retribution based on divine judgment. Except for divine grace, karmic laws are believed to supersede all other laws of nature and the universe. The obvious inference from this is that man probably cannot do much to effect any change in his karmic state, except if he appeals to divine grace. Indeed, God "alone can give new direction to the inexorable *karmic* determination" (Baba, 1971, p. 47).

Not only does the notion of karma absolve one to a limited degree from taking responsibility for one's behavior, which after all is only the result of karma from some now-forgotten other life, but the relationship of God to a disciple's karma is interesting. The following anecdote tells the story:

> One devotee, who seemed quite discontented to me, changed her attitude markedly after "initiation," when she received a Sanskrit name and the guarantee that the spiritual master would be forever afterward responsible for her behavior. (Levine, 1974, p. 43)

By all accounts, the members of these cults are nearly all white, middle-class, and college-educated to some degree, ranging from undergraduate dropout to profession-trained and even beyond. The average age is in the early 20s, ranging anywhere from 18 to 35. Most members are dropouts of one sort or another, although young professionals (lawyers, doctors) are known to belong to Divine

Light Mission, Hare Krishna, and the Baba-lovers. Without exception that I know of, members have previous experience with consciousness-altering drugs—this is a major point, to which I will return later. And often members have previous criminal records and/or psychiatric histories.

The cults clearly have a special appeal for very disorganized adolescents who have made at best a marginal adjustment to life. The very nature of such highly structured, regulated organizations suggests their usefulness to such a population, but I must confess I was startled to learn how very disorganized specific members actually were. One Hare Krishna woman in the New York temple is an ex-heroin addict, hospitalized nine times for psychiatric treatment and given ECT, who once nearly shot her husband with a loaded rifle kept "around the house." An even more pathetic story involves a male Hare Krishna devotee, also an ex-addict, who says:

> "A variety of sinful activities brought me here. Now when I'm on the street and someone says they're attracted to the temple but they're uncertain, and they mention doing things I've done . . . illicit sex, which I've done . . . drinking, which I've done . . . shooting heroin, which I've done, I don't know what to tell them."
> —Why not?
> "Because I don't know whether I'm sane." (Levine, 1974, p. 21)

The book, *Who Is Guru Maharaj Ji?* contains life stories of a similar nature, so many it is hard to choose. But for sheer desperation and depth of depression, *This Girl Will Die* is unequaled. Its author describes herself as having roamed India for four years, going on foot from ashram to ashram,

> weeping quite a lot, reading scriptures and mourning . . . [waiting] for the pit. Or whatever. I felt I had really had it, and there was nothing else I wanted to try, or any other place

> I wanted to go. [She meets a young sadhu, or disciple, who sends her to Guru Maharaj Ji's house.] I arrived at Guru Maharaj Ji's home, a beautiful white house with so many trees and flowers, a paradise, and I huddled on the front lawn, fearing. (Cameron, 1973, pp. 111–115)

It is worth noting that when the guru speaks to her after her long wait, her only response is to weep for 20 minutes.

The stories are numerous and contain many of the same elements: isolation, loneliness, profound depression, doubts about sanity, and, above all, total desperation. These are important attitudes and conditions to which we shall return. I cannot emphasize too much, though, the totality of the members' desperation—like one woman whom Cameron (1973) quotes: "Throughout my life, I have been searching for one person to give my life to" (p. 164).

For these people, the traditional institutions and helping organizations are clearly not going to be enough. They seemingly must have the total involvement, the endless routine, the compulsive chanting, and the ritual meditation to fill the almost unimaginable voids within themselves.

II

> Does it worry you to be alone?
> How do I feel by the end of the day?
> Are you sad because you're on your own?
> No, I get by with a little help from my friends
>
> Do you need anybody?
> I need somebody to love.
> Could it be anybody?
> I want somebody to love . . .
> I get by with a little help from my friends,
> Yes, I get by with a little help from my friends . . .
>
> The Beatles, *Sergeant Pepper's Lonely Hearts Club Band*
>
> © 1967, Northern Songs Ltd., England.

Back around 1967, as surely everyone remembers, there were hippies. These hippies—flower children, free spirits, the Love Generation—flocked in large numbers to San Francisco's Haight-Ashbury or New York's East Village or Cambridge's Harvard Square to live the life of dropouts from the straight world, a life where easy sex and extended drug use were the rule, and peace, love, beauty, and harmony the stated goals. California was the place to go, really —California, after all, is the land where the sun always shines, where surfers surf day and night, where movies and television come from. California, in 1967, was our Never-Never Land, the golden place where no one grows old and everyone is free. California, in 1967, was flowers and rock concerts, shared acid and free food in the park.

Also in 1967, there was The War: the Vietnam War, which went on and on and on, killing American draftees and Asian peasants, because a lot of generals in the Pentagon and supremely LBJ, our all-time evil stepfather, decreed that it should be so. 1967 was the good guys against the bad guys, bright youth against churlish age, the loving and pure against the miserly corrupt. Note the order: *we* were in the vanguard, *we* had the upper hand, and it seemed only a matter of days until *they* bowed before our gentle beauty and cheerful superiority. The straight world oppressed us and killed Vietnamese, but still everything was possible for us: we would silence guns by slipping daisies into their barrels; we would confound aggression by doing nothing, beautifully and magnanimously; we would change the world by loving each other and letting *them* be stunned into reform by our example. Hope was so deeply assumed that we never mentioned it. If we acknowledged our anger, we called it benign and believed we were happy in it. There was no limit to what we could do, and Frodo still lived.

Or so we saw it, The events of 1967 in large part prefigured the religious revival of the 1970s; in fact, they are in some ways one and the same movement, but with certain very significant differences. One enormous similarity is in the attitudes of the adolescents attracted to both movements, especially the affective attitudes. The kids attracted to hippiedom were troubled, unhappy, disillusioned, isolated, and alienated from the larger society; they were the desperate seekers, the kids who never quite fit in. It is essential, I think, to recall that real hippies were by no means the same as the much-publicized plastic, or parent-subsidized, hippies, the affluent suburban kids who on a weekend, say, would visit the Haight or the Village to be groovy. Real hippies were the panhandlers, the runaways who crashed in different pads every night, ate rarely, and used drugs almost constantly—rootless drifters, in essence, whose only ties were to the vague community of fellow wanderers (Lukas, 1967, pp. 1ff).

Like the cult members described earlier, the hard-core hippies were profoundly depressed adolescents with unhappy backgrounds and hopeless attitudes toward the future. My own best friend in high school was perhaps typical. Her father returned from the Korean War shellshocked to the point where her mother felt it necessary to divorce him; for a time afterward the family had to go on welfare, a serious blow to the mother's pride. The father committed suicide when my friend was ten, and the mother worked fulltime to support herself and her two children but drank increasingly and entertained a succession of men, with little success at hiding it from her children. My friend had three illegitimate pregnancies, resulting in two adoptions and one illegal abortion, dropped out of high school at 17, and ran away to Haight-Ashbury, returning only once to find her mother dying of cancer.

This pattern of early losses, inconsistent parenting, and troubled latency period is described superbly by one research team who studied young residents of Haight-Ashbury over a long period of time and who report, among other things, that their subjects experienced a high degree of "chaos and continual over-stimulation" including separation, divorce, and death resulting in broken homes, all through childhood and adolescence (Pittel et al., p. 18).

In a very poignant way the Love Generation's counterculture represents their effort to make their own reality, their own world. The choice of the term "flower children" can hardly have been accidental; indeed, the hippies strove to create and maintain a world of children only—children without parents, that is. "Don't trust anyone over thirty" always meant "Don't trust parents," just as the vague reference to "they" (as in "*they* won't let us . . ." or "*they* just want us to . . .") probably referred, really, to parents. For there is no question but that the flower children were acting in reaction to parents, dropping out of their parents' society. One study of some 30,000 Haight-Ashbury kids during the Summer of Love found the vast majority to be intelligent, college-educated, white middle-class kids trying to escape their backgrounds "less with a feeling of anger than with disillusionment and the sad conviction that their parents were unable to offer relevant models of competence" (Allen and West, 1968, p. 366).

One principal bond for hippies, besides their mutual escape, was drugs. It seems important to observe, though, that the use of drugs among adolescents and youth is and was probably much more prevalent than a lot of people would like to believe; not only hippies turned on to drugs, not by any means, not in 1967 or 1970 or now. I myself have a fairly large acquaintance with all sorts of people from all over the country, and I cannot think of one person roughly my age who has never used drugs of some kind at one time or another.

In this context, I was interested to come across a recent study whose authors were startled to learn that a very high proportion of public school teachers (hardly a counterculture occupation) under 30 were involved in a "liberated life style" which included drug use, liberal sexual attitudes, and fairly radical politics. Although I cannot say I am surprised myself, the study does corroborate the extent to which drugs have become a commonplace (Janus and Bess, 1973). I want to emphasize this point because it is my belief that, although most people seem to associate drugs almost exclusively with hippies and assume also that drug-taking was the predominate focus of their lives, the real nature of the truly hip life-style was something other than, if inclusive of, the drug experience, and that in using drugs hippies were in the mainstream of the larger youth culture and hardly in the minority.

There is, of course, no question but that variations in degree or amount of drug use do exist, and that hard-core hippies used more drugs more often than most users. I by no means intend to minimize the dangers of drug abuse, nor am I unaware of its serious adverse effects on the extremely troubled youths who turned to drugs and the hip life. I do, however, feel that drugs are less important as motivating factors than other common experiences for the population which has now turned to religion.

Before moving on to what I believe the real essence of the hip life to have been, I want to point out two aspects of drug use that are particularly relevant to the religious cults: one, the view of the psychedelic drugs as sacraments; and two, the mystical properties of acid. The origin of the sacramental use of acid and other psychedelics originates with the ancient Indian peyote ritual (see Castaneda, 1968). Any number of examples of mystical experiences while on acid can be found in the literature; the main theme seems to be that the user feels at one with nature and the cosmos (see Speck, 1972, pp. 163–166). The parallel between this kind of mysticism and that associated with meditation is obvious.

But the essence for me of the hippie experience is its life-style: the communal, tribal collections of children standing together against the straight world. The ideas behind communes and collectives sound awfully good: freedom, peace, equality, sharing, all-for-one and one-for-all; but the reality quickly becomes extremely threatening to the more disorganized and unhappy members. The grand design for the ultimate democracy that was envisioned is nowhere better described than in a science fiction novel which was extremely popular during the 1960s, a so-called underground classic called *Stranger in a Strange Land* (Heinlein, 1961). The book tells the story of a human male born and brought up on Mars, whose culture is spiritually advanced so that its natives enjoy enviable powers including telekinesis, total control of all involuntary muscles, mind-reading and ESP of all sorts, and the ability to destroy any object without leaving a trace. They also have no negative emotions and are purely rational, logical beings. The human/Martian comes to earth and founds a religion which involves learning all the above powers as well as the practice of free love, which is one of the religion's two sacraments—the other is the "sharing of water" by drinking together; this produces "water brothers," who are bound in eternal love and loyalty. The cult members live in groups where everything—water, food, thoughts, money, and sex—is shared absolutely equally by everyone, bound in eternal love.

This kind of group life was the model for the hip commune—and a terrifying life it seems, too: no controls on sexual behavior, no individuality, no privacy of any kind, no leaders, and no rules. The majority of communes set up on this model have long since fallen apart, partly because of the absence of leaders to see that things get done (in Heinlein's book the communards cleaned up by thought control, but the rest of us aren't that gifted); but probably also because the free life attracted precisely the kind of unstructured, poorly integrated person who was least able to function in the setting (cf. Speck, 1972, especially pp. 130–144).

Finally, Heinlein's book describes the spiritual brotherhood that was important to hip communes and prefigures the spiritual movement underlying all the religious cults of today. In this context it is important to recall the widespread hip fascination with astrology, Tarot cards, palmistry, *I Ching,* and the like, as well as the popularity of Eastern mysticism in the form of books like Hesse's *Siddhartha,* the Buddhist scripture known as *The Tibetan Book of the Dead,* and Kahlil Gibran's *The Prophet.* According to one author, the flower children

> reject the usual problem-solving techniques and replace them with problem-solving via mysticism, astrology and magic. They are disillusioned with the culture's solutions, but they are going to share a further disillusionment unless they can bridge the abyss between the reality and the fantasy. (Speck, 1972, p. 112)

In the summer of 1968, "Hippie" died and was buried. College campuses in Paris and New York erupted, two prominent public figures much loved by many young people were assassinated, LBJ had been dethroned, and Chicago's streets became the scene for youthful rebellion carried to the point of combat. The times had changed. Large numbers of American kids had apparently been radicalized and, concurrently, student revolt had taken on a new flavor of violence. A hard-core radical fringe became extremely prominent in the popular media, one which quickly came to typify to most people all student protesters—which could not have been further from the truth. Most student activists were of the petition-signing, peace-marching, Be-Clean-for-Gene variety; but with the birth of Yippie! and the Weathermen, the flamboyance of the few seemed to stick in the mind of the nation and come to stand for the many. One result of this distortion is that it is now quite difficult to talk about student protest in general, which like so many things exists in different forms but which seems to be comprehensible to most people in only one form: the worst.

The history of the student political movement is relatively nonviolent. In the very early sixties, politically activist students often worked with blacks under the nonviolent aegis of Martin Luther King, Jr., doing things like registering Southern blacks to vote, tutoring ghetto schoolchildren, sitting-in to protest institutional racism, and similarly benign activities. The black movement eventually turned separatist, though, as radical black leaders like H. Rap Brown and Stokely Carmichael challenged the essentially liberal Dr. King's leadership.

Students also served in the Peace Corps, VISTA, VISA, and the like, teaching impoverished peoples here and abroad new skills and otherwise trying to help them improve their lot. Work in the Peace Corps et al. was a much-esteemed alternative to straight, middle-class life in the United States, and most of its volunteers were probably dedicated to working within the system to change things. At some point in the second half of the sixties, though, it became the accepted opinion of most of this kind of student that the Peace Corps and its fellow organizations were tools of American imperialism, and another avenue for dissatisfied youth who wanted to work to change things was, in effect, shut off.

Meanwhile, the vanguard of student rebellion, Berkeley's Free Speech Movement, had fallen victim to repression at the hands of Governor Reagan and the California Board of Regents, a process which led ultimately to violence over People's Park and left Berkeley's streets to street people, "those who have dropped out of something—families, high schools, colleges, the Great Society—and are looking for something to drop into . . . begging for spare change, working occasionally, hustling for a place to crash, ripping off, dealing" (Stickney, 1971, p. 25). In Berkeley, protest was now more a matter of guns than of words; and Berkeley was where so much had begun, so very hopefully.

The political lives of students, however radical, were interwoven with one universal focus: the Vietnam War. The apparent endlessness of that war was the lever that changed student protest from its original, nonviolent orientation to a desperate search for stronger modes of confrontation and resistance, a switch which in turn tended to legitimize the violent few who were anxious to take over the New Left. As Keniston (1968) points out, the history of the New Left was one of "growing frustration, discouragement, anger, and what Robert Coles has aptly called the 'weariness of social struggle' " (p. 194).

Keniston also reminds us that failure and despair were inevitable, given the sheer scope of the changes the Movement was trying to make. For instance, the Vietnam Summer of 1967 was intended to bring about not just the end of the Vietnam War, but the end of the possibility for future wars as well. Other discouraging facets of Movement work are outlined by Keniston: the worker is rejected by those whom he is trying to help; and, perhaps hardest of all, the worker experiences "growing awareness that his own perspective, which seems so self-evident and right to him, is not shared by others" (pp. 195–196). As the activists felt more and more aware of their defeat and became more and more disillusioned, the Vietnam war itself was spiraling out in ever greater escalations. It is no wonder that the mood of committed youth turned from despair to rage—rage at the War, at the draft, at LBJ, at General Hershey, and ultimately, at the Establishment or adults/powermongers/capitalists/institutions in general. Hand in hand with the evergrowing rage, of course, was alienation, defined by Keniston (1968) as "an explicit rejection of what are seen as the dominant values of American culture" (p. 326).

The picture emerges of angry youths feeling ever more isolated from their society even as they grow angrier at their own impotence to effect the change they so deeply believe in. Somehow there is nothing more infuriating than to do in good faith what one knows to be right, only to be laughed off, ignored, put down, and even punished—as were draft resisters. The most awful part of student protest was the invisibility of the other side. I vividly recall a March on Washington to End the War when John Mitchell was still the much-despised attorney general; as the crowd passed the Justice Department, virtually everyone spontaneously made the classic obscene gesture—to a man who wasn't there.

If the authority responded at all, it was usually through a surrogate, as at Kent State, where a bunch of kids were suddenly fired upon by the anonymous Ohio National Guard sent in by Governor Rhodes. The prize for arrogance in this regard must go to Richard Nixon, though; after one large March to End the War he let it be known that he had spent the afternoon of the march watching football on TV. Much of the protesters' rage and alienation was certainly exacerbated by the absolute refusal of the authorities on whatever level—national, state, university— to respond, openly, directly, and in person.

One author discusses precisely this subject and draws the compelling connection between institutional authority and the parents of many campus radicals, whom he studied at Harvard. He found that the remoteness of leadership on all levels served to enrage and alienate students. He adds that

> an increasing number of young people come from back-grounds in which the family has virtually disintegrated. . . . A home in which both parents are available to the child, emotionally as well as physically, has become the exception rather than the rule. . . . The absence and uninvolvement of parents induces in the child repeated feelings of rejection and resentment. (Nicholi, 1970, p. 425)

He also found that the radical students showed (1) depression and excessively low self-esteem; (2) an intense sensitivity to the unresponsiveness of authority as discussed above; and (3) poor impulse control and an inability to tolerate frustration, as witness non-negotiable demands (p. 426).

Really, then, the violence of the SDS and other radical groups, made up as they were of the most radical, most frustrated, most precariously organized of the activist students, is entirely predictable. Rejection and rage, resentment and the feeling that one is left out, unwanted by the big people, seeing one's hard work doomed to failure and ridicule, not to mention the very real possibility for males of being drafted—all this and more can easily be seen to have so depressed, frightened, and infuriated student protesters that the step towards fighting back, meeting aggression with aggression, eventually became easy to take. The violence of the Weathermen, for instance, must certainly have made sense to its perpetrators in view of the massive violence being waged in the name of democracy every day across the world in Vietnam—not to mention the more abstract violence done to the poor and uneducated by giant institutions of the larger society, examples of which helped provoke the uprising at Columbia in 1968 (see Liebert, 1971, especially pp. 232–233).

The revolutionaries' main purpose, however their activities were designed, was to change the world—all of it, if need be. This is an enormously more active stance than that taken by the hippies, and that it should degenerate into violence and generalized, uncontrolled aggression can be no surprise. The real object of that aggression is clear, if we are to take the word of one of the three national officers elected by the SDS 1969 national convention: "Bring the revolution home, kill your parents, that's where it's really at" (Powers, 1971, p. 126).

III

I just want to ask a question
Who really cares?
To save a world in despair
Who really cares?
There'll come a time, when the world won't be singin'
Flowers won't grow, bells won't be ringin'
Who really cares?
Who's willing to try to save a world
That's destined to die

© Marvin Gaye, *What's Going On*

From the love-feasts of 1967 to the radical fury of 1969, we have come to the Jesus-freaks and Hare Krishnas of 1974; from sexual freedom and wanton aggressive acts we come to rigid, authoritarian cults dedicated to the spreading of obscure and ascetic religious practices—all in the space of six years, a remarkably short time. Oddly enough, in some instances the self-same kids who were hip or radical have turned to religion: much media attention has been paid to Rennie Davis, late of the Chicago Seven and now the chief American proselytizer for Guru Maharaj Ji; and a religious commune in Tennessee is run by one Stephen Gaskin, whose wife Maggie was a luminary of the early Haight-Ashbury scene (Wolf, 1968, pp. 81–93). No matter who the individuals were or are, the real question is why: What drives the same generation who sought almost limitless freedom to what is surely its antithesis, an exotic revival of that "old-time religion," bristling with rigid codes, strictures, and shibboleths?

To begin with, it is essential to remember that we are talking about adolescents, and late adolescents at that, who, for whatever reasons, are trapped in the struggle to separate and individuate themselves from their parents. Jacobson (1964) speaks of certain postadolescents whose problems stem from failures to resolve conflicts in the areas of object relations, identifications, and the process of identity formation, as a result of which they are unable to separate.

> Fighting their dependency trends, such persons may derogate their parents and turn away from them in adolescence, but as adults they continue to emulate and lean upon other persons and groups and unduly admire them until they again rebel, abandon them in rage and disappointment, and look for the next object to be glorified and emulated. (p. 201)

She suggests a kind of identity-shopping, which makes perfect sense in the case of kids who go from life-style to life-style, presumably hoping each one will turn out to be The One.

Quite clearly today's cult members are trapped in an extended adolescence, or they wouldn't need to shop for a ready-to-wear identity that often comes complete with new name and all. One author defines identity as "stability both of social behavior and of self-knowledge," and assumes by "self-knowledge" that the ego will prevail as the integrating force and that the affects will not directly influence behavior (Mitscherlich, 1963, p. 70). Now as we have seen, the hippies' and radicals' behavior was very much influenced by their affects, and one wonders about the affective state of the religious youth in this same context. A number of writers agree that the general mood of today's adolescents is one of depression and sadness. Speck's description (1973) is particularly eloquent:

> Clinically, adolescents seen today are simply not the same as the youth of the past two or three generations. They appear depressed and hopeless, but they admit it rather than blame themselves. They see the world situation as hopeless—but for dialogue, not therapy. They are suffering from real distress of the soul. (pp. 17–18)

Anthony (1970) describes the clinical, as opposed to the normative, depression in adolescence similarly, as "a sadness 'emanating from nowhere' " (p. 842).

The relationship between depression and mourning, between feelings of grief and sadness and the fact of separation and loss is well known and needs no amplification. What is particularly fascinating is the role religious conversion plays in changing that affective state by removing the need to worry, encouraging a happy mood, and altering the person's perception of the world: "learning the art of life which was defined by Thomas Jefferson as the art of avoiding pain" (Wilson, 1972, pp. 385–386). In *Young Man Luther* (1962), Erikson observes that not only Luther but his contemporaries as well characterized his mood just before he became a monk as "a state of *tristitia,* of excessive sadness" (p. 39). It is worth pointing out that the words invariably used to describe either the devotees of the Hare Krishna sect or the followers of Guru Maharaj Ji are "blissful," "joyful," "ecstatic"; in addition, the guru uses the irritating but significant come-on, "Everybody's going to be blissed-out!"

Another extremely useful function of the religious groups is their role in defining ethical values for their members. The prohibitions against sex, drugs, and stimulants described earlier are hardly without meaning to an adolescent trying to become an adult. They are even more necessary for adolescents who have previously come across the anxieties and the dangers inherent in free experimentation with drugs, promiscuity, and antisocial behavior, as had those whose testimonials to their newfound faith were quoted above. The consolidation of values is a central task of adolescence (Esman, 1972, p. 90), and it is a task which seems increasingly difficult to complete in a world devoid of meaningful, relevant models via government, schools, traditional religion, and even parents.

Erikson (1964) makes a tidy distinction between moral

rules of conduct based on fear of reprisals and recrimination, which are just about the only rules taught in our society, and ethical rules, which, he says, are based on ideals of a formulated good, a definition of perfection, a promise of self-realization (p. 222). The religious groups, for all their reliance on a vaguely defined, hastily imported Hindu mysticism, do hold up an ideal, a definition of perfection, a reason to try to be good; and that, frankly, is more than most institutions are willing to provide. "Do it for Krishna" is probably easier to swallow than "Do it or else."

The weakness of our social institutions, which have traditionally acculturated youth by providing them with principles and guidelines in carrying out their leadership function, is an unfortunate by-product of the increased mobility of people thanks to the Industrial Revolution in general and particularly the invention of the internal combustion engine. It used to be that families lived and worked more or less together, so children could see their parents functioning as adults in a variety of situations and were thus able to identify with them and internalize their rules comprehensively. This is no longer so, according to Mitscherlich (1963), who goes so far as to say that "the severity and the protraction of the crisis of adolescence" today is less the simple result of psychopathology of the individual and more the result of "the disappearance of the father imago so closely associated with the roots of our civilization, and of the paternal instructive function" (p. 141).

Mitscherlich puts particular emphasis on the structure of the nuclear family as it has contributed to this picture; not only do most children not see their parents performing a variety of functions (if they see them at all), but also they haven't the opportunity of seeing many other adults either, living as most of us do in tiny family groups isolated from extended family networks. Framo (1972) observes that children in nuclear families are often forced to accept roles which are constricting and all too frequently projected onto them by their parents, which brings to mind all the miserable kids one knows who feel forced to pursue an unwanted education or vocational choice because their parents want them to (there is an eloquent expression for this in current adolescent jargon: kids speak of their parents "laying a heavy trip" on them). One reaction to such a wholesale assignment of identity is

> to break away violently from the family, to "cop out" and become a hippie, with life being based on a refutation of the parents. This kind of individual will often suffer from the kind of symptoms described by the existentialists—alienation or lack of meaning or connectedness with life. (pp. 281–282)

The exotic mystical Eastern religions are at such visible and dramatic odds with the larger American culture that we can safely assume that to belong to one qualifies as a "refutation of the parents"; in fact, one premie (follower) said, with a big smile on his face, "Before I came to Guru Maharaj Ji I was a dope freak who had completely dropped out. And my parents liked that better than they like this."

If parents aren't effectively instructing their children in the ways of the world, who is? Their peers, says Mitscherlich (1963).

> In the absence of direct and immediate instruction in practical life under the paternal eye, and the consequent lack of dependable tradition in this respect, contemporaries orient themselves by each other. The peer group—that is to say, one's contemporaries at school and place of residence and work—becomes the guiding line of behaviour. (p. 149)

He adds that the result is people "for whom to a large extent only two standards of value exist—being socially with the trend, or popular, and being forgotten, out-of-date, worthless" (p. 150).

Anyone who has spent any time at all in the American public school system will know at once how crucial it is to be popular. My husband recalls deliberately failing a seventh-grade history test; he says this took a lot of effort but he did it because he didn't want to be the only one who always got good grades. It will be no surprise to learn that a study of students who had undergone religious conversion found that the converts had come to their new faith "through the influence of someone from [their] own generation—usually a recently converted roommate, sibling, or classmate" (Nicholi, 1974, p. 397).

Another, rather older study of adolescents found that when parents and peer groups disagreed on a given issue, the adolescents tended to turn to their peers 74 percent of the time and to their parents only 26 percent of the time (Rosen, 1955, p. 160). Mitscherlich (1963) says that

> The collapse of paternal authority automatically sets in train a search for a new father on whom to rely. . . . The weakness or fallibility of the father has to be made good and wiped out by putting in his place a new one of still undiminished strength. (pp. 300–301)

Mitscherlich might find interesting the fact that the new religious groups provide precisely what society does not: a very strong father-figure who is both a powerful authority and a strict maker of rules. The choice of the word "father" is justified by the fact that the religious cults are male-dominated without exception, and most of the leaders are advanced in years and display a most avuncular manner as well.

A lot of public comments have been made in recent years about the affluence of today's youth which frees them from the need to work for a living, thus affording them the supposedly golden opportunity to explore the endless possibilities open to them in the way of vocations, schools, places of residence, and so forth. It is undeniable that much of American middle-class youth do enjoy this affluence and its accompanying freedom of choice, but little is said about the terrifying effects of seemingly limitless freedom, especially on adolescents whose permanent sense of self is still poorly formed. Like Dostoevsky's Grand Inquisitor, one longs to ask, "Didst Thou forget that man prefers peace, and even death, to freedom of choice in the knowledge of good and evil?"

Dostoevsky knew very well the anxiety which comes not only of freedom of choice but also of the taking of responsibility for that choice; every condition has its price, and the price of freedom is accountability for one's behavior, a price which the poorly organized adolescent may not be willing or even fully able to pay. I think this has a great deal to do with the attractiveness of a religion whose leader will take full responsibility for his followers, or one in which karmic law rules supreme, changeable only through divine intervention. To one who is not at all sure who he wishes to be and what he wants to do, the thought that compelling forces beyond his control determine his course through life must be very reassuring—and yet sufficiently abstruse and remote not to evoke the image of the parents on whom he dare not continue to be dependent.

Fromm (1941) has a revealing concept, the "magic helper," or outside force to which man ties himself—a feature common to all religions—and he says that "the intensity of the relatedness of the magic helper is in reverse proportion to the ability to express spontaneously one's own intellectual, emotional, and sensuous potentialities" (p. 176). Speaking of people who are ripe for mass movements and who show the kind of blind obedience to magic helpers that we have seen in the religious cults, Hoffer (1951) observes that "people whose lives are barren and insecure seem to show a greater willingness to obey than people who are self-sufficient and self-confident. To the frustrated, freedom from responsibility is more attractive than freedom from restraint" (p. 109).

Too much freedom provokes anxiety in the youth of today, but possibly even more provocative of anxiety is the discharge of aggression. We saw in the political activists the paucity of internalized controls of aggression that may be characteristic of adolescents—certainly of the extremely disorganized adolescents who are likely to turn to repressive organizations—and indeed, the switch from Weatherman to Hare Krishna suggests a massive effort at damping and controlling that which previously ran wild. It is certainly significant that the bliss, joy, and love we are told characterize the religious movement and its denizens have no corresponding anger, resentment, or hate. Quite the contrary, in fact; one author speaks of how the Baba-lovers revel in their feelings—"Not one of them, though, 'revels' in his negative feelings: anger, envy or self-pity" (Needleman, 1970, p. 98). Presumably we are supposed to believe that a conversion carries the wonderful fringe benefit of eliminating the negative; but I must say I can only wonder where all the rage has gone since 1970, when the political movement ground to a resentful but cowed and dispirited halt after the gunfire at Kent State. Wherever it went, we can be sure there was and is an incredible lot of it, to require such massive denial.

The only outburst of anger I have seen in the religious cults occurred at Guru Maharaj Ji's Millenium in Houston in November, 1973, when groups of Hare Krishna people and Jesus freaks set up little bands outside the Astrodome warning visitors that the Guru was a dreadful charlatan and Krishna/Jesus had it all over him; some very minor contretemps resulted. It is interesting that love does not seem to extend itself to competing cults, but then, as Freud (1930) pointed out

> It is precisely communities with adjoining territories, and
> related to each other in other ways as well, who are engaged
> in constant feuds and in ridiculing each other. . . . I gave this
> phenomenon the name of "the narcissism of minor differ-
> ences." (p. 61)

One of the problems we all have with aggression is
that, according to Anna Freud (1972)

> We call a "good lover" one who is faithful to his objects, i.e.
> constant in cathecting them. In contrast, the "good hater"
> is promiscuous, i.e. he has free aggression at his disposal
> and is ready to cathect with it on a non-permanent basis any
> object who, either by his actions or his characteristics, offers
> adequate provocation. (p. 166)

So we don't learn to control aggression through restricting
our choice of objects, and in fact we are supposed to learn
the harmful effects on others of our aggression and modify
our aggressive expressions accordingly, choosing, say,
words instead of muscular actions. But even inhibiting aggression by empathy for the victim and insight into the
situation, which Mitscherlich (1963) observes is the civilized way, "runs counter to the ideology of authoritarian
superiority and its right to impose punishment" (p. 175);
and our society, clearly, is not about to change its ideology
or give up its penal codes overnight.

One method by which previous generations have discharged aggression is through wars, in which soldiers
fought directly and everyone else vicariously. But since the
first atomic bomb was exploded in 1945, the very nature of
war has changed radically; no longer is it a viable means by
which an entire people can project all its aggressive feelings
and act on them in a satisfying way, for the stakes are much
too high. Not only that, but as Erikson (1970) points out,
the communications systems we have developed bring the

reality of war into every livingroom, making the enemy look all too human; combined with a technology which makes possible the appalling absurdity of overkill, this produces new and very bewildering tensions in individuals and larger associations (p. 14).

At no time was this tension more dramatically demonstrated than during the Vietnam War, when most of the post-Hiroshima generation absolutely refused to support the venture, a defiant posture that must have been extremely confusing to older generations to whom war may have seemed hell, but a periodically necessary hell. I think it is no accident that the term "generation gap" began to be used incessantly at the time.

I have come to believe that the real possibility of total annihilation of the species is not just a source of anxiety for my generation but a major anxiety, one so paralyzing that we have learned to deal with it only by massive denial. I have asked a number of people my age what they associate with nuclear war, and their answers are extremely interesting: one person remembers carting canned food down to his parents' cellar at age twelve; another thinks that whenever he hears a plane at night, it's The Bomb; a third recollects planning to rape the first woman he saw after the sirens went off lest he die without experiencing sexual intercourse; several people remember bomb drills in school, huddled under their desks; and I myself remember compulsively reading every book I could find on the order of *On the Beach* or *1984*, as well as every book or article available on the subject of the Nazi extermination of the Jews—amazed and horrified, I guess, by the notion of wholesale slaughter of a people.

And this anxiety made the Vietnam War that much more unbearable; here were the old guys, the Establishment, casually bombing and strafing and mining Haiphong as if it were nothing—didn't they know how serious it was? The rage, the incredulity, the sheer terror associated with the situation immobilized some and stimulated others to fight desperately for Revolution Now! before it was too late. In a book appropriately titled *Bomb Culture* (1968), a young British artist describes the feeling:

> The decline of the anti-bomb movement in 1962 [one recalls that the ubiquitous peace symbol was originally the Ban-the-Bomb symbol] left us stranded in the unbearable. . . . We knew for certain that governments had nothing whatsoever to do with the morality they preached and enforced, that society had lost its appetite for life and looked forward to the death it had contrived (how many times had I stood on ordinary doorsteps with black and white leaflets, arguing down through the levels of the deterrent theory and lingering patriotism until the householder blurted angrily "Well what difference does it make if it does come? So long as we all go quickly the sooner the bloody better I say"), that we ourselves lacked even the will of colonial dissidents, that none of us was sufficiently alarmed about extinction to force the murderers to put down their weapons, that society commanded nothing but contempt, much less dedicated labour or respect for law, that love, honour, faith, selflessness were as false in ourselves as in our elders, that the only effective thing to do was what we daren't do—riot and destroy the death machine in a demonstration of serious protest, that the only thing we *could* do was sit in humiliation and wait for extinction. (Nuttall, p. 113)

The fact of the ultimate, total destructiveness of war has an effect on how one sees aggressiveness, of course; as Wangh (1972) points out, the students of the sixties "had learned early that aggression, if actualized, could become all-destructive" (p. 216). He also provides an interesting discussion of dropping-out, which he suggests provides a retreat from aggressive competition with one's agemates in school (p. 219); and by extension, clearly, dropping out more permanently into drugs or religious groups, say, enables the avoidance of all aggressive social competition.

But a moratorium from aggression and competition is not all that the religious groups provide in the way of protection from the major anxieties. Certain unique qualities of their mystical origins lend themselves beautifully to the narcissistic needs of the adolescent beset on so many sides by pressures and worries which he cannot deal with or even face. One useful concept is that of Nirvana (in Zen, *satori*), the ineffable bliss of total enlightenment. In an article linking the mystical experience to the prevention of suicide, Horton (1973), connects the experience of Nirvana to primary narcissism, the passively experienced oceanic feeling which he relates to the unconscious memory of the uterine abyss. He goes on to suggest that "residues of primary narcissism may represent the human being's last refuge in life's storms—short of suicide" (p. 296). Whatever use the mystical experience may have as regards suicide, it is assuredly a much-sought retreat from reality, if the numbers claimed by meditation groups are to be believed. Maharishi Mahesh Yogi's Transcendental Meditation organization in Los Angeles claims 300,000 American members now, with 15,000 more added each month (Campbell, 1974, p. 37)— and TM is just one outfit among many.

There's a funny thing about reality in the Eastern mystical sects, too; they don't believe in it. Reality is illusion— *maya.* And according to the Hare Krishna sect, our age, *Kali-yuga,* or the Iron Age, is a particularly deadly time of discord and early death, whose people are trapped in thoroughly illusory and odious materialism; every man is partly demonic as well. The end will come in only 427,000 years, when Krishna will appear on a horse to slay evildoers and bring them to salvation. The only recourse left us in this dreadful age is endless chanting of the Hare Krishna *mantra* (sacred formula or spell), hoping to make a dent in *Kali-yuga* (Levine, 1974, p. 12). The primitive reliance on magical thinking speaks for itself.

It is a sad commentary on our time and/or our youth that our world is so overwhelming and frightening that they prefer to wrap themselves in the security blanket of compulsive ritual, chanting to the "illusion" that is their lives. On the other hand, the world is extremely confusing, and to function in it seems to require a very strong sense of self and a good bit of self-direction—qualities not characteristic of disorganized, confused, even borderline adolescents. It is unfortunate that none of the traditional resources of society seems to have anything to offer these marginal souls and that they have had to turn to religious groups whose continued existence depends on handouts, a precarious fiscal policy at best, and one which renders the groups nearly as insecure as their members. It is perhaps reassuring, though, that these troubled children have found a haven at all, and one much less dangerous than its predecessors. What is not so reassuring, however, is that this very precarious existence is all that society has to offer to people in such need.

A reporter asked two ex-members of a particularly horrifying neo-Marxist organization why they had stuck it out for so long. One thought for a while and said, "Because we had no place else to go" (Montgomery, 1974, p. 51). He was right; they haven't.

Chapter 2

STUDENT-TEACHER INTERACTION IN AN URBAN SCHOOL

Joel Emanuel

During the fifth period one sunny morning, Mr. Y, a teacher on cafeteria duty, happened to glance out into the schoolyard. Through the windows of the basement cafeteria, which afforded an ankle-height view of the yard, he watched a youngster playing handball against the concrete wall. The ball dropped into a puddle, bringing the game to a temporary halt. What to do? The boy whose ball was in the water found an immediate solution; he picked up a textbook and skimmed it across the puddle to dislodge the ball. Unfortunately, the book failed to do its job and dropped into the puddle. Meanwhile, Mr. W had joined Mr. Y at the window, and together they watched as the boy picked up the dripping book and threw it at the ball once more. This time the book found its mark, at the expense of another immersion. The ball popped out of the water. "Did you see that?" exclaimed Mr. Y indignantly. "Well," replied Mr. W, "it doesn't really matter much, does it? After all, the book was wet already."

This is a typical occurrence.

I have been a teacher for seven years, during which time I have seen the student composition of my school shift from 50 percent middle-class students to over 90 percent lower socioeconomic status students. With this shift there has been a progressive erosion of the reading and mathematics achievement levels as well as the motivation to improve either. The children also show little interest in the world outside themselves. One student expressed her attitude in the following manner: "I don't see why I should give anybody in this room respect. After all, they ain't my mother. They ain't goin' to take care of me. They ain't goin' to buy me clothes or feed me. I don't need to be nice to none of them 'cause they ain't goin' to give a damn about me."

Disregard for the feelings and, in fact, the very existence of others is a natural consequence of the increased value attached to "autonomy" in recent years. However perverse such an interpretation of autonomy may be, this is what seems to have occurred. The student of today is deeply unaware of the need to be cooperative with others, either students or teachers. He doesn't even seem to be in touch with being cooperative with himself; some students appear to be unconscious of their very actions.

To cite a typical example: In class the teacher appreciates some degree of attention to his statements. As he speaks, he is interrupted by the talking of a student. He may turn to tell the student to stop talking. Increasingly, the student will respond, "I wasn't talking." Sincerely and earnestly, he means it. The student literally has no recognition of the fact that he was indeed talking. Psychoanalytically, such denial has been seen as indicative of two facets of the personality functioning independently of and even at odds with one another. The side of the student which wants to hear the lesson replies with "I wasn't talking" when reprimanded by the teacher, although the latter was actually

seeking contact with the side of the student—the self—
which denied his presence and talked to his neighbor. Such
transgressions of class rules and lack of awareness of the
teacher's feelings is not always intended to provoke anger.
Very often the student's response will be, "But I was just
asking him for . . ." or "I was just handing her a . . ." or "He
has my . . ." and so forth. Such answers express that aspect
of the student's personality which excludes the teacher as
a significant object and therefore has no consciousness of
wrongdoing.

This process of excluding others without awareness of
its effect was originally described as narcissism by Freud
(1914) in a paper entitled "On Narcissism: An Introduction." He characterized it as a turning of one's power for
relating to the outside world with love (libido) back onto
oneself. Spotnitz (1972) offers a different interpretation. It
will be recalled that the myth of Narcissus concerns a
hunter who spurns the love of a wood nymph. The heart-
broken nymph invokes the gods to punish cruel Narcissus
by causing him to fall in love and have no love returned to
him. The gods hear the nymph's plea and punish Narcissus.
One day, after a particularly fatiguing hunt, Narcissus rests
on the shore of a beautiful lake. On gazing into the lake he
sees his own reflection; but not knowing it is his own image,
he presumes it to be a water nymph of surpassing beauty.
He pleads with the nymph to allow him to embrace her, but
each time he tries to grasp the lovely creature she disap-
pears. Narcissus remains, transfixed by his elusive image,
until he finally dies of starvation and thirst.

Spotnitz advances the interpretation that Narcissus,
rather than attack the frustrating image, turns his hatred
upon himself. Narcissus mistakenly believes that he is unworthy and starves in the attempt to make amends to a
cruel and unyielding object. This interpretation, applied
psychoanalytically, is essentially different from that of
Freud, who saw narcissism as the turning of love away from

the world and inward upon the self. By contrast, Spotnitz believes that narcissism represents hatred for the outside world, or object, that is not permitted expression. The narcissist fears the consequences if that hate is ever permitted to be discharged outwardly; that it will kill. The individual becomes incapable of relating to the outside world because of the hate that he fears will escape. Rather, he turns it inward upon the self and presents a confused and helpless image to the world. In the most extreme cases the narcissist attacks his own mind with such success that he renders himself psychotic and nonfunctional.

I propose that this mechanism goes far to explain the withdrawal and learning dysfunction that we observe in the contemporary ghetto classroom. As part and parcel of this narcissistic preoccupation of our students we also note the phenomenon of communal possession destructively expressed. Because of an extended family situation, in many instances, and the overcrowding in home, school and ghetto community, the child's ego boundaries are fluid. This demonstrates itself in the concept of nonpossession. Nothing that the child owns means anything to him. He accepts the loss of a coat or jacket with some regret, but this feeling soon fades under the normal pressure of everyday life.

The child will work for weeks on a shop project, yet when another member of the class accidentally drops and breaks it the owner of the destroyed piece will simply throw it away, seemingly dismissing the fruit of his labor without a second thought. A student complains about the ugly condition of the school building and is found a few minutes later writing his nickname on the desk with a felt marker; when asked why, he says, "Well, my name isn't the only one on the desk." When asked why he just punched in a stairwell windowpane he may reply, "It was broken already." This ubiquitous sense of possession is not the healthy communal property ownership known in some parts of the world. It is a mental attitude more on the order of, "If it's mine, I can destroy it."

These observations are not intended to expose or to deplore the atrocities committed against schools and teachers by destructive students. A much more critical result of the narcissism prevalent in the schools is the danger of losing our whole school system to it. For teachers are similarly infected. The teacher enters upon his career as relatively sane and as well balanced, presumably, as anyone else in the humanistic professions. But after a time he also undergoes a metamorphosis. For no teacher can be exposed to over 100 narcissistic personalities each day without some alteration in his character, and the degree of his frustration operates in direct ratio to the zeal with which he enters upon his task.

I have noted the transformations that teachers undergo in the public school system. The first stage of metamorphosis is the utter terror that overtakes each new teacher. The teacher feels as though he will die if he enters the building one more time. And, in fact, the teacher does either survive or die. By "die," I mean that he dies professionally; he leaves the ghetto school or the school system itself. If he survives, the metamorphosis has begun. The first sign is the shell that the teacher builds to protect himself. He becomes increasingly callous to experiences and events that would turn most peoples' stomachs. He appears deaf to curse words currently in vogue or obscenities coined for the occasion. He doesn't seem to be affected by fights or temper or any claim to compassion that the children make on him. He replaces sensitivities with a feeling of security in his job and his ability to do it each day.

Deeper changes occur in the ensuing years. The veteran teacher is a different person from the novice. Through his daily association with the students he has begun to change his modes of behavior. The veteran doesn't seem to be able to follow the simple tasks that are set for him. He finds it difficult, for example, to fill out his attendance sheet each month. For him, a job that should take about ten minutes ends up consuming the better part of a week. He can't complete the student records that have been given into his care. This job, which should take some hours, takes the teacher ten months to accomplish, if he does it at all. The teachers eventually show the same resistance as the children to doing required jobs. They hide from the assistant principals (APs) and cannot manage to get to class on time. They become the adult incarnation of the very resistances the children manifest to frustrate them. Why is this possible?

The children share the common syndrome called transference. This phenomenon occurs whenever two people are associated for any length of time. A views B as some early and significant figure in his life and deals with B in that manner whether or not B's behavior warrants it. This is plainly a loss of reality for A, the person with the transference. Our students develop transference problems with the teachers. They view the teacher as the parent counterpart. Since they can't be punished (starved, beaten, abandoned) by this teacher-parent, however, they have no fear of living out their wildest feelings in the classroom. They tune the teacher out and occupy themselves with their inner lives, which are many times more exciting than the real world. How does this affect the teachers?

The teacher has trouble at first in dealing with the feelings of being made to disappear. He feels he is losing his mind. Then he finds a solution. He develops countertransference reactions. Countertransference response is the teacher's reaction to being canceled out by the students, especially when the students ignore him as an individual. The teacher tends to let himself float along with the students' narcissistic preoccupations and thus loses sight of his own frustrating reality at times.

The student collective, in actively blocking out the anger it feels toward the harsh world, presents a confused and detached personality to the world outside. This onslaught on the teacher's sensitivity is too much after awhile. Involuntarily—sometimes spitefully—the teachers fall prey to the pounding that their minds and feelings have to take day in and day out. They join the students in their way of thinking; they become extensions of the childrens' narcissism. They often make life choices that are detrimental to their own best interests. I have seen young men buy houses that they can ill afford to maintain. I have seen grown men play childish pranks on one another during and after class; hardly a good example for the young minds that they are trying to shape. In fact, their own minds have been reshaped. In great numbers teachers try to escape the oppression that they feel through vacation travel. But, since they must return to the classroom the solution is shortlived.

Thus teachers and children both regress into the fun and games of fantasy. The teachers literally meet their students on the students' level. This is not a matter of choice. It is an insidious and largely unconscious process that takes place in one level of the system after another. First the teachers react to the children, then the APs react to the teachers and the children, then the principal reacts to the APs, the teachers, and the children, and finally the Community School Board, composed of the childrens' parents, reacts to all of them in the same way that the children do.

I offer no solution to the situation. It seems obvious that the condition must be corrected if there is to be any education in the schools. I feel, however, that the best answer would be some analysis or analytic group experience, for all teachers. Even under optimal circumstances this seems largely impractical. The best that can be hoped for, perhaps, is psychologically oriented education for the supervisors to enable them to relate to the teachers in a maturational mode. In this way we may get some adult teachers back into the community and the classrooms to deal with such problems closer to their source.

Chapter 3

DISCUSSION: NARCISSISM AND OTHER DETERMINANTS OF BEHAVIOR IN URBAN SCHOOLS

Samuel S. Rubin, Ph.D.

Readers who have worked with ghetto children will recognize the student-teacher interaction that Mr. Emanuel discusses in the preceding essay. Apathy and lack of relatedness, poor cooperation and motivation, absence of respect for the individuality and autonomy of others, as well as indifference and destructiveness toward property are typical reactions among ghetto students with whom teachers must deal. Similarly, the teacher's difficulty in reaching such students—the inability to affect the lives of those who do not want to or cannot relate—are common problems in modern American education.

The author employs Spotnitz's (1969; cf. Chapter 20) concept of narcissism as hatred turned upon the self, in contrast to Freud's concept of narcissism as libido turned back upon the ego, to explain his observations. According to Spotnitz, narcissism unconsciously intensifies when love objects are lost, and hatred for the outside world is not permitted expression due to fear of the consequences.

Spotnitz's theory of narcissism is similar to Freud's first theory of masochism (1905–19), in which masochism was seen as a transformation of sadism (Nagera, 1970). In the paper "Instincts and Their Vicissitudes," Freud (1915) formulated that "masochism is actually sadism turned round upon the subject's own ego." Freud's second formulation of masochism (1919–24) saw it as a regressive phenomenon deriving from an unconscious need for punishment. In the paper "A Child is Being Beaten" (1919), he describes this form of masochism: "It is not only a punishment for the forbidden genital relation, but also the regressive substitute for that relation, and from this latter source it derives the libidinal excitation which is from this time forward attached to it." Freud's third formulation of masochism (1924–37) was the theory of the death instinct. In this later conception, Freud also postulated primary as well as secondary masochism and distinguished the three forms of erotogenic, feminine, and moral masochism.

Although Spotnitz's formulation of narcissism is not identical with Freud's first theory of masochism, it is similar enough to warrant useful differentiation from it. In both theories—Freud's formulation of masochism and Spotnitz's theory of narcissism—anger and aggression are turned inward on the self. For Freud, however, masochism is the passive form of an instinctual drive (aggression), which was originally cruelty to an external object, transformed into a "passive instinct of cruelty" turned on the subject's own ego. For Spotnitz, the internalized hatred is also originally directed toward the outside world, but the hatred is turned against the self rather than the outside world not because of any transformation of instinctual energy but rather because the individual fears the consequences of discharging the aggression outwardly.

Rochlin's (1973) conception of narcissism, while related to Spotnitz's, seems more sophisticated. Whereas Freud's second formulation of narcissism, noted above, sees egocentric aims as opposing the social condition and narcissism serving as the regressive substitute for forbidden genital relations, Rochlin sees social needs as always operating, even in instances where people appear to "thrive on isolation." According to Rochlin, the injuries to self-esteem that occur due to loss of love objects can be repaired only through relationships with another. The narcissistic state, therefore, is one in which loss of self-esteem occurs and, here in some measure agreeing with Spotnitz, Rochlin concludes that aggression always issues as a result of damaged narcissism. The lowering of self-esteem which "mobilizes aggression" may result in aggression turned on the self and, as unrelieved aggression, further compromise self-esteem. This causes depression, a sense of self-defeat, and a "brittle indifference to others." Increasing demands are made on relationships to the point where the relationships themselves may be broken off because of the verbalized aggression, causing neurotic conflict and aborting social relationships. Thus, these two modern theorists both conclude that narcissism and aggression are related concepts.

Returning now to our discussion of Emanuel's observations, we note that he characterizes withdrawal and learning dysfunction as narcissistic mechanisms. No doubt there is some validity to this contention. The American black has internalized the concept of inferiority and has indeed suffered a consequent blow to his self-esteem and narcissism. But withdrawal and learning dysfunction in the ghetto schools cannot be understood only on this basis. Other issues, both socially and analytically relevant, also pertain.

The present writer and A. Pisciotto have examined some of the larger issues involving loss of self-esteem among blacks from a psychoanalytic point of view in a book entitled *Racial Interaction in School and Society* (1974). There we analyze the ways in which social and historical conditions determine the white man's attitude toward the black man and the black man's attitude toward himself, and the perpetuation of these attitudes due to the dependency of each group upon the other. Projected feelings of sexual superiority from one group to the other and feelings of inadequacy have attended black-white interactions over the several hundred years of this relationship in the United States. Such fantasies and feelings have their roots deep in Western civilization and have an historical existence in the institution of slavery in a country in which "all men are created equal."

> The interplay between the two groups—an interplay of projected fantasies of sexual superiority of one group toward the other and unconscious homoerotic feelings—has prevented men of both races from attaining a sense of adequacy. When inadequacy feelings and infantile fantasies come to the surface, anxiety is stimulated in both groups. It is difficult for both black and white men to face their feelings about themselves and the ways in which these feelings are projected onto the other group. (p. 41)

Thus the black man's self-esteem is damaged as part of the developmental process and both apathy and aggression result.

But injured narcissism is not the only reason for the expression of aggression:

> The black man, searching for a new position of independence and equality with reference to the white man, both economically and psychologically, must experience similar anxieties, fears, and perhaps even a yearning to return to the safer though noxious position of dependency. Let us look at what the black man must do in order to change his position in society. He must face and deal with those very conflicts about self-image, self-esteem and self-concept . . . particularly in connection with sexual stereotypes. He must face the challenges of adulthood. The old stereotypes and feelings must be dealt with, and changed. To confront these feelings

> must inevitably stimulate anxiety on the part of the black
> man not only because it is not a pleasant picture he must
> look at but also because there must be fear of not knowing
> where to turn to create a new image of himself. (p. 50)

Other issues which relate to the causes of learning dysfunction among blacks result from the very nature of our schools themselves and their failure to "educate" ghetto students. Professor Jencks (1969) of the Harvard Graduate School of Education takes the position that our schools fail minority groups because they do not teach minority groups such middle-class virtues as self-discipline and self-respect and not because they fail to teach subject matter. Silberman (1970), by contrast, proposes that the minority group child's failure to learn in school "produces the behavior problem of the slum school . . . and not the behavior problems that produce the failure to learn." Rubin and Pisciotto conclude, "In our opinion, it is fruitless to argue which is the cause and which is the effect. Probably both factors operate together." In any case, black students have failed to internalize many white middle-class standards which are taught in school and which are the basis for our educational system. The problem arises out of the social condition as well as psychological deprivation.

Another chronic problem noted by Emanuel is the deportment of students in the classroom. The white teacher frequently perceives the black student as gyrating, agitating, or physically provoking, disorderly, etc. What the white teacher is often unable to understand is that blacks often use nonverbal body language which to them is incomprehensible. While white children communicate nonverbally as well, they are more adept at verbal communication. And even when black students communicate verbally, cognitive problems arise between white teacher and black student. English for blacks is a different dialect from that used by middle-class, white teachers. Emanuel provides vivid examples of "black English." A number of studies have appeared recently by psychologists, educators, and students of linguistics on the nature of the language spoken by black people in the United States today. Many of these works see black English not as a corruption of English but as a valid dialect with a history and structure of its own. The fact that the languages of the two groups differ not only suggests one reason for the distance of the two groups but also symbolizes the psychological distance between the two groups.

Another issue in black failure in our schools is discussed in a growing body of literature on what is referred to as the self-fulfilling prophecy, the expectation of failure which most black students acquire early in their school education and which snowballs as they rise throughout the various school grades. Whiteman and Deutsch (1967) point out that social disadvantages associated with poverty often result in learning difficulties in the early grades. They go on to make a point that through

> early failure or difficulty in academic tasks, the child's self-confidence may be impaired so that learning becomes more difficult and unrewarding. A lower achievement level may even feed back on the development of the original abilities. In any case, lowered abilities may produce lower achievement, lower achievement may induce diminished self-confidence, which in turn feeds back upon the achievements, and so on. (p. 112)

Here again, one can notice the importance of self-esteem and the problems with self-esteem in the school behavior of blacks. Injured narcissism may well produce aggression which is turned on the self and which may create narcissistic withdrawal by the student.

But the sociological factors should not be ignored. It is the feedback process between the black student's expectation of failure and the white teacher's expectation that the black student will fail that creates problems in the teaching-learning process. According to Silberman, teachers communicate to the working-class child what the teacher himself expects the child to be, and these expectations become self-fulfilling prophecies. Lack of motivation to perform school tasks, environmental deprivation, poor language background, lack of relevant curriculum, and negative teacher expectations all contribute to the failure of the black child in school. Thus, to explain lack of interest in school on the basis of purely narcissistic withdrawal seems to oversimplify a very complex issue, although this by no means mitigates the importance of narcissistic withdrawal as a vital element in the process.

"The phenomenon of communal property destructively expressed" also understates the problem. To assume that property has no meaning due to "fluid ego boundaries" seems naïve. Lack of value for property might be better explained by a theory of narcissism in the following way: If feelings of inferiority or loss of self-esteem are narcissistic injuries and lead to aggression towards the self in relationships, the child who suffers narcissistic injury—that is, loss of self-esteem—may well treat objects (property) in the same way that he treats himself; aggressively, hostilely, and destructively. A child who impassively throws away an object on which he has worked for weeks when it gets broken by another child is not simply functioning as a product of extended family situations in overcrowded homes. He is also expressing the same lack of esteem for his possessions that he may feel for himself. He may also be discharging the same destructiveness in his attitude toward property that he internally feels for himself.

From an experiential and descriptive point of view, Emanuel graphically describes the process by which a new teacher approaches the ghetto situation and eventually becomes a hardened veteran. He explains the teacher's loss of interest and withdrawal as transference-countertransference phenomena, thus using this phrase—which is usually applied narrowly to psychoanalytic situations—in the broad sense that Meerloo and M. Nelson (1965) use it. According to Emanuel, the teacher then becomes the parent who cannot be punished. While this formulation may in part be true, and is certainly true for many white students, it ignores the larger social factors at work both in black student-white teacher interactions as well as other social forces which have been noted elsewhere (Rubin and Pisciotto, 1974). Emanuel's statement that the ghetto child lives out his wildest feelings in the classroom does not jibe with the theory he espouses, that narcissistic withdrawal is occasioned by "the fear of expressing aggression due to its consequences." If both of these conditions occur—which may well be true—he calls no attention to and offers no explanation of this paradox.

Nor is his description of what he refers to as a teacher countertransference (withdrawal by the teacher which parallels that of the students)—while poignant and familiar—an inevitable occurrence. White teachers such as Gloria Channon (1968, 1970) have written extensively on their work with black students, and the richness of their perceptions and creativity defy challenge. Silberman (1970) also stresses the responsibility of the white teacher's attitude toward the black student. According to Silberman, private schools in New York and Chicago are showing that ghetto blacks, with all their problems, can be motivated learners in school. The most important factor affecting black performance is the teacher's conviction that the student can learn and the teacher's full acceptance of responsibility for the student's learning. The veteran need not inevitably withdraw.

Not to underestimate the immensity of the problem confronted by the white teacher in a black ghetto school, it would seem to this writer that withdrawal might occur most severely with teachers psychologically predisposed to sustain narcissistic injuries in response to what they perceive as lack of interest, motivation, and success of black students. Teachers less narcissistically invested would undoubtedly be able to work within the framework of that harsh reality which is the ghetto school and bring to it some kind of creative answer to what outwardly appears as an impossible situation.

Psychoanalysis for all teachers seems like a panacea easily suggested but difficult to achieve; but in addition to understanding the psychodynamic, social, and historical problems involved in working with ghetto blacks, I would heartily agree that a teacher of such students must come to terms with the ways in which he invests his energies, his own narcissism, and his reactions to what are felt as narcissistic injuries. For what may often be experienced by individuals as narcissistic injuries may well result from historical and social conditions whose roots lie deep in the history of our country.

Part II

NARCISSISM: THEORIES AND THERAPIES

Chapter 4

NARCISSUS AS MYTH, NARCISSUS AS PATIENT

Hyman Spotnitz, M.D.

While searching for a proper vehicle for illustrating what it is like to work with an extremely narcissistic patient, I got to thinking about Narcissus himself. I refer, of course, to the handsome youth who, by pining away from love of his own reflection in a pool of water, assured himself of a permanent if somewhat fragmented existence in the annals of psychoanalysis. At the risk of appearing ungrateful to the source of one of our most felicitous terms, I began to wonder how he might function in the treatment relationship and how I might apply myself to help him resolve his problems. An account of the initial phase of this fantasied experience is presented here.

The reader may be startled by some of the facts that Narcissus divulged during the period on which this report is based—the 45 sessions that were conducted during his first year of treatment. Unlike the encounter itself, however, none of this information was spun out of my imagination. It was all recorded 2,000 years ago, in the earliest accounts rendered in the Classics of the life of Narcissus.

When I investigated these versions many years ago, in connection with an analysis of the myth (Spotnitz and Resnikoff, 1954) I discovered much information about Narcissus that was not reported by Ovid, whose *Metamorphoses* is the source of the story of Narcissus that has captured the fancy of generation after generation of schoolchildren, provided an object lesson for countless moralizers, and inspired great poets and other creative artists. The case history presented initially is based on this familiar version but encompasses other biographical data extracted from the relatively unknown versions.

PRELUDE TO THE ENCOUNTER

I received a phone call from a woman who asked if I would see her 16-year-old son, Narcissus. She was very concerned about him, she said, because he seemed suicidal to her. He had abandoned his usual activities and would have nothing to do with other people. He had lost interest in his friends, yet seemed to be languishing for love. He spent the whole day moping at home and would stand before the mirror making queer grimaces. She voiced fears that he would destroy himself and again asked with great anxiety if I would see him.

I immediately indicated that I was willing to see her son. I suggested that she ask him to call me himself and arrange for an appointment.

Narcissus phoned me a few days later. He said he would like to come in and talk to me. Would I have time to see him? I asked, "When would you like to come in?" He specified a time that was not available. I asked him to call again the following week to see if we could find a mutually convenient hour. After several similar attempts an appointment was set up, and the young man was given specific directions for getting to the office and finding my waiting room. He entered it 15 minutes after the appointed time and said that he had been wandering around the city searching for my office.

THE INITIAL INTERVIEW

Sitting down opposite me, Narcissus said that he had come in response to his mother's urging, not because he wanted help for himself. He was convinced that nobody could help him; he saw no hope for himself. "Nothing can be done for me," he said despondently. "I can't get my mind off myself. I am in great torment. I feel I am going to die."

He gave me a brief family history. He had always lived with his mother; he knew very little about his father; there were rumors that his parents had not been on speaking terms; his mother never talked about his father. Narcissus thought his father might be dead, but was not certain about it. His mother, aside from being very worried about him, seemed to be in good health.

I asked him whether, in view of her worries about him, he would be willing to come to the office once a week so that I could relieve his mother's anxiety. After a period of indecision, Narcissus agreed to come once a week.

Narcissus was asked when he would be willing to lie on the couch. He agreed to do so immediately if that was desirable.

On the couch he talked freely about his misery. He couldn't eat; he couldn't sleep. He had terrible thoughts and frightening dreams. He felt that he was about to die. As a matter of fact, at times he felt that he was already dead. He was very concerned with his horrible feelings. Over and over again he mentioned how unpleasant it was to be thinking about himself all the time and to be suffering from such thoughts and feelings.

The thoughts that disturbed him also seemed to disturb his mother, he said. When I asked why his mother was disturbed, he replied that she had always made a great fuss over him. He didn't care about her very much. She was not very important to him at the present time. What really concerned him was himself.

At the end of the interview, Narcissus asked if he had conducted himself well on the couch.

I rejoined, "Do you think I performed well during this interview?"

The question seemed to surprise him. The idea that I figured in the situation was apparently far from his mind. He was supposed to be doing all the talking.

NARCISSUS ANSWERS SOME QUESTIONS

In the course of his first year in treatment, the youth continued to talk about his woeful state. Despite his gloom he made no demands on me and frequently seemed oblivious to my presence. Had he been permitted to go on talking without making any attempt to establish verbal contact with me, I suspected that he would have become psychotic and have had to be hospitalized. To prevent further regression, I interrupted his monotonous monologue in each session by interposing a few questions. These interventions had nothing to do with his own ego functioning; they directed attention to other persons and external realities. And each of these object-oriented questions (Spotnitz, 1975) was geared to a subject he had just referred to.

In the third session, for example, when Narcissus mentioned that he had not touched his lunch that day, he was asked to describe the meal his mother had prepared. He wasn't particularly interested, he replied, but if I really wanted to know he would tell me. I also asked how his mother had reacted to his not eating lunch.

Questions about his contacts with other people or about his daily routines annoyed Narcissus. He said that he did not see how they would help to relieve his misery.

Other interchanges are reported below in the sequence in which they occurred.

In the tenth session, when he talked repetitively about his preoccupations, I asked him if his mother questioned him about them. Often she tried to get him to talk about them, he said, and this made him very angry.

HS. When did she start worrying about you?

Nar. Before I was born, probably the very moment she found out that she was pregnant. I am the product of a rape. The attitude I sense in her is that the offspring of her chance encounter with someone she hated and never saw again is bound to end up badly.

HS. How does she demonstrate her anxiety?

Nar. I've already told you how terribly upset she gets when I am absorbed in myself.

HS. Why does this upset her?

Nar. How should I know? But I've heard that she took me to Tiresias—you know, the famous oracle—and asked him if I would live to a ripe old age. He answered in his usual cryptic way. All he told her was that her son would have a long life "if he ne'er know himself" (Ovid, p. 149).

HS. What did Tiresias mean?

Nar. How do I know? I was just a baby at the time and don't recall anything about the incident. I'm only telling you what Ovid wrote about it. I don't even know if my mother understood what Tiresias meant. She hasn't talked about that; she just nags me about keeping to myself.

In the eighteenth session, Narcissus complained that his mother persisted in her efforts to get him involved with people. He was becoming known as proud and heartless, she told him. But he couldn't care less if that was his reputation, he said. He had good reason to keep to himself. Experience had taught him to shun close relationships because they always led to trouble.

HS. What kind of trouble?

Nar. Various kinds. Particularly with girls who find me

sexually exciting. I'm indifferent to them and wish they'd leave me alone. Being physically attractive is a real curse. I don't understand why my mother, of all persons, doesn't recognize the risks involved. So I try to avoid girls.

HS. Have any girls sought you out?

Nar. One tricked me into a meeting one day. But why waste time talking about it?

HS. What trouble did she give?

Nar. Well, if you insist, I'll tell you what happened. She was a wood nymph, a total stranger who came upon me when I was hunting with several other boys. Without any encouragement—I didn't even know she was there—she fell in love with me. She pursued me silently until I got separated from the other boys and began shouting to help them locate me. Each time I called, "Let us join one another," I heard an answering "join one another." These answers became so clear that I thought my companions were getting closer. But just as I expected to see them, the nymph suddenly rushed toward me from a clump of trees and tried to fling herself into my arms. Infuriated by this trickery, I pushed her away and told her sternly, "Hands off! embrace me not! May I die before I give you power o'er me!" (Ovid, pp. 151–152)

Hs. How did she respond to this rebuff?

Nar. It seemed to stun her. All she could say was "I give you power o'er me!" Then she turned away in shame and ran into the woods to hide. I spurned her so roughly because I felt that she had deliberately deceived me. I learned later that she was Echo, and that she had lost the power to speak freely. (According to Ovid, the nymph had prevented Juno from discovering her husband disporting himself with Echo's friends by wagging her tongue long enough for the party to break up. When the goddess found out why Echo was holding her up with idle chatter, Juno punished her for this mischief. The nymph has been reduced to repeating the last words she hears.) Since my meeting with her, she has been hiding in the woods. They say she is wasting away there and is still in love with me.

HS. Who says that?

Nar. I'm just repeating what Ovid reported.

HS. Has she made an effort to meet you again?

Nar. That one meeting should have been enough for her. Let her wither away in her lonely cave and forget me! Or she can go on wailing for me as long as she has a voice.

In the twenty-third session, Narcissus said that treatment hadn'd helped him get his mind off himself. A girl had invited him to a party that week, actually pleaded with him to come. He could not convince her that he did not want to come and had finally hung up the phone on her. She was as persistent as Echo, and he did not feel responsible for his rudeness. "After all," he continued "I could have treated Echo as my father treated my mother, but I didn't harm her in any way. I don't accept blame for her plight."

HS. Who blames you?

Nar. Well, she gets an awful lot of sympathy from other girls. More than she deserves. But it's easy for them to identify with her.

HS. Why do they identify with her?

Nar. I've scorned them too. Any girl who tries to waylay me lives to regret it.

HS. Have any boys annoyed you?

Nar. A little. Some boys take it for granted that, since I have no use for girls, I'm fair play for a homosexual relationship. I've had to teach them to keep their distance.

HS. How do they react to your rejection?

Nar. More aggressively than girls. They're more persistent, too. And when I finally convince them that I am totally indifferent, they seek revenge.

HS. What kind of revenge?

Nar. Why talk about it? No one has threatened me directly. All of this is hearsay. Some say that two of the youths I rejected pleaded with the gods to avenge them.

HS. How did they do that?

Nar. One suitor whose passion left me cold lifted his hands toward heaven and prayed, "So may he himself love and not gain the thing he loves!" (Ovid, p. 153) I don't know why Ovid referred to his prayer as "righteous" or how he learned that Nemesis heard it.

HS. Who was that youth?

Nar. I don't remember his name. Many fools have courted me.

HS. Who was the other youth?

Nar. Amenias. He made so many advances that I was never able to forget him. The only way I got rid of him was to get him to commit suicide. I sent him a sword to help him do it. But I didn't expect him to do it so dramatically.

HS. How did he kill himself?

Nar. With my sword, of course. And right in front of my house. He called on the gods to avenge him and blood-ied my doorstep. What a commotion!

HS. Did the death of Amenias upset you?

Nar. Not at all, and I don't know how people got that impression. Probably from Conon's report of the incident (Smith, 1904). He wrote that I was tormented by repent-ance for Amenias as well as by love of myself, and that I eventually ended this double torment by killing myself.

HS. Did anyone else report that you killed yourself?

Nar. A stupid question! Surely you know that death wishes have been directed to me since the moment I was conceived. Probos wrote that I was killed by one of the male suitors I spurned (Smith); but people are more fascinated by Ovid's theory. But why do you keep on asking me what other people say about me? You can see that reports of my death are false. Asking me to repeat them doesn't reduce my suffering. What are you up to?

In the thirty-second session, Narcissus said that in his mind he had been talking to me all week long, and this made it harder to find something to talk about when he

came to the office. Deciding what to talk about first when
he had many things on his mind was another problem. His
mother had upbraided him when she caught him looking at
himself. He was sick of being told that he was wearing out
the mirror. To escape her sharp tongue, he decided to get
out of the house. Some boring neighbors tried to draw him
into silly conversations, but as quickly as he could he made
for a quiet grove in the park where no one would disturb
him. There was a pleasant pool where he had often
quenched his thirst after a long walk. The water was cool
and unruffled. On that last visit, he had spent several hours
stretched out on the grass and just looking at his own
reflection. That was the only place where no one intruded
upon his misery.

HS. Has anyone else described the place?

Nar. Aren't you satisfied with my description? I've
been there many times. If you insist on confirming it, read
Ovid. He wrote quite a bit about it and identified it as the
spot where I became so preoccupied with my reflection that
I could not eat or rest. At least Ovid credits me with doing
a thorough job of obliterating myself, even my body. No
traces of it could be found by those who wanted to brandish
torches at my bier. I deprived them of the pleasure of
giving me a funeral. All that they found was a little white
flower, and that was why they gave it my name.

HS. Did Ovid identify what you were gazing at in the
pool?

Nar. He implied that I was gazing at my own reflection,
but he did not say that I recognized it immediately as my
own image. Other reports of my alleged death at the pool
challenge that notion.

HS. Who challenged it?

Nar. Come off it! Must I spend the whole session telling you what other writers imagined? I'll just give you an
illustration of the far-fetched theories they came up with.
Pausanias ridiculed the idea that I saw my own reflection in

the water and unconsciously fell in love with myself. Pausanias repeated another story: that I was mourning the death of a twin sister with whom I had fallen in love and who looked very much like me. So much so that I could imagine I was seeing her when I gazed at my own reflection. And I did this to alleviate my grief (Pausanias).

HS. What did your sister die of?

Nar. Have I mentioned having a sister? Why do you bother me with these stupid questions? If you think that they will help me get my mind off myself, I can tell you that it won't work. I don't care what they say about me.

In the forty-third session, Narcissus complained that he was getting nowhere in treatment. He had given me the information I asked for, but this was not helping him. He still suffered intensely, and was as preoccupied with himself as he had ever been.

HS. I haven't done anything for you yet.

Nar. Why haven't you? Are we just wasting time? Why should I go on talking here if nothing will be accomplished?

HS. Have you asked me to do anything for you?

Nar. (after a brief silence) Come to think of it, I haven't asked you for anything yet.

HS. Then what am I supposed to do?

Nar. I guess I didn't ask for anything because I was sure you couldn't help me. So what's the good of asking for anything?

HS. What then is the purpose of your coming here?

Nar. Perhaps I've been coming just to prove that nothing can be done to help me.

HS. What a success! But now that you've proved I can't do anything for you, where do we go from here?

Nar. Can you really do something for me?

HS. What should I do for you?

Nar. Help me accomplish something. I'd like to do something worthwhile in this world.

HS. How am I supposed to help you do that?

Nar. I'm not interested in telling you how to do your job. If you really don't know how to help me, ask your own analyst. A competent doctor knows how to treat a patient. You're just a bastard!

HS. I know how to treat you, but I want your impressions, even your guesses.

Nar. I hate you too much to help you in any way.

THE ANALYST'S IMPRESSIONS

The first year of my fantasied encounter with Narcissus was accompanied by highly contradictory impressions of the youth.

He seemed at first to be a mild and gentle personality who was completely wrapped up in himself. His vague appeal for help in mastering this problem and his air of resignation were as charming as his appearance. His excessive gratitude for mere audience and his failure to make demands served to convey this message: I am the helpless victim of a cruel destiny, defended against whatever buffeting I may be exposed to only by my ability to love myself. This theme was adhered to, though elaborated somewhat differently each time he returned to the couch. It seemed endless and each repeat made it duller to listen to. I became aware that my initially sympathetic attitude was being diluted with impatience as I waited for new themes— progression.

The appealing demeanor that I observed at the beginning of our relationship gradually eroded as Narcissus was questioned about other people. I was shocked to discover the resentments, anger, and rage that slumbered behind his attractive facade. In our interchanges, as I have illustrated, he demonstrated great pleasure in provoking hostility, and in damaging other people and himself. He unconsciously fought against revealing this secret—the gratification he derived from being an agent of destruction —by appearing to be completely absorbed in himself.

I also observed that the more annoyed he became when I questioned him about other people, the more freely he talked about them. And the more freely he expressed his anger, the less preoccupied he became with thoughts of suicide. As his rage was deflected from himself to others, he became more murderous.

As the year ended, Narcissus impressed me as a youth whose past experience had filled him with hate. Although he utilized self-preoccupation to hide this hate, actually he liked to express it by exciting others and provoking them into violent behavior.

When I recognized what he was really like, I experienced great annoyance and anger. When I thought that I might be mobilized to an act of violence, I experienced strong anxiety. At such times, I thought it would be better for both of us if the encounter were terminated forthwith.

This frequent temptation was outweighed, however, by the determination to change Narcissus. I was resolved to help him master his tendencies to destroy himself and to engage in the destruction of others (Spotnitz, 1969). His exciting beauty could then be used to promote his own best interests while giving unalloyed pleasure to many people.

THERAPEUTIC PRINCIPLES

The first year of the hypothetical case reported here illustrates the author's initial approach to a patient functioning on the preoedipal level. The interventions described are encompassed in the theory of the technique that I refer to as "modern psychoanalysis." The sequence of events that unfold when treatment of the schizophrenic patient is conducted in this way has been schematized as ten discrete steps (Spotnitz, 1969). These psychodynamic developments, which usually overlap, are outlined below in the chronological order in which they began.

The relationship with Narcissus was structured to permit the youth to attach to the analyst feelings that he developed for himself and others during the process of ego formation. In other words, the analyst's interventions in the first phase of the case favored the development and silent analysis of a narcissistic transference (step 1).

The origin and history of the youth's attempts to establish contact with the analyst were studied. The responses to the patient's so-called contact functioning were motivated primarily by the need to control the intensity of his immediate resistance to progressive communication (step 2).

The analyst, as narcissistic-transference object, typically experiences strong feelings of anxiety, anger, and annoyance. Acting on these feelings would make it impossible to preserve and consolidate the tenuous relationship with a preoedipal patient like Narcissus. The recognition and silent study of the analyst's narcissistic countertransference resistance (step 3), as indicated, were engaged in throughout the fantasied encounter. The application of this therapeutic principle is not limited to the early phase of a case; it is, rather, a general guide.

Similarly, the effective influencing of narcissistic transference by joining or reflecting the patient's attempts to get in contact with the analyst (step 4) continues through subsequent phases of the case.

The steps mentioned above are illustrated in my description of the initial interview and interchanges that occurred during the first year of the treatment of Narcissus. Assuming that this treatment were continued, the next operation would be the working through of his narcissistic transference resistance (step 5). This would involve processes of liberating him from his tendencies to be self-preoccupied and his unwillingness to give the analyst responsibility for effecting significant change, and resolving his resistance to discharging hostile feelings in language.

Having been helped to re-experience the emotional charge of his earliest object relations, Narcissus would then begin to relate to the analyst more consistently as a separate and distinct object (step 6). The analyst studies the object transference—that is, the regular oedipal-type transference. (The term "object transference" is commonly used in modern psychoanalysis to differentiate this phenomenon from "narcissistic transference," in which the analyst is related to as part of the self or like the self.) The ensuing events would adhere more closely to the basic model of psychoanalytic technique. However, occasional backsliding into his narcissistic maneuvers would probably be observed, challenging the analyst to resort again to the type of interventions that were therapeutically effective earlier in the case.

Predictably, with the establishment of object transference, the analyst would at times be related to as the mother of Narcissus; at other times he would be related to as the father the youth had never known. There would also be occasions when the analyst would be related to as an infant while Narcissus behaved as though he were his own parent.

As he studied these transference manifestations, it would be incumbent on the analyst to recognize and investigate his countertransference resistance (step 7). When serving in the father role, the analyst might be inclined to attack, ignore, or respond indifferently to Narcissus. In the mother role, the analyst might feel timid, fearful, or seductive. Complementary feelings might be induced. Thus, when related to as the infant who was abandoned by his father, the analyst might feel hungry for affection and eager for contact. Or he might feel sleepy, self-preoccupied, or non-communicative when Narcissus behaved like his own mother.

Eventually, the object transference resistance would be interpreted and the patient would be helped to work it through (steps 8 and 9). In the process the self-gratifying and mutually gratifying operations that dominated the earlier stages of the case would be sacrificed, giving way to the search for understanding. Narcissus would demonstrate more positive attitudes towards others, and become a more outgoing person. He might fall in love with a woman and discuss the possibility of marrying her. Since his parents had not married, he would communicate great anxieties about committing himself to the marital state.

The resolution of resistance to termination of the analytic relationship (step 10) would complete the sequence of events.

To conclude: In explaining, all too briefly, the rationale of the interventions illustrated in the fantasied encounter and the therapeutic principles that would have guided that hypothetical case to its conclusion, I have incorporated findings that a comparative study of the Narcissus myths helped me to formulate. When the results of that study were reported (Spotnitz and Resnikoff, 1954), my experience with schizophrenic patients had already suggested, despite the traditional linkage of the illness with self-love, that the primary problem to be worked on in these cases is internalized aggression. After assembling sufficient clinical evidence to confirm that impression, a working hypothesis and operational principles were formulated to help these patients achieve emotional maturity (Spotnitz, 1969). Inasmuch as that early study of different versions of the story of Narcissus contributed to these developments, it seemed appropriate to draw upon the myths for symbolic representation of schizophrenia.

Chapter 5

THE NARCISSISTIC COURSE

Ben Bursten, M.D.

I

A previous paper of mine (Bursten, 1973b) distinguished four types of narcissistic personalities—the craving, paranoid, manipulative, and phallic narcissists. While these personality types do not appear in pure form, I have seen sufficient numbers of people who exhibit predominantly the features of one or another of these types to justify separating them into these diagnostic categories. When we examine this array of personalities from the point of view of sensuality we see a progression from the oral emphasis of cravers through the anal and anal-phallic emphases of paranoid and manipulative personalities to the mainly phallic features of the phallic narcissists.[1]

---

1. I prefer Klein's (1969) term "sensual" to the more commonly used words "sexual" or "instinctual." This represents a departure from my previous paper in both my terminology and my thinking.

The same paper suggested that early in life, certain people embark on a course which will lead them to become narcissistic personalities. The particular type they will become rests partly on the vicissitudes of their sensual development, partly on the degree of their self-object differentiation, and partly on the values of their families. In that study, I put forth the view that the array of narcissistic personality types represents a continuum, blending at the more primitive end with the borderline personality and at the more advanced end with what I call "complementary personalities" organized around the Oedipus complex. That view will be modified in the present paper.

Now, when I suggest that early in life certain people embark on a narcissistic course, I am approaching the subject from the point of view of development. And, since much of what I have to say will be an attempt to describe what goes on in the mind of the infant, it can only be speculative; direct observation is of limited help. It is here where psychoanalytic data are of great value. But it is here, also, where two types of assumptions must be made explicit. First, there are the assumptions underlying the genetic point of view (Hartman and Kris, 1945; Rapaport and Gill, 1959) which assert that the psychological condition of the adult rests in great part on her/his maturational and psychosocial history. Second, there are the assumptions underlying reconstruction (Freud, 1937; Ekstein and Rangell, 1961; Novey, 1968, pp. 41ff) which assert that the psychic material available to the analyst today can give rise to an accurate portrayal of the psychic contents of some forgotten yesterday. In some instances, such as with affect-laden early events, direct observation can be helpful. Thus, a theory based on reconstruction of specific types of events, such as tonsillectomies at age five, can be supported by seeing the effects such tonsillectomies have on other children. Theories having to do with reconstruction of parental attitudes are harder to support because such attitudes may be more difficult to detect in our direct samples of other families. And other very early mental events such as degrees of self-object confusion, are reconstructed only on the basis that these states do occur and are reportable in older patients and that they make a kind of reasonable sense in our understanding of development, but they are not amenable to direct verification in the very young infant. Nonetheless, despite the necessity for making these assumptions and the limits on our ability to verify our theory, conceptualization of the developmental course leading to the narcissistic personalities can have both heuristic and clinical value.

I shall set the stage for such a conceptualization by referring to other formulations of the events leading to predominantly narcissistic character patterns. From the standpoint of sensual development, it seems to me that there are three possible views of the narcissistic course. The first is that of a theory of developmental arrest of the oral stage. We can dismiss this one immediately. I have never seen a purely oral character; they do not exist. Even these people who have predominantly oral traits show some characteristics of other stages as well. The array of narcissistic personalities I have described in my previous paper indicates that narcissists undergo sensual development beyond the oral stage.

More consistent with the clinical data is the role of orality described by Abraham in 1924a. In this paper he developed the view that subsequent libidinal (sensual) stages may be "built upon the ruins of an oral erotism whose development has miscarried." In this view, then, while there is no developmental arrest, a narcissistic course might be set by a failure of a satisfactory oral resolution, so that oral conflicts leave their imprint on subsequent development. This view has been expanded by Erikson's (1950, pp. 44ff) discussion of epigenetic development. Essentially, this view posits a specific narcissistic course charted by the fate of infantile orality and its associated modes of relating to the world.

However, in another paper Abraham (1925) suggested a different view. Following Alexander (1923), he concluded that "the definitive character developed in each individual is dependent on the history of his Oedipus complex." This view emphasizes regression. While it does not overlook the importance of earlier sensual stages, the implication is that their impact is to serve as points to which, in Abraham's terms, the libido regresses when the Oedipal problems are unresolved.

The concept of libido has given rise to another formulation of the narcissistic course—"the transformation of object libido into narcissistic libido." (Freud, 1923, p. 30). This formulation, emerging from Freud's classic papers in 1912 and 1914, separates two lines of instinctual development: those instincts which aim for relationships with differentiated objects and those which are aimed toward the self or objects which represent the self. The latter is the narcissistic libido. According to Kohut (1966), there are two lines of development of narcissism from the cathexis of an undifferentiated self-object (primary narcissism)—the vicissitudes of the cathexis of the narcissistic self (later called "grandiose self" (Kohut, 1971) and the vicissitudes of the cathexis of the idealized parent imago. As Kohut (1971) traces these pathways, there is considerable emphasis on the cohesion and stability of the self and the degree of its differentiation from objects. However, it is important to keep in mind that in this formulation, narcissistic libido is a type of instinctual energy; it "does not refer to the target [self or object representation] of the instinctual investment" (Kohut, 1971, p. 39n).

Kohut (1971, p. 220) postulates "two separate and largely independent developmental lines." The first, corresponding to Freud's (1914) line "leads from autoerotism to narcissism to object love." This line, as Kohut states, roughly corresponds to Mahler's (1967) progression "from autism to symbiosis to individuation." It also corresponds to Jacobson's (1964, chapters 3 and 4) description of self and object development during infancy. There are differences in emphasis, however. Kohut emphasizes the libidinal development while Mahler and Jacobson emphasize the structural aspects of self-object differentiation both in a transactional and intrapsychic sense. Kohut's second line of development "leads from autoerotism via narcissism to higher forms and transformation of narcissism." This separate line of development, not resulting in object love, would be the course traveled by narcissistic personalities.

These formulations postulate the earliest state to be that of primary narcissism (Kohut, 1971, pp. 63f; Jacobson, 1964, p. 15) with the subsequent narcissistic events being secondary. Balint (1968, Part II) takes a different view. Starting with primary (object) love, development proceeds to the two-person situation which may give rise to a "basic fault" (pp. 18ff). This is conceived of as a deficiency state arising from a lack of fit between the neediness of the child and the ability of the milieu to care for these needs. This can result in themes which we will recognize as belonging to narcissistic personalities:

> It is definitely a two person relationship in which, however, only one of the partners matters; his wishes and needs are the only ones that count and must be attended to; the other partner, though felt to be immensely powerful, matters only in so far as he is willing to gratify the first partner's needs and desires or decides to frustrate them; beyond this, his personal interests, needs, desires, wishes, etc. simply do not exist. (p. 23)

Finally, I shall consider one other narcissistic line—that presented by Bibring (1953) and discussed by Rapaport (1959a). This is a line of narcissistic aspirations on which self-esteem depends. While Rapaport maintained that Bibring's formulation is an "important step toward specifying the conception of autonomous ego development" it is clear that his line is closely attached to the epigenesis of zonal sensuality. On the earliest level, there is the need to get or have supplies which sustains self-esteem; later, mastery and the wish to be good bolster the self-esteem; and still later there is the wish to be admired, to be the center of attention, and to win competitively.

These formulations run the gamut of the uses of the term "narcissism" described by Pulver (1970). If we consider Kernberg's (1970) description of narcissistic personalities—"an unusual degree of self-reference in their interaction with other people," a great need for supplies and oral rage when they are disappointed, grandiosity and the need to be admired, and a coldness in their relationships with others which he traced to a "defensive fusion of the ideal self, ideal object, and actual self-images"—we can see the persistence of the features of several developmental lines in the character of the narcissistic personality. Our task, then, is to describe a course of development which takes these various formulations into consideration, and which gives us some basis for understanding the differences between narcissistic and other types of personalities. In addition, I hope to throw some further light on the role of sensuality in the various personality types.

II

Rapaport (1959b) noted that psychoanalytic theory is rooted in empirical observation. The subject matter is behavior which is "broadly defined and includes feeling and thought as well as overt behavior." Theory is inferential and may exist at different levels depending on the distance from the observables. Along similar lines—but resulting in a different theoretical position—Klein (1969) wrote about

"Freud's two theories of sexuality." One is a clinical theory which relates various experiences of the individual. The other is a translation of this clinical theory into a "quasi-physiological . . . model of an energic force that 'seeks' discharge." Fifty years earlier Freud (1914) had made the same point. While he did not shrink from speculating about "ego-libido," he acknowledged that "these ideas are not the foundation of science, upon which everything rests: that foundation is observation alone. They are not the bottom but the top of the whole structure, and they can be replaced and discarded without damaging it."

Of the formulations of the narcissistic course which I have reviewed, those resting on oral sensuality, self-object differentiation and self-esteem, are, I believe, on the level of clinical theory, closely related to observables. Narcissistic libido, and with it the concept of primary narcissism (or primary love) requires a much higher order of inference, and I propose to set both these concepts aside.

The experience of oral sensuality is readily available to most of us in our adult life. Although the role we assign to it in infancy is largely inferential (reconstructed), that role can be supported by direct observation of sucking behavior in the infant.

Observation of the different degrees of self-object differentiation come directly from our psychotic patients who report their confusion to us. We see transitory episodes of boundary blurring also in the analysis of narcissistic personalities. One patient was not certain if he were moving his arm or mine; another felt that our minds were one. Dreams of mystical union and merging have been reported by several of my patients. Outside the analytic situation, dreaming and hypnagogic states afford us all the opportunity to experience self-object confusion. While the direct data we get from observing children may not be quite so clear as in the case of oral sensuality, it is reasonable to infer that the infant may likewise experience various degrees and qualities of self-object differentiation.

Experiences of the importance of self-esteem and its regulation hardly need documentation here. Feelings of pride and shame, of self-importance and diminished worth are common both in our analytic patients and in everyday life. Whether the very young infant experiences self-esteem fluctuations, as implied by Bibring (1953), is a matter of theoretical inference; they are difficult to support by direct observation of preverbal infants, although they are easily seen in somewhat older children.

It is on the basis of observables such as these, then, that my formulation of the narcissistic course will be built. When we come to the concept of narcissistic libido, however, we have no observables. No one has ever felt libido or experienced it. It is not a mental phenomenon; it is a concept used in an attempt to understand mental phenomena. It is significant in this regard that while we may speak to our patients about oral sensuality, self-object confusion, and self-esteem, we do not talk with them about their narcissistic libido; they would not know what we were talking about.

Joffe and Sandler reviewed the relationship between narcissism and the libido concept in 1967. They, too, emphasized clinical observables. While retaining the energy concept, they suggested that it is of diminished usefulness in the approach to narcissism. "We would suggest that the clinical understanding of narcissism and its disorders should be explicity oriented towards a conceptualization in terms of a metapsychology of affects, attitudes, values, and the ideational contents associated with these." Similarly, Pulver (1970) has discussed the many problems we encounter when we employ the drive concept of narcissism.

The concept of narcissistic libido is tautological in the manner that Holt (1967) has described the libido concept in general: "The only data by means of which it can be assessed are the very ones it is invoked to explain." For example, hypochondriacal concern is "explained" by narcissistic libido, and it is cited as data from which the concept is inferred. The same situation obtains for the relationship between narcissistic libido and seeing objects as extensions of one's self. Thus, narcissistic libido is not useful as an explanatory concept.

For these reasons, I shall not employ the concept of narcissistic libido. How, then, can we deal with hypochondriasis or objects related to as extensions of the self?

Phenomena such as hypochondriasis are in themselves observables. We can bring them into the narcissistic fold by talking about an interest in the self, a preoccupation with the self, a focus of attention on the self, etc. These are phenomena which our patients (and we) are capable of experiencing. There are no energic implications in these terms—no different types or quantities of energy, no energy transformations or regressions, concepts such as fusion, neutralization etc.

Relating to objects as extensions of the self is also something we can easily observe, as when we swell with pride at the accomplishments of our children. I believe this is related to the psychology of possessiveness, the anal sensual underpinnings of which are well known (Abraham, 1921). However, from the standpoint of self-object differentiation, there is a dilemma, because while the relationship is as one might relate to part of her/himself, the object is perceived as a separate object. The economic conceptualization, which I do not hold, is that this object is invested with narcissistic libido. Rose (1966) has suggested that early self-object blurring is retained, presumably unconsciously, while the blurring does not extend into normal waking consciousness. I shall return to this topic in the next section of this chapter.

Now, with regard to primary narcissism, it is generally accepted that the very young infant has no conception of inner versus outer or self versus object. It is this primitive state which is usually called "primary narcissism." Various objections to the usage of this concept have been raised by

Balint (1968, pp. 61ff), Pulver (1970), and Jacobson (1954), although in 1964 (p. 15), Jacobson chose to retain the term but without its usual conceptual reference.

Technically, primary narcissism does not refer to a state of self-object undifferentiation. It refers (Freud, 1940) to a very early state of the ego "in which at first the whole available quota of libido is stored up. . . . It lasts until the ego begins to cathect the ideas of objects with libido, to transform narcissistic libido into object libido." Since I have set aside the concept of narcissistic libido, such a concept of primary narcissism has lost its meaning. The boundaryless state can stand as a concept in its own right, without narcissistic implications. While it is probably true that in this state, "the infant is as yet unaware of anything but his own experiences of tension and relief, of frustration and gratification" (Jacobson, 1964, p. 15), this awareness is not narcissistic, for the infant has no locus (inner or outer) of these experiences. In the mind of the infant, these are experiences, if you will, but not "his" experiences.

What I conceptualize, then, is development from a boundaryless state to the infant's very early, tentative fluctuating conceptualization of inner and outer, self and object. To the degree that this infant can organize any interest or focus on self and object we may then begin to speak of narcissism. I believe that this does away with the questions raised by Balint (1968) about whether there is primary narcissism or primary (object) love. Neither is primary, and when boundary does begin to develop the infant has developed the capacity for both simultaneously.

III

Having set aside the concept of energy, I can no longer define narcissism in terms of the nature of the instinctual charge (Kohut, 1971, p. 26) or even in terms of the cathexis of the self (Hartmann, 1950) and "self-objects." Instead, I shall define it simply as an interest in (or focus on) the self. Narcissistic personalities have a very intense interest in their selves—so much so that they often can see others only as extensions of themselves, or existing for the purpose of serving themselves. With this definition in mind, we can rephrase the question of the narcissistic course. We can ask, "Why do these people need to have so high an interest in themselves?" Perhaps the answer is that they cannot take themselves—their selves—for granted; they constantly need to confirm their selves.

What I am discussing, lies, I believe, in the realm of experience—conscious in the young infant and often subliminal in the adult. It is the sense of self, a feeling of integrity and adequate differentiation from the environment, and a feeling of historical continuity so that—as one psychotic woman put it—"Today, I am the same person who had this other experience [some time ago] . . . it happened to *me.*" Further, there is the sense of the self as actor —a feeling of volition, and a sense of sharpness of consciousness. I believe that the abilities which underlie these various feelings are all intimately related (Bursten, 1973, p. 73). A borderline patient reflected on the change in her sense of self from when she had been feeling poorly: "Now I can do something. I think of it and I go ahead and do it. [Before], I couldn't get it into focus. It was like there were a lot of things, but nothing was clear."

Kohut (1971, pp. 15ff and 152f) has emphasized the importance of the cohesiveness of the self and the danger of fragmentation. To the degree that this refers to the realm of experience, it is very similar to what I call the sense of self. However, this sense of self must be distinguished from the self-representation (Sandler and Rosenblatt, 1962). The latter term, although it would include the sense of self, refers also to other aspects of selfhood such as identity, evalutation of the self, goals, ambitions, etc. Self-representation answers such questions as "Am I good?" "Am I adult?" "Am I a member of the group?" etc. Sense of self answers the more basic question "Am I?" or "Is there an I?"

The mirror has many uses in psychology, myth, and metaphor (Shengold, 1974). The significance of the mirror described by Elkisch (1957) illustrates the basic question of the sense of self—"Am I?" It is a reflection of the soul, the essential being. A middle-aged woman whom I would classify as borderline and whose symptomatology well fit Hoch and Polatin's (1949) description of pseudoneurotic schizophrenia, recounted her experiences on getting divorced. She felt lost and bewildered. She felt alienated from everyone—there was no possible way that she could relate to them because she did not feel anchored. "This is going to sound stupid," she told me, "but for about a week I wanted to look in the mirror but I couldn't. I was too scared. I was afraid I wouldn't see anyone in there."

Now, in this example, the mirror image was not herself (her soul); it was a reflection of the existence of her self. She was subjectively experiencing a loss of self; she wanted to confirm its existence by the reflection, but she was afraid. This use of the mirror is homologous to the infant's use of the empathic mother. This concept of empathic mothering is somewhat different from that derived from Freud (1926) which describes the mother's satisfying *"a growing tension due to need"*—tensions which seem to lie in the realms of sensuality and hunger. The infant's earliest use of empathic mothering is, I believe, to fortify and help confirm the fragile sense of self coming from within by the reflection from the mother. Prior to this time—and I cannot even attempt to date it—empathic mothering is needed for the infant's biological survival, but the infant makes no psychological use of it and is not aware of it. In contrast to Loewald (1971), I do not believe that empathic mothering prior to early self-object differentiation has any psychic significance for the infant other than to result in the cessation of diffuse distress when biological needs are satisfied.

If this be so, it follows that the earliest phases of self-object differentiation and the concomitant earliest sense of self do not derive from the infant's experience of minimal frustrations (Tolpin, 1971). I speculate that the earliest capacity to sense the self and concomitantly to have a sense of boundary, however fleeting, is a maturational phenomenon, based on biological development of the rudimentary perceptual and organization skills which underlie the sense of self. It is only when biological development has reached this point that empathy can be used to reinforce the rudimentary sense of self. This is the significance of separating the self from the reflection of its existence in the mirror. The earliest sense of self arises from within—a consequence of biological development; it is exceedingly fragile and is reinforced—by empathic mirroring, sensory stimulation, including maternal soothing and especially kinesthetic sensations (Bursten, 1967), disappearance and reappearance of the familiar, etc. The biological aspects probably play the predominant role in the ability to sense the self (and objects) for quite some time, and only gradually do the confirmers become more effective.

Therefore, "good-enough mothering" (Winnicott, 1953) is not just a function of the the mother; in some infants, the biological substrate(s) of the sense of self may be so unreliable that much stronger maternal confirmation may be needed in order for a firm sense of self to be developed. A mother who might be quite adequately empathic for one infant may be insufficient for another.

Just how empathic mirroring reinforces the sense of self is not at all clear. Another homologue of this situation is seen in psychotic patients. In the treatment situation, it has often become clear that these patients need to sense that we understand them. One such patient had been exceedingly upset as he started to apply to graduate school. He began to withdraw, to lose his sense of continuity, and to experience the intrusion of disconnected thoughts which had almost hallucinatory quality. Over a week's time, he told me that his parents, while verbalizing approval of his decision, were expressing concerns about the costs. His friends, too, seemed upset by his decision. One began to express doubts about his own career. Others wondered why he wanted to do all that studying. Over several sessions, I became aware that any remark I made was missing the point. I could not reach him and I told him so. He thought about this for a bit and he acknowledged feeling estranged from me—unconnected and distant—literally and visually. Then he said, "I think you don't want me to go either." I had endorsed his plan all along and, thinking that he needed my approval again, I gave it to him. However, he remained distant and fragmented until I said, "I'm not upset about your going to graduate school; I know what it's all about. I've gone already." He smiled and reintegrated and said, "I didn't need you to do anything about it. I just needed to know that someone could understand."

Whatever the mechanism may be wherein this kind of empathic mirroring confirms the sense of self, it could well serve as the foundation for two of Freud's (1914) narcissistic paths: "A person may love . . . (a) what he himself is . . . (b) what he himself was." You will note that I omitted Freud's parenthetical phrase "(i.e. himself)" when referring to a person's loving "what he himself is." Of course narcissists love themselves; it is the thesis of this paper that they have to in order to confirm their selves. But the mirror image is not the self. Having set aside the concepts of narcissistic and object libido, I do not consider objects of the narcissistic relationship as self-objects. In this case, the empathic mirror is an object which confirms the existence of the self. It is a separate object, like other objects, except for its mirroring, self confirming attributes. This need for empathy, I believe, underlies what Kohut (1971, p. 115) calls "the alter-ego transference or twinship." In the analytic situation, the patient will look for her/his reflection in the analyst. At times one's need to see this reflection—or one's wish for it—will cause the patient to "assume that the analyst is either like him or similar to him."

Lacking the actual alter-ego, the patient fantasizes it. A narcissistic person with strong manipulative tendencies fancied himself as a person of great artistic and cultural taste. From the outset, he expressed contempt and criticism for the way my office was decorated. I was in good company—his former analyst had "abominable" taste, his lawyer's office was "dreadful," etc. In this particular hour, he again depreciated my pictures, some figures I have on a table, my color scheme, etc. I asked him why he cared, why my taste was so important to him. The question took him aback for a moment. Then he recalled how, when he was four or five, he had been ill and frightened. His mother came into the room and sat by the bed. She didn't have to say anything; her being there made him feel better. "If you only had good taste, we could communicate—we wouldn't even have to use words because you'd have the same background and the same values as I do." We discussed his need for mirroring and, perhaps, my understanding this need gave him the empathic response he had sought in the decor. For the first time, as he left, he said, "I do like your shirt." Thus, after his angry disappointment in me, he found some resonance, after which he was able to make me a man of at least some taste.

As development proceeds, additional methods of confirming the sense of self come into play. One of these is the fantasy of omnipotence and grandiose control of others. In my current view, this fantasy is not based on primary narcissism or largely on inadequate self-object differentiation, economic, and structural considerations, but on childhood fantasy which had been pressed into the service of confirm-

ing the self at a time when the sense of self was still insecure. The toddler who shakily discovers that it can do
something to something can easily develop the wish and
fantasy that it can do everything to everything, that it is the
center of the world and that everything belongs to it. This
is the basis of Freud's fourth narcissistic path—that of loving "someone who was once a part of the self"—and the
more general narcissistic practice of relating to people as
if they were extensions of oneself. These people are not
self-objects in any structural or economic sense; they are
perceived as separate objects. The narcissist's feelings of
possessiveness and control or the feeling of pride in the
object as part of the self are based on childish fantasy (see
Schafer, 1972), a fantasy which was fostered to help confirm an uncertain sense of self. That is what Kohut (1971,
p. 114) refers to as "merger through the extension of the
grandiose self" although I do not see the relationship as
one of "(primary) identity." Rather, there is a fantasy of
merger, usually unconscious, while the predominant state
of self-object differentiation is quite adequate.

The process of confirmation is a major task of the
separation-individuation phase of infancy. The biological
substrata of the perceptual organization necessary for a
firm sense of self probably undergo continuous maturation
during that period, and the mother is used in a variety of
ways to assist it when it falters. Because the earliest attempts to sense the self take place when oral sensuality is
at its height, orality becomes a stage on which later struggles to preserve the sense of self are enacted. Beyond this,
however, the fantasies of taking in (Abraham, 1924b; see
also Schafer, 1972) support the sense of self as within the
body, and fantasies of the effects of eating help confirm the
sense of self by the illusion of partaking of the mother's
bigness and power. One patient, a craving person, needed
to support his specialness by hoping that I would waive my
fee. He dreamed that he was in a restaurant expecting soup

and cookies, but he was disappointed. Then, he was served a pill; it was wheat germ—"very potent stuff."

By contrast, however, we should bear in mind that not all feeding fantasies confirm the sense of self. A phallic narcissist, who had always been afraid to get too close to his mother, dreamed that someone had a bottle of fertilizer to make grass grow, but the fertilizer was too concentrated —it was dangerous. In his associations, he thought of his mother. "It's like if I get too close to her, I'll catch something from her and my insides will be eaten out by the fertilizer." This can be seen as a biphasic dream. Initially, the food is nourishing, self enhancing, then it is repudiated as dangerous—self-destroying. In a like manner, this man repudiated "softness" and "dependency."

At times oral fantasies support the idealized images of the parents. Thus, if incorporation confirms the sense of self by enhancing it, the potent stuff must come from a potent person. One does not have to invoke the concept of vicissitude of narcissistic libido to understand that to the little infant, mother and father are indeed powerful and grand. They are bigger, more skilled (and more danger-ous), they can gratify, and in oral fantasies, they can supply wheat germ and fertilizer. It is these fantasies which under-lie Freud's third path to a narcissistic object. "A person may love . . . what he himself would like to be." This path is, of course, reinforced by parents who encourage their children to "be like me."

Now, the need for a powerful supplier can, at times, result in a loss of the sense of self and confusion between self and object, such as in ecstatic states or religious union with God (Rado, 1928; Reich, 1960; Bursten, 1973a, Chap. 6). This type of merger with the idealized object (see Kohut, 1971, p. 55 and 153) contrasts with the "merger" through extending the self, because here there are actual perceptual and organizational distortions. They may well be based on the infantile experiences of the oral triad (Lewin, 1950, Chaps. 5 and 6) which link oral sensual fantasies with loss of the sense of self (sleep phenomena). More often, however, the supplier is seen as a distinct object; whatever merger fantasies there may be do not intrude into consciousness, although attitudes based on these fantasies may be appreciated.

Of the many other ways the sense of self may be confirmed in infancy, I shall mention one more—enhancement of self-esteem. This is the area of what Kohut (1971, pp. 115f) calls "the mirror transference in the narrower sense." This is the use of the mirror in Lichtenstein's (1964) sense although he deals with a concept of a more archaic use of maternal mirroring than I am describing here. This is the gleam of approval, the signposts which tell the infant how to be in relation to what the mother needs or wants. On the adult level, this is not the use of a mirror to ascertain the very existence of our self; it is looking in the mirror before we go out in order to make sure we look all right, to make sure we meet with our or our parent's (see Shengold, 1974) approval.

We have already seen how an idealized and exalted parent figure can raise a person's self-esteem by having the power "rub off on him"—feeding fantasies leading to a grandiose enhancement of the self. The self is further and importantly enhanced by parental approval. This is Bibring's (1953) line of narcissistic aspirations as discussed by Rapaport (1959a). In contrast to their view, I am not certain how early in life self-esteem levels per se can be appreciated. It is certainly there in what Mahler (1967) calls the "practicing" and "rapprochement" subphases of infancy, where the infant actively seeks (and gets) the approval and admiration of the parent. The earlier emotional refueling probably has more to do with other modes of confirmation of the self, such as empathic mirroring, obtaining supplies, sensory stimulation from the mother (soothing, etc.), than with approval and self-esteem. However, with growing independence and individuation—that is, with increasing stability of the sense of self—these earlier methods of self confirmation may tend to recede somewhat and self-esteem as a method of enhancing the sense of self becomes increasingly important. Further, when the infant is able to grasp the concept of being worthy, the possibility of receiving these other modes of confirmation depend on the approval of the person from whom they may come. It is for this reason that self-esteem issues, which rest on first the reality and later the fantasy of reunion with the parent, are so central to the narcissist (Bursten, 1973b).

Now, in several instances I spoke of enhancement of the self. I am assuming that enhancement confirms the sense of self, although just how it operates is not clear to me. Direct sensory experience (up to a point), such as wrist-cutting, confirms the sense of self by focusing attention on the "I" who now feels something. The enhancement achieved by the fantasy of ingesting "grow power" from the powerful parent or the feeling of greater worth and self esteem when praised do not have direct sensory quality. It may be that the sense of self is confirmed because the infant thinks about itself in these situations—it is the center of its focus. Additionally, enhancement may rest on an underlying fantasy of bigness and, just as wrist-cutting is a sensory intensification to the point of self-awareness, so may bigness fantasies be a kind of intensification (certainly a magnification) to the point where the faltering selfhood may be appreciated.

Several of these confirmatory modes were revealed in the dreams of one of my narcissistic patients, a young salesman. He frequently had difficulty in writing his sale presentations and otherwise pursuing his career. His father had always been a disappointment to him while his mother had kept him closely attached to her, and even as an adult, he had the frequent fantasy that she would die or disappear if he became too independent. In one dream, he was riding a motorcycle and was afraid that he would not be able to round the corner. He then saw Marjorie (a friend) and he was relieved and gleeful. She was naked and beckoning to him, and he could not take his eyes off her breasts. Finally, he looked away and saw a raucous family behind a brown screen hanging on a clothesline. He wanted to get as far away from this screen as possible.

Associations to the dream were quite helpful and will be presented in the order in which he gave them. He had been worried that Marjorie was more friendly to a sales-woman colleague than to him. The brown screen reminded him of a Polish joke about putting toilet paper up to dry. His depreciated father had Polish ancestry, whereas his mother's family had come from Germany (higher on his social scale). As a child, he used to fantasize having a distinguished German name and being a spectacular athlete in order to win his mother's admiration. I asked him about rounding the corner and he said that he was afraid he would fly off into space. "I didn't want to leave the earth."

The role of Oedipal themes in narcissistic personalities will be discussed shortly; at this juncture I shall examine the dream from the standpoint of narcissistic concerns. The initial fear is the loss of his anchor—his sense of self and his bearings—if he becomes separated from mother. But mother is there, with ready, beckoning breasts, and he is further assured because he is more special than his younger sister. Again he is in danger because of inner impurity which might make him unworthy (see Bursten, 1973a, Chap. 6), but (from the associations) he gets mother's power and wins her praise, thus probably elevating his own self-esteem.

Some time later, there was a long period during which the analysis did not seem to move along. The man's work was also suffering; he did as little actual work as possible and spent most of his day meeting friends and discussing his past successes. He was constantly seeking praise. We came to speak of this activity as "seeking readings"—feedback to tell him how he was doing. He was quite distressed that I did not give him any readings; it was humiliating, much as he felt humiliated by his father. And in another sense, by "withholding praise" I was his mother separating from him. One day he reported that he had been talking with a friend who had just terminated his analysis. He was planning to celebrate by going to an amusement park. While the friend thought roller-coasters and "whip" rides were exhilarating, the patient had found himself becoming unaccountably uneasy during the discussion. I pointed out that the discussion had struck a chord with him. Separation from his mother and alienation from me raised fears of losing his bearings. "It's like you're afraid you'll lose track of where you are or even who you are. You're afraid you'll go crazy."

Probably both because of the content of this comment and the fact of my empathic mirroring, the next day he brought in the first dream in many months. He was pulling away from the curb in a car. Then he was in an auditorium, but things were very fuzzy. He went to a supermarket where he saw a dark-haired woman. It was Marjorie who said, "He (the patient) is a good salesman." He became very angry at this. At this point in the hour the patient stopped recounting the dream and he had a sudden thought: he decided to show one of his old written presentations to his boss—in essence, he decided to bolster his self-esteem by taking another reading. He then went on to say that he was angry at Marjorie because she spoke of him in the third person, as if talking to someone else who really counted rather than speaking directly to him. The dark-haired woman reminded him of someone else—a movie star who had just re-entered a mental hospital. He laughed nervously as he diagnosed her case as "terminal insanity." By coincidence (?), I sneezed at this point. He panicked momentarily and said, "I thought you were blowing up," and then (sadly), "I didn't want my mother to get pregnant."

The dream follows the discussion of the day before. Separation leads to disorientation and (in the dream) actual disperception. Such perceptual and organization difficulties echo the "basic" loss of the sense of self. Again, he tries to bolster the faltering sense of self by eating (*super*market), but he is deprived of two-person closeness (see Balint, 1968, pp. 21ff) and he becomes angry (see Kohut, 1972). At that point, the dream, through another association tells us that, in part, the two-person closeness was interfered with by the coming of his younger sister, although talking about him in the third person also has the flavor of mother talking to father. The reaction to my sneeze is particularly interesting because while "blow up" points the way to his mother's pregnancy, and his loss of her, it also echoes the movie star's "terminal (terminating) insanity." And as such, it mirrors his own disperceptions and insanity—his own loss of sense of self. In characteristic fashion, he attempts to pull himself together by taking a reading.

IV

As you can see, several of the factors present in part I of this chapter figure prominently in the establishment of a narcissistic course. No one of these is pre-eminent; all of them serve the crucial task of confirming the sense of self. Self-esteem and the approving reunion which underlies it may tend to become more prominent because, as I have noted, the possibility of receiving the other confirmers seems to the child to rest on her/his being worthy.

The confirmers I have enumerated are extraordinarily complex and I do not pretend to have accomplished more than a sketch of them; there are many nuances I have not considered. Also, confirmation of the sense of self goes on in many different ways long beyond the infantile period. However, the sketch I have drawn will be sufficient, at least, for me to proceed with my formulation of the narcissistic (and other) course(s).

The crucial consideration for the various courses is the ability of the person to maintain a sense of self. This sense of self rests on "basic" biological perceptual and organization factors which are supported by psychological and psychosocial confirmers. We can somewhat arbitrarily distinguish three levels of this ability:

1.   The sense of self is maintained with great difficulty and considerable instability, so that there are frequent lapses.

2.   The sense of self is maintained with somewhat less difficulty, so that the confirmers are usually successful in preventing lapses. However, the sense of self is still sufficiently vulnerable that the confirmers play an extremely important role in its maintenance.

3.   The sense of self is so secure that the confirmers are of relatively less importance.

These three levels represent a developmental continuum, although not everyone achieves the highest level. They also represent, if you will, a diagnostic continuum with level one corresponding to the borderline and schizophrenic course, level two, to the course of narcissistic personalities, and level three to the course of complementary personalities.

This conceptualization implies a deficit rather than primarily a conflict root of not only schizophrenia (see Arlow and Brenner, 1969; London, 1973; Gunderson, 1974), but also of narcissistic personalities. However, the deficit does not lie in withdrawn cathexes but in the ability to maintain the sense of self. Despite the fact that I postulate a deficit, I also postulate a continuum as outlined above. Among the various courses, then, there is a difference in degree of ease in maintaining the sense of self. Where conflict does enter in is in the ability of the person to employ the confirmers where needed or in the ideational elaboration of fantasies. Thus, the phallic narcissist mentioned earlier could not use feeding (fertilizer) to assist in confirming his sense of self because he fantasized that anything coming from mother was too dangerous. A person on level one whose conflicts deprive him of the comfortable use of confirmers is more apt to lose his sense of self and be psychotic. Another possibility for the role of conflict is that the physiological concomitants of anxiety or other affective states may sufficiently alter an unstable biological substrate so that the sense of self is endangered.

What determines the various levels—the various courses people will travel? I can think of three possibilities:

1.   In infancy, the biological substratum of the sense of self lags and it remains unstable or undeveloped throughout life. Possibly its tenuous development is disrupted from time to time by metabolic changes. If the maldevelopment is very severe, the confirmers will not be sufficient to restore the sense of self and a borderline course will be maintained. With less severity, self-confirmers will need to be consistently pressed into service and the narcissistic course will ensue.

2.   In infancy, the biological lag is sufficient that an undue emphasis had to be placed on confirmers in order for the sense of self to be maintained. Even after the biological substrate(s) is secure, the infantile confirming patterns persist because they have been so well learned.

3.   Even if there has been no particular biological lag, parenting may have been so poor that the sense of self remains fragile, either because the confirmers have become involved in dangerous fantasies or because they have proven unreliable.

These possibilities are not mutually exclusive, of course. It remains for future research to parcel out which of them, or which combination of them operate in which cases.

The emphasis in my approach is not that the sense of self (and with it the appreciation of self-object differences —reality) is built up primarily on infantile disappointment and lack of gratification because mother is not available (Freud, 1911b; Tolpin, 1971) but rather that it is the very presence of the "good enough" mother that help fosters the sense of self and the appreciation of reality which are biologically coming of age. It is this that may be reflected in Wexler's (1971) therapeutic approach to schizophrenia where the technique is not based on graded frustrations, but on maintenance of contact and communication by a caring therapist—techniques which can confirm the sense of self.

Keeping in mind the continuum outlined above, we may now understand the role of zonal sensuality. It is not as I had suggested in my previous paper (Bursten, 1973b), a primary determinant of borderline versus narcissistic versus complementary. Rather it stands, if you will, apart from that continuum. All people on whichever course undergo reasonably sequential stages of zonal sensual development and can have conflicts reflective of primarily any stage. This will lead to various personality types (Bursten, 1973b). This conceptualization helps us understand how one person with strong anal characteristics might be a paranoid personality while another might be an obsessional personality, with others falling somewhere in between. Both personality types share many traits in common (Shapiro, 1965, Chaps. 2 and 3), but the paranoid person's anality is pressed into the service of narcissistic repair (Bursten, 1973b) in order to confirm his sense of self, while an obsessional character has less of a need for self-confirmation and is probably on the complementary level.

The Oedipal level is not a matter of zonal sensuality and should not be considered on the same continuum. Rather it seems to develop at a particular time in both the sensual and the stability-of-self continuua. The sensual level is primarily phallic, but if the sense of self is stable enough, the infant can break away from needing the two-person self-confirming situation and enlarge his horizons. As the infant develops complementarity, the sensuality of the genitals no longer inspires only exhibitionistic attempts to obtain admiration (self-confirmation); attention can turn gradually to a less narcissistic love with all its Oedipal implications. For an infant on a narcissistic course, exhibitionism and phallic narcissism remain.

While it is helpful to separate the patients on a narcissistic course from those on a complementary course, for their lives and their analyses are quite different, I do not subscribe to the view that narcissists cannot have Oedipal conflicts—or that they only have pseudo-Oedipal conflicts. There is nothing pseudo in the mind; everything counts and nothing is fake. Having set aside the concept of narcissistic versus object libido, I do not see relationships defined by the predominant type of cathexis available. The narcissist is held on level two by a relatively unstable sense of self. However, it is quite conceivable that, from time to time, the sense of self is sufficiently stable that the patient can turn her/his interest outward for awhile. This is genuine, not pseudo, although since the basic deficit is still present, it will not be long before she/he will have to return to self-confirming activities. The salesman described earlier had many periods of typical Oedipal thought and conflict. I would say they were just as genuine as those seen in complementary persons. However, once he became aware of Oedipal competition he faltered because father's penis in his memory was shockingly huge. This narcissistic blow was enough to disturb his sense of self, and he had to retreat to his more usual narcissistic maneuvers.

Now, what I have presented is merely a framework of degrees of stability of the sense of self. On this framework must be hung the role of the affects, the process of taming of infantile sensuality, the role of cognitive development, and the impact of family patterns and values. And, from another vantage point, the nature and the role of the biological substrata remain to be worked out.

Chapter 6

THE EXISTENTIAL PSYCHOTHERAPY OF ALIENATED PERSONS*

Frank A. Johnson, M.D.

I

The use of the term narcissistic personality or character has been established in the psychoanalytic literature since the 1930s. Historically, it stems from Freud's original division of clinical conditions into the psychoneuroses, the *actual* neuroses, and the narcissistic neuroses. Freud's meaning of narcissistic neurosis subsumed some conditions which were later incorporated into yet an additional category of the character neuroses. In the early 1900s, however, the term "narcissistic neuroses" was used by Freud to include a number of regressive psychotic and borderline conditions which were not amenable to psychotherapeutic techniques

---

*This chapter is a portion of a working paper presented at the Eighth World Congress of Sociology, Toronto, Ontario, August, 1974. Other portions have been abstracted from chapters 2 and 14 of *Alienation: Concept, Term and Meaning,* edited by Frank A. Johnson, Seminar Press. 1973. We are indebted to Seminar Press for permission to publish these excerpts. *Ed.*

in use at that time (see Rosenfeld, 1964). These included some overt schizophrenic conditions as well as latent schizophrenia and what later would be considered schizoid (or narcissistic) personality. In the past 30 years, the meaning of the term narcissistic neurosis or narcissistic personality began to be more definitive of a borderline state of functioning typified by severe but nonpsychotic estrangement from both self and social environment.

The term narcissistic personality has also been complicated by the sharp distinction within psychoanalytic theory between primary narcissism and secondary narcissism. Clearly, the use of the word "narcissistic" in Freud's taxonomy, and in its later use by other psychoanalytic authors, carries the implication of narcissism in the sense of a primary, objectless ego state. Kohut and Kernberg have clarified the nature of what they define as pathological narcissism (Kohut, 1971; Kernberg, 1974). Additionally, Kernberg (1972) has depicted a series of stages during early childhood where faulty incorporation of internal objects occurs in certain selected varieties of narcissistic personality.

In common parlance as well as in its mythological derivation, the word "narcissism" is used to suggest a relatively superficial and fatuous self-absorption, which is more suggestive of hysteroid or immature adaptations. In these connections, the word is associated with demands for gratification and cherishment based upon the continuation of a compensatory overvaluation of self. Etymologically, of course, the problem is that the latter connotations of "narcissism" are distinctly different from those which are connected with primary narcissism. In centering on the semantic connected to the process of "splitting," the Bleulerian term "schizoid" evades some of this confusion. Again, regardless of terminology, there seems to be a genuine consensus concerning the nature of these conditions. There also is agreement concerning the technical difficulties involved in the psychotherapeutic treatment of such states.

This present chapter is concerned with looking into comparative advantages and disadvantages inherent in the use of existential and ontoanalytic treatment procedures with severely alienated persons. These factors will be examined by way of contrast with more traditional psychoanalytic techniques. Before discussing some technical aspects of the use of existential psychotherapy, it is necessary to discuss some of the terminologies which have been applied to malignant states of isolation and self-estrangement.

The clinical portrait of Alienated Man—it is to be understood that I use the word "man" in its generic sense, so that references to "Alienated Man" and "his" experience of "himself" are abstractions that stand for individual men and women—has received attention from psychiatric and social-psychologic sources including especially Fairbairn (1954), Kohut (1971) and Lifton (1971). Other terms designating what I here call Alienated Man include "schizoid personality," "narcissistic personality," "Protean Man." (Cf. Fairbairn, 1954; Kohut, 1971; Fromm, 1961; Lifton, 1971; Daly, 1968; Laing, 1960; Riesmann, 1961; Jourard, 1964.)

While there is a fairly close consensus at a descriptive level concerning the nature of Alienated Man, opinions about the genesis and internal structuralization of such states remain controversial. Following Guntrip (1961, 1969, 1971),[1] the concept of "splitting of internalized objects" can be used to explain various schizoid and narcissis-

---

1. Guntrip's work is especially thorough (1961, 1969, 1971) and based on Ronald Fairbairn's Object-Relations Theory; cf. Fairbairn (1954). Various objections to Fairbairn and Guntrip's modes of explanation have been leveled from orthodox psychoanalytic writers. Stein (1967) has summarized some of these; Guntrip (1969) has responded to some earlier criticisms.

tic conditions. Internalized objects are held to be representations of outside experiences that are incorporated by the infant and child in the process of longitudinal development. According to Kernberg (1972), the "splitting" of internal representations is described as a complex process involving a variety of unsuccessful attempts at incorporation occurring during infancy and early childhood. To a certain extent, there is a separation or splitting which is basic to the very process of creating internal representations of external phenomena. A second, more pathological, splitting is that process whereby internal representations of the outside world are fractionated into partial representations as a reaction to either tenuous or threatening experiences with external objects. Speculatively, the goal of this latter splitting is to allow the child to continue relating in a positive way with his otherwise perplexing or overwhelming environment. Splitting of this kind, if done in a wholesale way, is held to account for the presence of an abundance of dissociated, internalized partial objects.

In the most severe narcissistic states, many objects in the environment must be selectively processed and divested of their threatening quality in order for the individual not only to survive but also to continue interacting. Phenomenologically, the onus of this excessive use of selective decontamination is twofold. First, the individual— simply because of the frequency with which he performs these functions—becomes acutely aware of himself as a processor of threatening external phenomena. Second, those negative internalizations which are fractionated from the original external objects accumulate as a frightening series of disconnected and noxious feelings, memories and experiences.

Since these are disorganized, through being split from their original objects and contexts, they later become diffusely identified with the self. As such, they constitute a vaguely substantiated but extremely powerful reservoir of negative feelings concerning the operations of self (Johnson, 1973).

As already suggested, these severe states of estrangement have been described by a number of authors using a variety of different nosologic terms, most commonly either "schizoid" or "narcissistic" personality. Regardless of terminology, there has been a consensus that these conditions do not represent clear psychosis.

II

The development of existential psychiatry and ontoanalysis is intellectual heir to the phenomenological formulations of Edmund Husserl and Martin Heidegger. Generic features of Husserl's phenomenological approach that have influenced the nature of existential psychotherapy include his continuing search for the foundations of meaning ("essences") in "pure consciousness" and the use of reduction as a setting-aside of formal "organizing principles," patterns, or other (in his view) extraneous explanations of being. [See Johnson, (1974) for a statement of some of the relations between phenomenology and existential therapeutic procedures. For the contributions of Karl Jaspers, see Havens (1967). Because his definitive volume on general psychopathology (1923) was only belatedly available in English, Jaspers' effect on the American existential and ontoanalytic movement is less evident than the contributions of Binswanger and Minkowski. For a review of the contributions of these latter, see May, Angel and Ellenberger (1958), May (1959), B. Nelson (1961–62), Ellenberger (1970), Wyss (1966), and Havens (1972).]

In order to set a context on the issue of treatment of severely estranged patients, some operational principles ascribed to the existential analytic procedures will be summarized here. These will be listed in comparison to conventional ("Freudian") psychoanalytic treatment procedures. The operational principles consist of:

1. An emphasis on subjectivity rather than objectivity.
2. A more intimate quality of participation between analyst and analysand. This difference in quality of participation affects the ways in which the statuses of the participants are constituted as well as the significance of the "material" revealed by the patient; Havens (1974) comments, "In (psycho)analysis, the associative material being followed does not reveal its meaning to the patients. It only gradually reveals its meaning to the analyst" (p. 4).
3. A search for "essences" rather than for historic traumata.
4. A deemphasis on epigenetic theories of development, with their references to "stages" or "fixations," in favor of an emphasis on the contemporary and contemporaneous.
5. A different attitude toward unconscious determinants— they are not usually given the structural or motivational typifications which flourish in traditional psychoanalysis.
6. A shared emotionality between patient and therapist that is designated as central to the procedure.
7. An aversion to any conceptualizing which might interfere with understanding the *Being* of the patient.
8. A relative avoidance of causality in the explanation of behavior.
9. A somewhat different weight given to the process of (mutative) interpretation.
10. An acknowledgement of certain spiritual—even mystical—aspects of human communication. (Freud's rejoinder to Binswanger's attempt to introduce the concept of spirit into psychoanalysis is quoted by Needleman, 1963: "Dear Friend! A sweet surprise, your letters! ... In reading it I rejoice over your beautiful prose, your erudition, the scope of your horizon, your tact in disagreement. ... *But of course I don't believe a word of what you say.*")
11. The expectation that persons are in some ways inevitably unique (idiodynamic, idiosyncratic, "unknowable").

Some of the differences between traditional and existential procedures are in terms of emphasis—or, perhaps, priority. Also, it should be suggested that some of these differences may be more ideological than real; the objective procedures of these two schools may differ less than the explanations of their procedures. Whether practical or ideological, there are major differences in the explanations for therapeutic change emphasized in existential and traditional treatments.

The earliest explanations of change occurring through the process of psychoanalysis were semantically embedded in the very term which Freud used to describe his new procedure. As Benjamin Nelson (1965 b) has emphasized, psychoanalysis was analogized, as it were, to chemical analysis. That is to say that the curative consequences occurred as simple, prima facie resultants of the (analytic) method— just as a pure metallic substance might be separated through the reduction of a metallic salt or ore. Although Freud obviously intended the term psychoanalysis to be understood metaphorically, the term nevertheless suggested that previously fused complexes (or conflicts) would be reduced (separated, "healed") through a process of analysis. Somewhat more refined attempts to explain the process occurred later; for example, the term "psychosynthesis" was used as a catch-all generalization during the early 1920s. It was coined to suggest the opposite of "psychoanalysis"—specifically to indicate a process of *fusion* of previously separated or unintegrated phenomena. Freud (1924) derided the term: "I cannot imagine, however, that any new task for us is to be found in this psycho-synthesis. If I were to permit myself to be honest and uncivil, I should say it was nothing but a meaningless phrase." Later, the significance of the "mutative" interpretive process (which separated past from contemporary experiences) was felt to explain the acquisition of insight and the curative thrust of psychoanalytic procedures (Strachey, 1934). James Stra-

chey's presentation to the British psychoanalytic association in 1933 (c.f., Strachey, 1934) reviewed the historical
modes of explanation accounting for therapeutic change in
psychoanalysis. Despite its time of publication, this critical
article is still useful. Additionally, a great deal of weight
has been given within psychoanalysis to the resolution of
the primordial parental relationships through the objectification of the transference experience with the therapist
(Glover, 1958).

In contrast to these explanations, therapeutic change
in existential analysis is more commonly depicted in terms
of the healing or reparative nature of the therapist's total
communication with the patient's Being. Minkowski's explanation of this is typical:

> Rather, it is radically human encounter that comes into play,
> encounter that is called upon to act as the foundation for
> spiritual presence between two human beings—once again,
> as far as is possible for us. This encounter allows us to
> engage in dialogue with one of our fellow men who is open
> to us. This dialogue is by no means merely a spoken or
> written communication, nor an exchange of points of view,
> nor still less a discussion, indeed a dispute; it seeks rather
> to reach the other precisely as a "thou", to touch and move
> him to vibrate in the richest, deepest strings of his being—
> and in so doing, to create a union between persons, each
> capable of communing with the other. (Minkowski, 1969,
> p. 14)

Minkowski furthermore accentuates the therapeutic capability of the psychoanalyst as being "gifted with special
intuition." He sees this as different from the traditional
analysis, which he describes as more of a "penetration."

Havens (1974) has discussed the process of therapeutic change in existential analysis in terms of "being and
staying with the patient":

> The critical tests are only two, however difficult they may be
> to class conclusively: Has the therapist tried to be and stay;

more specifically has he practiced the phenomenological reduction and translated his empathic experiences?

Second, has he had success in this, as measured by affective responses to the patient? (p. 6)

Havens has discussed this kind of change (through intimate, intuitive connection) as different in focus from the "therapeutic alliance" of Greenson, the "symbolic realization" of Sechehaye or Alexander's notion of a reconstructive therapeutic relationship. Such a description of change —which Havens renders very thoroughly—nevertheless seems wanting. Clearly the changes which are described are not equivalently shared between the therapist and the patient. The direction and thrust of such changes are on behalf of the patient. Additionally, it is quite clear that mere communion ("being and staying") are not therapeutically sufficient by themselves but require a translation or interpretation in order to be effective.

Part of the problem of elucidating the more interpretive aspects of existential technique is the tendency of existential therapists to avoid descriptions and terminologies which sound harshly objective. Some writers from existential psychiatry demonstrate an understanding of these and other problems. They are aware of the dangers of sentimentalization and pseudo-camaraderie which may afflict therapeutic relationships that strive for informality and intimacy. They also call attention to the issue of vagueness— even vapidity—which may be a concomitant of aversion to the conventional, interpretive (analytic) process in psychotherapy. They are also aware to some degree about deluding themselves concerning their actual ability to escape categorization. Vespe (1969) has discussed the latter problem.

> It appeared to me that existential theories and interpretations could become as absolute and totalistic as Freudian ones and could be as falsely applied to the patient's experience with the result that their phenomenological reality was

distorted rather than disclosed. Further it appeared to me
that as existentialists we seem so averse to conceptualizing
our knowledge and formalizing our procedures that after
some thirty years the existential movement in psychotherapy
is in need for some kind of laxative! How fertile will existential psychotherapy be and how relevant will it become if its
meaning cannot be grasped or communicated? Admittedly,
one of the greatest virtues of the existential approach is that
it remains open and flowing. But the obvious danger is that
in being everything it is at the same time nothing.

Additionally, there has been a concern that the transcendental communicational union, characterized by the
detection of Essences or "Spirit," should not be corrupted
into a mystical, magical, or "religious" experience.

III

In this section I am concerned to synthesize critical elements of phenomenology, existentialism, ontoanalysis, and
psychoanalysis with a view toward suggesting that the reification of Alienated Man can lead, at times, to biased and
unproductive psychotherapeutic ventures.

The term "reification" is used here in its conventional
meaning of the inadvertent concretization of something
which is basically abstract or which does not have corporeal
or physical substance (e.g., the reified idea that a "personality" is a *thing*, rather than a loose psychological construct
summarizing a host of observations regarding human behaviors, motivations, dispositions, intentions, etc.). The
process of reification, especially as described by Berger and
Luckman (1966), is ubiquitous. Reification becomes a
problem in psychological and social scientific disciplines
when professionals may unintentionally manufacture
(reify) the very phenomena they propose to study or cure.

Some of the literature concerning Alienated Man—as
stereotype and caricature—has already been noted. Other

social philosophic, sociologic and literary descriptions have been summarized elsewhere. (See Johnson, 1973, especially the contributions of Gelfant, MacQuarrie and Stanley.)

Alienation themes in Western theology have emphasized man's separation from himself and his Creator. Later this separation was transliterated by Rousseau to man's separation from his natural paradise through the ravages of civilization, and the effects of industrialization and technicism. Stimulated by both the theological and secular depiction of man's existential separateness, literary themes have rendered portraits of separation, loneliness and the problems of transcendence. In the past 40 years, such themes have highlighted the alienation experience in terms of the phenomenology of disconnected heroes and heroines. Although subjectivistic orientations originated much earlier (Kafka, Joyce, Dostoevsky, Gide, etc.), their extraordinary popular acceptance has been most apparent in the past several decades. In their most recent forms, the subjective states of loneliness and separation are frequently accompanied by the hero's conscious recognition of purposelessness, moral relativism, and even absurdity concerning his existence. In these contemporary versions, Alienated Man is cast in opposition to antagonistic social and natural forces over which he exercises little control. Of course, Alienated Man is not monochromatic or stereotyped; he appears in various roles, statuses, and colorations.

In addition to a terrible awareness of separation, of overwhelming opposition and a sense of absurdity, the depiction of Alienated Man often includes a belief in the insubstantial quality of action. It is a halcyon sign, therefore, that contemporary Alienated Man apprehends his own facticity, and, at times, is paralyzed by such apprehension. Whether seen in literary versions (Prufock, Ulysses, Raskolnikov, Mersault) or in clinical renditions, a central concomitant of the alienation experience is the relative purposelessness of action and even of existence itself. As a corollary, there is a focus on the relative impossibility of personal substantiation.

Alienated Man is portrayed as thrown into fragile, temporal associations within a denaturalized social milieu. He is overwhelmed by the inexorable social demands and rituals which grant him slight significance and little option in the control of his own destiny. In populous, civilized societies, he finds himself surrounded by manufactured objects whose separateness from him appears to outweigh their relevance. In addition to such objects, he is surrounded by a surfeit of superficial ideologies—religious, commercial, nationalistic, scientific. From these he selects opinions and beliefs as if they were costumes donned to portray certain agreeable states of conformity, rather than used to identify or refresh any internal sense of integrity. His recognition of facticity is reiterated in descriptions of the process through which he encounters reality. Encapsulation themes abound; he is described as compartmentalized in roles as spouse, parent, worker, lover—even as a player or recreator. In the usual portrayal of Alienated Man, the sum of all of his roles somehow does not add up to a self. The situation is, perhaps, worse than Berger and Luckmann (1966) suggested; persons may be less than the total of their parts.

Looking inward to some sense of personal integration, Alienated Man is confronted with the inconsistencies and deficiencies in his various roles. From inside looking outward, the phony aspects of social performance and the sensed discrepancies between his various roles elicit feelings of inauthenticity and meaninglessness. Looking further into himself, he discovers a systematically regulated repertory of functions. Some of these moderate his interpretation of the actions of people around him; others function to carry out appropriate reactions to these people on the outside. However, neither his interpretation of others nor his actions toward others seem authentic or meaningful. Fleeting memories of innocence and spontaneity are painful; when recalled, they are ascribed to the delusions of childhood which were later shattered by the recognition of separateness and insignificance.

Ultimately, Alienated Man sees himself as just another, standardized, manufactured, thing. The very self-consciousness that Alienated Man has about his own functioning convinces him of his synthetic nature and, hence, of his inauthenticity. Sensing these deficiencies in his existence as inevitable, he resigns himself to seeking meaning out of isolation and despair themselves. He makes an attempt to enjoy or appreciate himself as an intriguing system of parts. Ultimately, he ends up sitting in his own private theater; at once the projectionist and the sole audience. In this theater he sees his behavior on an imaginary screen ("social reality") outside of himself, but rarely feels as if he is actually there on the screen, since he is so distracted by the production, direction, casting, and filming of his projections.

In severe schizoidal conditions, the deficiencies in meaning connected with social experiences are transferred from the outside to the arena of internal "reality" where they, ostensibly, may be more carefully modulated. The search for meaning, then, becomes formulated as questions concerning the smooth operation of his (synthetic) parts. Needless to say, the operation of such "parts" is often disjointed and erratic. Anxieties previously cued from contacts with social reality now are cued when the internal machine fails to perform satisfactorily. Recoiling from insubstantiality of outside contacts, Alienated Man comes to discover deficiencies in his existence signaled by the imperfections of his internal life.

As described previously (Johnson, 1973), ontological concerns are central to the experience of self-alienation. Although the problem of onotological insecurity has been beautifully expressed by Laing (1965, 1967), the implications of the degree to which falseness and inauthenticity are goals rather than concomitants has not been confronted. It would seem that the schizoidal disguise is not merely a side-product or resultant of social pressures, but rather an essential ingredient that makes performance possible. The portentiousness of any action—significant or insignificant —is, as it were, divested of its threat by pretending that it never really quite happens. The sense of facticity or inauthenticity, therefore, becomes a *touchstone for action* (Johnson, 1973). Knoff (1969) has previously identified the complicity of the estranged person in his own estrangement.

The individual is awed by his realization of the facticity of his own, and presumably others', existence. He is distracted by the sound of his own internal machinery, which diminishes his capacity to comprehend or feel others. He is so concerned with his own interior filtering, processing, and reacting equipment that he finds little time to examine the actions, qua actions, of others. He prefers to see these actions as a complex of blips on his own radar equipment. Possessed with a high degree of objectification and consciousness within himself, he becomes beguiled with his own reactions to phenomena rather than with the phenomena themselves. He begins to consider himself a locus of processes which are themselves disconnected from other processes, both within himself and outside. This sense of disconnectedness accentuates his awareness of separation from others. Descriptions both from fictional and "real" alienated individuals frequently feature terms such as "capsules," "shells," "coverings," "layering," etc. Metaphorically, such heroes live in "caves," "niches," "cocoons," "containers," and "bell jars." Separation is commonly perceived as a nearly concretized barrier between persons, as if individuals lived behind walls or communicated electronically with each other while living in adjacent plexiglass containers.

A corollary feeling of falseness and facsimile pervades this disturbed sense of being. Hence a whole series of descriptions are replete with the idea of inauthenticity, both in fictional and "real" experiences of alienated persons. People are seen as disguised or hiding behind masks. As Laing (1965) comments, the schizoid feels as if he is an actor, player, or impersonator, but never a person. Concepts of sincerity, self-confidence, or authenticity seem absurd and irrelevant. Relationship to others is accompanied by such intense self-consciousness that any kind of action seems overwhelmingly synthetic, hence phony or "plastic". Like "sincerity," *spontaneity* appears to be a meaningless word, since the schizoid person is so wretchedly aware of the mechanisms underlying his specific actions. It is, therefore, inconceivable to him that interaction could ever be construed as spontaneous. Even in situations where spontaneity and abandon are difficult to abolish (such as while playing or copulating), the severely alienated person may still feel that he is acting as an automaton.

The exquisitely schizoidal person becomes, as it were, an amateur sociologist studying his own operations. He looks on himself as a collection of roles rather than a self. He is able to expound on the nature of his perceptions, integrations, and reactions. However, the tragedy is that in contrast to the use that sociologists make of role playing (as an analytic device), the alienated person begins to believe that that is all he is—a dessicated structural model. He sees himself as a puppet cued by social circumstances which exact ritualized performances from him. His irritation about the inevitability of this is counterbalanced by one major consolation. This consists of his narcissistic affection for his own machinery—that is, his own processes and parts. This becomes the most stable and reliable domain in his encapsulated onotological scheme. He enjoys the splendid private awareness of his own internal equipment, which he feels—most of the time—that others cannot see. Life, then, becomes a series of private mental pictures which generate excitement partly because they are secret from others.

IV

Before discussing treatment I wish to suggest that alienated persons are not necessarily in need of psychotherapy simply by virtue of sensing themselves alienated. Many states of alienation may represent highly advantageous adaptations to contemporary roles and institutions, and even grossly maladaptive states of alienation may not necessarily compel consideration of treatment. But on the basis of the preceding description, I wish now to pose some problems that a narcissistic personality might encounter in analytic therapy.

Since the schizoidal person by (self) definition considers himself to be an aggregate of idiosyncratic consciousness existing apart from others, the problems of therapeutic intervention are especially challenging. So I will review a number of these problems in the light of the techniques of existential psychotherapy and existential analysis which might be applied to the treatment of some alienated persons.

The Problem of the Encounter Itself

Given the terrible sense of isolation, the notion of having a successful, real encounter with other individuals appears rather dim. Therefore, the idea that one can have a reparative, constructive interchange with another person (therapist) seems especially unlikely to the alienated person.

Aspects of this problem have been cogently summarized by Daly (1968) in approach-avoidance terms. Daly sees the alienated patient vacillating between strong compulsions to affiliate, immediately followed by feelings of repulsion. He has defined this vacillation in terms of dependent, ideational, and hysterical modes of adaptation.

The Paradox of Subjectivistic Competence

Less experienced therapists are often baffled and misled by the discrepancy between the alienated person's lucid awareness of an internalized social reality (as an idiosyncratic incorporation) which coexists with a nearly complete miscomprehension of the nature of the external social substance. Before the schizoid comes to treatment, he has already developed a totalistic "bracketing of the world" (see below).

The Concentration on Solipsism

This problem harks back to the difficulties in establishing intersubjective consensus. In the severely alienated person, there is very little belief in the validity of experience outside of the self. All experience (prosaic, momentous, transitory, durative) is relentlessly subjected to idiosyncratic interpretation. All experience, therefore, is conceptualized simply as occurring internally, and hence can only be what the individual experiences or feels. This becomes what Sartre has described as the "Reef of Solipsism" (1963, p. 223).

The Gravitation Toward Negativistic Hypotheses

There is a relentless movement toward dramatic and negative imagery in many narcissistic persons who seek treatment. Sometimes the type of imagery is devoted to self-terrification and, perhaps, simultaneously used to ruffle the therapist's attempts to remain calm and compassionate. Such negativity can also be attributed to the malignant sense of detachment that the schizoid person possesses, which, in its terrible objectification, may permit a melodramatic and surrealistic depiction of reality. In the actual clinical versions of such horror stories, this negative imagery is often transparently connected to an internal sense of extreme turmoil and "badness". One of the most malignant aspects of this negativity is its global and unselective application. It is as if the answer to the general question concerning "How are things?" is usually, "Absolutely terrible!" Since such negativity is fairly close to consciousness much of the time, it becomes relatively stabilized and ego-syntonic. It is, therefore, at least partly divested of some of its terrible force, both toward the patient, as well as toward the therapist. Thus, notions of conspiracy, threat, and immanent disaster (all of which are common), do not acquire the typically paranoidal coloration which they might in a person who did not, in a way, enjoy such negativity.

An additional factor connected with the gravitation toward pessimism and doom is the conspicuous quality of atemporality. The various kinds of historical traumata which are connected to this negativity seem to have just happened, even if they took place years ago. It is as if the badness and terrors of previous experience have not mellowed over time but remain as intact, eidetic memories which reach out and touch contemporaneous reality. Furthermore, this negativity frequently gravitates toward ontological questions. Even apparently mundane behaviors or goals become contaminated with absolutely ontic significance. Technically, the handling of this much negativity poses some real difficulties for the nondirective, existential therapist, insofar as the patient may well use the therapist to amplify his already exorbitant, negativisitic sense of being.

The Experiencing of Exorbitant Anxiety

The experience of anxiety in schizoidal persons, of course, varies, as it does with any person. However, the quality of the experience of anxiety—regardless of the type of experience—is distinctive. Again, experiences of anxiety readily get connected to frankly ontological issues—questions of existence and nonexistence—which may be aroused by the most superficial circumstances or threats.

The Tendency to Deny Process and Intentionality

It is somewhat of a paradox that while the schizoidal person is so terribly aware of his internal representations, he is at the same time remarkably naïve concerning any autonomous direction or the control of his mental processes. He takes the guileless position that his train of consciousness is automatized, and that there are no intentional implications to the fact that his thoughts so frequently feature destructive, terrifying and pessimistic themes. One of the most useful interventions in the treatment of schizoidal persons is the capability of the analyst to assist in the patient's understanding that his own "pure consciousness" is not inexorable and spontaneous (as if it were a film or tape placed inside his brain), but rather is the product of a process. Furthermore, it is useful to point out that the thrust of such processes is causally related to certain deleterious and scary consequences. For example, it may never have occurred to a schizoidally depressed person that sitting around all day imagining that his genitals are falling off may contribute to a sense of terrible anxiety about any real sexual encounter.

Lacking space for clinical illustration, it is difficult to convey how naïvely the schizoid denies connection between his negativisitic fantasy life and the difficulties he encounters in the world. Partly, this naïveté exists since the alienated person predicts future action by a comparison with an ensemble of dissociated partial-objects that have little semblance to contemporaneous action. Furthermore, in rarely carrying out new and genuine encounters, the schizoidal person does not become involved in behaviors which refute his previous experiences.

V

The foregoing section summarized some of the dimensions of the alienation experience as it is encountered in psychotherapeutic situations. The schizoidal position poses special problems of technique for therapists identified with various schools and persuasions. In the typical psychoanalytic situation, the naïve therapist might be misled to think that the patient's copious discharge of negativity—the brutalities of childhood, the terrors of connections with other persons, etc.—is being used to aid recovery, rather than to reify the person's "badness." Therefore, the traditional emphasis on relating past traumas to contemporary difficulties can be a serious technical error in the treatment of the severely alienated. Certainly putting such a patient on the couch can be a disastrous invitation. Commonly the patient will occupy himself by flashing a series of mental slides onto the ceiling reminiscent of Hieronymus Bosch, Edgar Allen Poe, Frankenstein, and *The Portrait of Dorian Gray.*

Contrastingly, the existentialistic and ontoanalytic psychotherapist can be seen as bringing some advantageous skills both in establishing a relationship with the alienated person, as well as averting certain technical difficulties. Some of these advantages will be summarized here along with a listing of other hazards that are inherent in existential procedures.

The Handling of Intentionality in Treatment

It has already been suggested that the existential therapist's deemphasis of causal hypotheses may be very beneficial to persons who have already overdeveloped a frightening personal history. In focusing on the pursuit of meaning rather than looking for ambiguous and global causes, the existential process in itself can be a refreshing change for the schizoid person. Intentionality is more directly confronted in the sense of the immediate, here-and-now reality, rather than in terms of the past. The contemporaneous treatment process can thus operate to divest prosaic action of its more auspicious, cosmic consequences:

> Shall I part my hair behind? Do I dare to eat a peach? I shall wear white flannel trousers, and walk along the beach. (Eliot, 1934)

The melodramatic and terrifying quality of eating a peach can be divested of its ontic consequentiality, partly through the assertion that the intentionality of eating a peach is fused in the (munching, sucking, dripping) phenomenological experience of actually eating the peach. As a technical maneuver, looking for more complex intentionality or significance in eating a peach becomes defined as extraneous —ultimately as patently ridiculous.

The therapist in this instance would be acting to deny an auspicious reification of any particular action. Similarly, the therapist would be divesting the act of its ontic significance by asserting its simple legitimation as a particular (ordinary) activity (See Berger and Luckman, 1966, p. 167–8)

The Use of Phenomenological Reduction in the Treatment Situation

In contrast to the use of intentionality—which is quite salubrious—the phenomenological reduction poses some problems in the existential treatment situation. The schizoid has already bracketed his world. Concentration on his being (as a central reality) is a tactic in which the alienated person needs no instruction. Therefore, a therapeutic process which focusses on contemporaneous consciousness raises some hazards in terms of collapsing into its own methodology. Just as the more traditional psychoanalyst-explorer may reinforce the quality of the schizoid patient's violent past, the phenomenological psychiatrist may also misinterpret the patient's dazzling capacity to visualize reality in terms of existent, ontic immanence.

Looked at in another way, the problem for both the ontoanalytic and the more traditional psychoanalytic therapists is somewhat the same. It is as if the patient were stepping out of the pages of Kafka, Camus, Riesman, and Laing. It is as if the patient were in fact a proof of all those typifications which we currently hold to be true. It is as if the patient were a pure instance of what we have been told to expect that contemporary man must be—disconnected, terrified by global destruction, ravaged by his family and society, uncomforted by a belief in a superior being, and so on.

In a microcosmic sense, the therapeutic situation may turn into what Keniston (1960) has described as a negative mythologizing:

> Every age, too, has its characteristic balance between positive, educative, hortatory, constructive, imperative, visionary, utopian myths, and negative, deterrent, cautionary, warning, direful, destructive and counter-utopian myths. In some periods of Western history, images of violence, demonism, destructiveness, sorcery and witchcraft have prevailed; in others, myths of blessedness, justice, cooperation, and universal concordance with divine order have dominated. . . . Few would disagree that our own time is one of predominantly negative, deterrent or even satanic myths. Our dissociated fantasy is fantasy of violence, cruelty and crime, presented ostensibly as a warning, but often acting as a stimulant. (pp. 185–186)

Robert Daly (1970) has also called attention to negative mythology in an article concerning the "Spectres of Technicism":

> Belief in the spectre of technicism may appear in still other forms in the lives of individual persons. Instead of being a

> force which one must dread and defend against, this spectre
> may become that ultimate reality in which one trusts and
> from which one draws hope and meaning. It may assume the
> semblance of a faith in the life of the individual. ... This
> life-way and the communities of faith which make it possible
> deserve the close attention of practitioners and scholars who
> would understand the religious meaning of many lives in the
> modern era. (p. 429)

The particular hazards in the existentialistic-onto-analytic method for such negativisitic mythologizing is connected to the thrust for the procedure to develop a "bracketing of the world," and to deemphasize any conventional, subject-object distinctions. Although the de-emphasis of the Cartesian dividedness of subject-object may well be a refreshing insight for some individuals ("sick" or "well"), the schizoidal person does not benfit from such a distinction. The alienated person has already "solved" the problem of subject-object relatedness by reducing everything to a fusion of subject and object within himself. Regrettably, an existentialistic procedure which reinforces this solution only leads to the reification of separateness, despair and hopelessness.

The Use of Intuition in the Analytic Situation

The development of closeness, empathy, and presence (May, 1959) in the therapeutic situation is extremely helpful to schizoidal individuals. One of the bridges through which the schizoid may begin to escape from his stark isolation is through the empathic connection made with the therapist. This may allow the beginning of a nascent sense of an ongoing intersubjective concensus. It may dawn on him that, in fact, experiences outside of himself do have some semblance (of one kind or another) to the internal phenomena which he heretofore has envisioned as idiosyncratic and unique to himself. This schizoid person who each day braces himself for a *Gotterdämmerung* of terrifying experiences may begin to realize that most actions are simply not that terrifying. Again, the particular bridge for such realization may be furnished through the long deferred and usually avoided sharing of empathic communion with another significant person.

SUMMARY

In this chapter, some of the derivations and uses of alienation themes have been related to social scientific, psychoanalytic and literary depictions of Alienated Man. The implicit negativity which is inherent in the concept of alienation has been discussed along with the tendency for the unintentional reification of the concept within sociology and psychiatry. The literary and philosophic descriptions of states of separation and estrangement have been compared to the clinical terminologies of "schizoid" and "narcissistic" personalities. Some of the historical derivatives of these latter terms have been discussed along with a brief presentation of hypotheses concerning the genesis and structuralization of these conditions.

The technical difficulties inherent in the treatment of narcissistic personalities have been summarized, partly through the use of a comparison between traditional psychoanalytic procedures and existentialistic methods. Techniques of the latter approach can be seen as beneficial in these conditions insofar as they focus on contemporaneous experience. Similarly, the emphasis on an existential communion between analyst and patient and the importance of an articulated empathy are seen as providing both an intellectual and emotional bridge for the severely estranged patient.

On the other hand, existentialistic-ontoanalytic procedures, with their bracketing of the world and ambiguity in subject-object distinctness, may unintentionally collaborate to intensify the patient's notion of his own isolation and idiosyncrasy. Furthermore, in preferring a less objectified and interpretive thrust, existential procedures may unintentionally reify the patient's convictions about his inherent "badness" through averting more conventional psychoanalytic techniques which focus on the historical separation of the past from the present.

Despite these hazards, it is the author's opinion that the addition of phenomenological and existential emphasis to traditional psychoanalytic technique possesses some distinct advantages for the treatment of narcissistic personalities. In addition, the impact of phenomenology on psychiatry in general can be seen as providing a very necessary counterpoint to prevailing Western psychologies whose thrust has been toward the more scientific, reductionistic, and causal-motivational. Phenomenology has succeeded in refocusing attention onto the immediate nature of lived experience in an effort to comprehend otherwise elusive dimensions of personal and social reality. In many ways, such a focus acts as an antidote against pseudo-objectification and other forms of compartmentalization of human experience.

Part III

EGO, WORLD, EGO IDEAL

Chapter 7

RENÉ DESCARTES AND THE DREAM OF REASON

John H. Hanson

Toute époque de la pensée humaine pourrait se définir, de façon suffisamment profonde, par les relations qu'elle établit entre le rêve et la vie éveillée."

Every epoch of human thought defines itself, to a great extent, by the relationship it establishes between the dream and waking life.

Albert Béguin, *L'Ame Romanttique et le Rêve*

I

René Descartes has long been recognized as one of the founding fathers of seventeenth-century science; with Bacon, Galileo, and others. Descartes revolutionized the nature and scope of scientific inquiry and gave an impetus to rationalism which lasted for centuries to come. Descartes was no chemist, astronomer, or physicist, however—his chief contribution to the "advancement of learning" was his methodology. The Cartesian rhetoric of discovery brought to the fore the scientific observer, that executive intelligence which examined the eventuality of the world from a point without, a motionless onlooker to the spectacle of atoms in motion.

In the twentieth century, where uncertainty and relativity have become irreducible components of scientific logic and where the very rationality of intelligence itself has been called into question by psychoanalysis, Descartes can no longer appear as the simple philosopher of "bon sens"; the lucidity of the *cogito* clouds over when examined in terms of more complex dynamics of the personality than those the author of the *Discourse on Method* was willing to accept. The genius of Descartes's accomplishments cannot be denied, but they must be situated in a culturally specific context and re-examined through the more comprehensive theories of mental life which we now possess. It is only then that we will be able to make our final escape from what Erik Erikson has called "the Cartesian straitjacket" (Erikson, 1962, p. 453).

It was "Descartes's merit in having established an ego-strength and an ego-freedom in his work, through which the development of modern science first became possible" (von Franz, 1968, p.137). Such *rousseauisme* characterizes the work of Husserl (*Cartesian Meditations*) and Lewis S. Feuer's brilliant analysis of the dreams, "The Dreams of Descartes" (*American Imago*, 20: 3–26, 1963). Both writers use Descartes as the departure point for a philosophy of ego process rather than unconscious restructuring. Husserl's Descartes is a combination of Novalis and Comte, while Feuer frankly admits that his own analysis of the dreams fails to take into account the fact that "the next step remains: to show how the specific ideas of Descartes' philosophy, his unique emphases and standpoint, were linked to the character of the underlying anxieties suggested by his dreams" (Feuer, 1963, p. 26)

Descartes's philosophy may be described as a tactical gain made at the price of a strategic loss. His system carried within it numerous disabilities, the most prominent of which were a rigid mind/body dualism and an equation of mental life with what Oswald Spengler called "the sovereign waking-consciousness" (Spengler, 1965, p. 347). Cartesian philosophy was an expression of perfect instrumentality and little else. Culturally, it cast aside the achievements of its predecessors, foremost among which were "the oneness of the reality which included the observer" and "the ancient doctrine of correspondence, in which the idea of a meaningful teleological order in nature still had a place" (von Franz, 1968, p. 83). As Alfred North Whitehead points out, the basic success of Descartes's thought depended on "the concept of an ideally isolated system" (Whitehead, 1948, p. 47), a position which led Arnold Geulincx, a student of Descartes, to explain the separation of mind and body in his master's thought by comparing *res cogitans* and *res extensa* to "two watches wound up at the same time" (von Franz, 1968, p. 86).

Another consequence of the rationalist dominion over mind and nature was a veritable loss of reality; as Maritain paraphrases Descartes, It is not reality which will require science to be true, it is Science that will require reality to be 'scientific,' and to produce its credentials" (Maritain, 1944, p. 50). While mediating experience of nature through the use of mathematical symbolism, Descartes excluded from his model of the mind everything but the mediate data of consciousness, making his own potent contribution to the seventeenth century's "ever-mounting slag-heap of rejected awareness" (McLuhan, 1969, p. 293).

It is intensely paradoxical, therefore, that Descartes's philosophical career should have begun on November 10, 1619 with a series of three dreams—a fact to which Auguste Comte referred with annoyance as a "cerebral episode" (Maritain, 1944, p. 15). The dreams have received little consistent interpretation from either philosophers or psychoanalysts, the former contenting themselves with describing Descartes's nocturnal inspiration as a variety of "crise mystique," the latter abandoning their efforts at explication with a series of inferences concerning erotic imagery and the personal character of the dreamer. Most importantly, no interpretations attempt to adequately discuss the relationship between the nature of the self and the experience of dreaming which lies at the heart of Descartes's philosophy.

René Descartes begins the third of his *Meditations on First Philosophy* by announcing to the reader:

> I shall now close my eyes, stop up my ears, turn away all my senses, even efface from my thought all images of corporeal things, or at least, because this can hardly be done, I shall consider them as being vain and false; and thus communing only with myself, and examining my inner self, I shall try to make myself, little by little, better known and more familiar to myself. (Descartes, 1972a, p. 113.)

The movement of his thought is away from the world; it is "extra-mundane" (Van Den Berg, 1962, p. 92.) in direction and dual in purpose. To meditate on first philosophy is to turn the body away from the impingements of the external world and, thereafter, to turn away from the body itself to enter a pure mental space ("my inner self"). Descartes's reality of the clear and distinct is attained through an initial derealization: by the denial of the senses and the erasure of their presence in the mind. *Cogito ergo sum* arises from an initial negation; the omnipotence of thought is founded in a denial of the body. The body is replaced by a reflection of the ego upon itself within the cocoon of reason.

The inner voyage of the *cogito* is an ascent of the "reasonable soul" to the extracorporeal, a narcissistic *Leibestod* or bodily death which the mind survives. A sense of otherness and death fills Descartes as he reflects upon his being:

> But I shall rather stop to consider here the thoughts which
> sprang up spontaneously in my mind, and which were in-
> spired by my own nature alone, when I applied myself to the
> consideration of my being. I considered myself, firstly, as
> having a face, hands, arms, and the whole machine made up
> of flesh and bones, such as it appears in a corpse, and which
> I designated by the name of body. (Descartes, 1972a, p. 104)

The word "body" is a descriptive term for an external,
nonliving object which is defined mechanically. It is a possession, an attribute rather than a life-center. Descartes's
description is the idea of a body and has been compared
with justice to the depersonalized body schema described
by Victor Tausk's patients as an "influencing machine"
(Brown, 1968, p. 120). "Cartesian man," writes Maritain,
"had lost his body: he has delivered it over to the universal
mechanism, to the energies of matter regarded as forming
a closed world . . . man's body ceases to be regarded as
human by essence" (Maritain, 1944, p. 181).

Yet another turn of Cartesian rhetoric places the *cogito*
even beyond the contemplation of the machine:

> I thereby concluded that I was a substance, of which the
> whole essence or nature consisted in thinking, and which, in
> order to exist, needs no place and depends on no material
> thing; so that this "I", that is to say, the mind, by which I am
> what I am, is entirely distinct from the body, and moreover,
> that even if the body were not, it would not cease to be all
> that it is. (Descartes, 1972a, p. 54)

If the origin of the *cogito* lies in the negation of the body,
then what is the origin of the body? Descartes answers that
"there is nothing that has a permanent place except in so
far as it is fixed by our thoughts," (Descartes, 1955, I., p.
260) and that "we perceive bodies only by the understanding . . . we conceive them in thought" (Descartes,
1972a, p. 112). Thought is primary and procreative; it
"conceives" the body. In accounting for his personal exis-

tence, Descartes attributes both his physical being and his individual ego not to earthly parents but to a spiritual creator, bodiless and rational. The Cartesian stance of radical doubt is a refusal to know in a carnal as well as a cognitive sense. Of his origins, the philosopher writes:

> But perhaps that being on whom I depend is not what I call God, and I am produced by my parents, or by some other cause less perfect than God. Far from it, for, as I have already said, it is very obvious that there must be at least as much reality in the cause as in its effect. (Descartes, 1972a, p. 128)

The body is a material composition, its being an external event; Descartes decides that, like Athena, he has sprung fully formed from the mind of God. The philosopher's birth is a family romance without a mother:

> As for my parents, from whom it appears that I derive my birth, although all that I have ever believed about them be true, nevertheless this does not mean that it is they who conserve me, or who made me and produced me in so far as I am a thinking thing, since all they did was to put certain dispositions into this matter in which I judge that I, that is to say my mind, which alone I take now as being myself, is enclosed . . . from the mere fact that I exist, and that the idea of a sovereignly perfect being, that is to say, God, is in me, the existence of God is very clearly demonstrated. (Descartes, 1972a, pp. 129–130)

This world of discrete objects and distinct perceptions is a world of repudiated interaction: con-ception, con-sciousness, and co-gitation are all seen as autochthonous (Thass-Thienemann, 1967, pp. 77; 264; 97; 40–41). The *cogito* is enclosed: it cleaves to itself and it is cleft from the body, for "body, by its nature, is always divisible, and . . . mind is entirely indivisible" (Descartes, 1972a, p. 164).

In defense of his position, Descartes writes to his student, the Princess Elizabeth of Bohemia:

It does not seem to me that the human mind is capable of conceiving at the same time the distinction and union between body and soul, because for this it is necessary to conceive them as a single thing and at the same time to conceive them as two things; and this is absurd. (Descartes, 1970, p. 142)

Descartes is willing to entertain the absurd, however, in a few speculations on aspects of experience which are not divided and distinct but "con-fused," joining together the *cogito* and the machine. Of bodily sensations which momentarily overpower the ego, he states:

For in truth all these feelings of hunger, thirst, pain, etc. are nothing other than certain confused ways of thinking, which arise from and depend on the union and, as it were, the mingling of the mind and the body. (Descartes, 1972a, p. 159)

These "confused ways of thinking" he attributes to the survival of "the prejudices of childhood":

For in the first years of life the mind was so closely allied to body that it applied itself to nothing but those thoughts alone by which it was aware of the things which affected the body; nor were these as yet referred to anything existing outside itself. . . . And as all other things were only considered in as far as they served for the use of the body in which it was immersed, mind judged that there was more or less reality in each body, according as the impressions made on body were more or less strong. (Descartes, 1955, I., pp. 249–250)

Needless to say, the philosopher had little tolerance for the ambiguities of infancy. The "principal and most usual mistake" in his perceptions, he feels, "consists in my judging that the ideas which are within me are similar in conformity with things outside me" (Descartes, 1972a, p. 116); such judgments are the product of "a blind and rash

impulse" (Descartes, 1972a, p. 118). Although he has decided to "apply myself seriously and freely to the general
destruction of all my former opinions" (Descartes, 1972a,
p. 95), he finds that "these old and customary opinions still
recur often in my mind" and "occupy my mind against my
will and, as it were ... dominate my mind" (Descartes,
1972a, p. 99). Descartes contemptuously compares these
old, nondualistic ways of thought to the dream of "a slave
who was enjoying in his sleep an imaginary freedom" (Descartes, 1972a, p. 100).

It is in sleep that the mastery of the *cogito* is challenged
by the enslaved body, and at one point Descartes anxiously
reflects that the dissolution of the self-conscious ego in
sleep might result in his total annihilation. In self-consciousness, Descartes sees an activity which

> cannot be detached from me. I am, I exist: this is certain; but
> for how long? For as long as I think, for it might happen, if
> I ceased to think, that I would at the same time cease to be
> or to exist. (Descartes, 1972a, p. 105)

Like Daniel Paul Schreber, the paranoid judge whose delusions Freud analyzed, Descartes feels that his reason encap-
sulates part of the divine and must be maintained by
"enforced thinking" (Freud, 1911, p. 406).

During sleep these compulsive structures are relaxed,
and it is in the fall into sleep and the dream that the origin
of the *cogito* is to be found. Descartes himself speculates in
this direction; in his third Meditation he wonders whether

> there is in me some faculty or power, even though I do not
> yet recognise it, able to produce these ideas without the help
> of any external things, and, indeed, it has always seemed to
> me until now that, when I am asleep, they are formed in me
> in this way without the help of the objects they represent.
> (Descartes, 1972a, pp. 117–118)

If Descartes's intimation is followed, then it might be expected that there are important structural analogies to be made between the processes of cogitation and dreaming. Descartes himself justifies this line of inquiry when he states that he "discovered the bases of a wonderful science" Descartes, 1963, p. 52) during the dreams of November 10, 1610. The dreams were recorded and commented upon by Descartes in a small piece entitled "Olympica"; the text was preserved by Descartes's biographer, Adrien Baillet (Wisdom, 1947, pp. 11–18). The three dreams have received attention a number of times in psychoanalytic literature as biographical indices to unconscious conflicts in the philosopher's life, but, as will be seen, they have never been adequately examined as the structural prototypes for Cartesian first philosophy.

In the first dream, Descartes

> saw phantoms which terrified him to such an extent that, thinking he was walking through the streets, he had to tilt over on his left side so as to continue on his way, because he felt a great weakness in his right side that prevented him from holding it up. Being ashamed to walk thus, he made an effort to hold himself erect.

A "gusty wind" sweeps about him, spinning him about several times on his left foot. Seeking refuge from his discomfort, Descartes spies "an open school" and makes his way towards it to pray. (It has been suggested that this school represents La Flèche, the Jesuit *lycée* where the young Descartes received his education.) He passes a man, and, realizing that he has not greeted him, turns to make amends for his discourtesy. The wind, however, prevents his return, and "at the same time he saw in the middle of the court of the school someone else, a man who addressed him by name." The speaker inquires of Descartes the whereabouts of a "Monsieur N.". The man states that he has something for N. "Descartes imagined it was a melon he had been given from some foreign country." At the same time, the dreamer is surprised to see that, while he is still "bent and unsteady" in the diminishing wind, the speaker and a group of people gathered about him "were upright and steady upon their feet." At this point he awoke from the first dream.

Previous commentators on the dreams have hastened to equate this first dream with a "primal scene fantasy" (Wisdom, 1947, Schönberger, 1939). A man, or phallic double, goes down a street, enters an enclosure; another stands firm and erect "in the middle of the court." The faults of their interpretations lie not in their conclusions but in their lack of corroborating associations from the dreamer himself. When Maxim Leroy wrote to Freud, requesting that he interpret the dreams, Freud refused to do so for this very reason (Schönberger, 1939, p. 44). For the reader of Descartes's works, however, the search for the phantoms may be continued in the philosophy. The disturbing apparitions are described by Descartes himself in a later work, "The Search after Truth by the Light of Nature"; the passage is interesting in its combination of the elements of the first dream:

> I declare to you that those doubts which alarmed you to begin with, are like those phantoms and vain images which appear in the night by the uncertain glimmer of a feeble light. Fear pursues you if you flee, but if you approach and touch them, you will find nought but wind and shadow. (Descartes, 1955, I., p. 315)

The second dream is in some ways a condensed reading of the first. After the initial dream, Baillet writes, Descartes awoke and

> had even at that moment a feeling of distress, which made him fear that this was the work of some evil spirit which

perhaps wished to ensnare him . . . he prayed to God to
protect him from the bad effect of his dream.

Descartes awoke and meditated after each dream, in
fact, and in the two hours preceding his second dream, he
pleaded to God "to preserve him from all the evils that
could threaten him in punishment for his sins, which he
recognised were serious enough to draw thunderbolts on
his head."

Descartes spent time "in divers thoughts upon the
good and evil of the world. Then came immediately a new
dream." In this dream, the philosopher is indeed punished
for his sins, for, just as he had feared, "he thought he heard
a sharp and resounding noise which he took to be a peal of
thunder. It gave him such a fright that he awoke instantly."

The second dream was sightless but was followed by
a tracerlike cloud of sparks which the dreamer saw before
him on awakening. Descartes often saw sparks when he
awoke, explains Baillet, and might have been disturbed by
a storm. Stephen Schönberger notes that sparks or flashes
often signify the sight of parental intercourse (Schönberger, 1939, p. 44), but again, while this conclusion is
psychoanalytically orthodox, its short-circuit effect denies
Descartes the opportunity to speak for himself. In his essay,
"Les Météores," he begins his explanation of thunder with
a description of contemporary mythologizing of natural
processes:

> Although clouds scarcely exceed the summits of some
> mountains and one sometimes even sees them lower than
> the tops of our bell towers, still, since one must turn his eyes
> towards heaven to look at them, we think of them as being
> so high that even poets and painters see them as the throne
> of God and pretend that He uses his own hands to open and
> close the doors to the winds, to sprinkle dew on the flowers
> and to hurl lightning against the rocks. That makes me hope
> that if I explain their nature here so that one will no longer
> have occasion to admire anything about what is seen or

> descends from above, one will easily believe that it is possible in some manner to find the causes of everything wonderful above the earth. (Vrooman, 1970, pp. 123–124)

A recent biographer of Descartes, J. R. Vrooman, writes of "Les Météores" that it "explains thunder as the result of a higher cloud falling upon a lower one, which creates a loud sound because of the resonance of the air" (Vrooman, 1970, p. 124). Behind the depersonalization, the logos of thunder is still divine, still the conjunction of Father Sky with his underling. Another subtle erotization of motion occurs in *Rules for The Direction of The Mind*, where Descartes writes as the mechanical physicist:

> I shall observe that while a stone cannot pass to another place in one and the same moment, because it is a body, yet a force similar to that which moves the stone is communicated exactly instantaneously if it passes unencumbered from one object to another. (Descartes, 1955, I., p. 30)

We might speculate that motion without change of place is coitus, from *co-ire,* to go together or move together, unencumbered, exactly, and instantaneously. The word Descartes uses in the *Regulae* for "unencumbered" is "nuda" (Descartes, 1955, I., p. 30)—a conventional philosophic term but significant—and in a portion of "Olympica" preserved by Leibniz, Descartes writes at the end of his dream narratives that "instantaneous activity signifies creation" (Descartes, 1963, p. 62).

A second meditation preceded the third dream. Descartes looks about his room "to catch a glimpse of the objects that were nearest him." Thereafter

> on this last occasion he wished to have recourse to reasons drawn from philosophy; and he drew conclusions that satisfied him, after observing, on opening and shutting his eyes alternately, the quality of the images.

Again falling asleep, "in a calm state of mind," he dreams that he finds two books on a table. The first is a dictionary, whose discovery delights him; the second is the *Corpus Veterum Poetarum Latinorum.* He opens this second volume to a poem by Ausonius which opens with the line "Quod vitae sectabor iter?" ("Which way shall I choose?"). A man indicates to the dreamer another poem beginning "Est & Non" and praises it. Descartes identifies the one by Ausonius and attempts to locate it in the anthology. He at first discovers the dictionary, then "no longer complete." On finding Ausonius he is unable to find the poem beginning "Est & Non" but recommends the poem beginning "Quod vitae." The man begs to see it, but Descartes's attention is distracted by the sight of "several small engraved portraits" which cause him to remark on the beauty of the book, although it is no longer the edition he recognized. "At this point the books and the man disappeared and went out of his thoughts, without however waking him."

The third dream continued with an interpretation. Descartes

> judged that the Dictionary meant nothing but all the sciences assembled together; and that the anthology of poems entitled *Corpus Poetarum* showed in particular and in a more distinct way Philosophy and Wisdom joined together.

Upon awakening, Descartes continued his allegorical interpretation of the dreams, taking the first two as divine admonitions relating to his past and the third—"which had nothing but was very pleasant and agreeable"—as a prophecy concerning his own future.

II

The temporal values attached to the dreams by Descartes are not to be ignored, for it was during the years following the dreams that his universal science attained its greatest import. But it is difficult, psychoanalytically, to concur with the dreamer's dismissal of the first two dreams as relevant only to his past. The third dream and the dreamt interpretation which followed it represent the most highly defended and abstract part of the series; as he interpreted the third dream, Descartes was unsure "whether he dreamed or mused." These final dream thoughts, in fact, can be seen as part of the amnesiac process which, to a varying degree, accompanies all dreams to consciousness. The only associations which remained to the dreams of the school and the thunderclap lack the discursive complexity of the third set of associations. Descartes identified the "ill wind" as an evil spirit "that tried to throw him forcibly into a place where he intended to go voluntarily." God sent the spirit to prevent his advance, only permitting his entrance into the school chapel at his will. The thunderclap "was the signal of the Spirit of Truth." Then followed the third dream musing, which was almost exclusively allegorical in content.

It is possible to see in the first two dreams reconstructions of past and repressed events; Descartes hints at this in his mention of "past sins," and it would not be difficult to see in his entrance into a "holy chamber" (the school chapel) and the thunderclap and sparks which follow as the results of the punishment of a curious young boy who receives a blow to the head by an angry father. Pardoxically, the "primal scene" can be seen as a variation within the basic structure of dreaming. Coitus is a progressive metonomy of the basic regressive structure of dreaming; as Geza Roheim points out in his study, *The Gates of The Dream*, "the primal scene may be a 'second edition' of the basic dream" (Roheim, 1969, p. 40). Falling asleep and dreaming, as will be seen, are two stages in a dialectical process, one aspect of which is cast in the form of parental intercourse. For "in seeing the primal scene, i.e., the father entering into the mother, the dreamer is really repeating the basic dream, i.e., himself entering into the mother" (Roheim, 1969, p. 29).

Descartes, however, has left his readers with the contention that the thunderclap was a visitation by "the Spirit of Truth." Are the first two dreams to be dismissed in favor of the third, thus satisfying the conditions for a nonpsychoanalytic, allegorical interpretation; or are the implications of the third dream to be dismissed and the contention made that two primal scene fantasies were followed by a near-waking state in which the philosopher thought out problems related to his scientific speculations and which was essentially unrelated to the previous material? With Descartes, we must ask: *"Quod vitae sectabor iter?"*

Psychoanalytic discussions of Descartes's three dreams have been divided between these two alternatives. The vast majority of interpretations offer little meaningful insight into Cartesian philosophy and have seen Descartes's writings as little other than unrelated byproducts of a fixated imagination. One writer, however, is willing to entertain the possibility that when Descartes said that during the night of November 10, 1619, he had discovered the foundations of his system that the philosopher was, in some sense, making an accurate statement.

In his *Dreams and The Uses of Regression,* Bertram Lewin is unique among the psychoanalytic commentators on the dreams in choosing to draw a structural analogy between

> Descartes's dualistic view of the world [and] the view that we commonly find in an ordinary well-projected visual dream, where the dreamer is exactly what the observer is supposed to be and tries to be in the Cartesian system, that is, *res cogitans,* the pure and irrelevant spectator, the external observer. (Lewin, 1958, p. 18)

Thus, the pains experienced by Descartes during the course of the first two dreams (which Lewin analyzes as the effects of an incipient migraine attack) result in '"the philosopher's efforts to solve the problem of how one may preserve sleep in the face of intrusive bodily pain and discomfort" (Lewin, 1958, p. 40) and prompt Descartes to remove his ego from the source of pain and to elaborate the same condition of bodily derealization in his philosophy. The analogy is forceful, but it is based on a rejection of erotic symbolization as "too generalized." Lewin's interpretation follows the same lines as his view of the dreams; both result in the exile of the body in order to create an essentially extracorporeal interpretation of psychic phenomena.

If the idea of overdetermination is to mean anything, then we can no more sacrifice the generalized information of the dreambook to the elegance of Lewin's reading of the mental ego than we can, on the other hand, dissolve the integrity of the case history in a too facile reading of repressed material. If the value of the dreambook and the case history is to be preserved—and they are the two great "genres" of psychoanalysis—then these two interpretative dimensions must be successfully reconciled. In the instance of Descartes's three dreams, the reconciliation remains to be made. If the language of dreams is to be interpreted meaningfully in terms of Descartes's own idiom of representation, then another approach to the process of dreaming is needed. Lewin's reading of the three dreams is attractive in its structural analogies to Cartesian philosophy; but at the same time it makes the mistake of treating the erotic content of the dreams as a sort of night residue, just as, in another over-reduction, Wisdom and Schönberger dismiss the biographical Descartes in favor of the archetypical slumbering child.

If the structural reading of the dreams is relevant—and it is—then it would have to comprehend the erotic as well as the "mental," the ego-alien as well as the ego-syntonic. Such a description of dreaming is found in *The Gates of The*

Dream, in which Roheim argues the existence of just such a structure, which he calls "the basic dream." Roheim's interpretation of the dream sees the condition of ego separation in the "successful dream" not in the static form that Lewin does but as one stage in a dynamic process. Roheim's rereading of the dream as a dynamic structure permits a rereading of Descartes's dreams. And, by extension, it makes possible a re-evaluation of the psychoanalytic meaning of Descartes's philosophy.

"In sleep," notes Roheim, "we close our eyes—regress from the object world. The dream consists of a series of images—a move towards an imaginary object world" (Roheim, 1969, p. 107). The motive behind the dream is a defensive action against the fear of annihilation or ego loss. The series of "pictures in the head" (Lewin, 1968) or the movement towards visualization "is caused by an attempt to regain a partial contact with the environment" (Roheim, 1969, p. 107). The dream-picture provides the illusion of a being-in-the-world; it is at once a distraction from the impingements of the world and a transient, hallucinatory madness—"our nightly psychosis," as Freud refers to the dream at one point.

The fall out of the world, the regression from outer reality, is magically countered in the dream, which provides a progressive movement into a world of illusion, a silent series of pictorial representations. The fall into the nothingness of sleep (which Roheim calls "the hypnagogic fantasy") is alleviated by silent pictures. The function of visualization in the dream is anxiety-reduction; the fear of annihilation, of being swallowed up in nothingness, is assuaged by a cunning deceit.

It is in this dual movement of sleep, both regressive and progressive, that the model of Cartesian thought may be found. A movement away from the sensual world is succeeded by the formation of a "world-picture." As his *Meditations* attest, Descartes always bore a troubled rela-

tionship to the questions of insanity, dreams, and decep-
tion. In his famous "demon argument," he is haunted by
the thought that his laboriously constructed relationship
with the universe and God is merely a diabolic trick. What
if his method is only a black art and his clear and distinct
perceptions "only illusions and deceptions which he [the
Devil] uses to take me in?" (Descartes, 1972a, p. 100).
Descartes's God guarantees the validity of his creature's
perception because he has placed a seed of his omniscience
in him, and all the qualities which the philosopher values
receive their absolute expression in the divine. Only
through this identification can Descartes combat the
thought that his extramundaneity is an illusion, the work of
a shape-shifter, or, as Spenser called him, Archimago. The
Cartesian flight from the world depends for its success on
a cosmic Dreamer, a keeper of appearances who, like the
philosopher, exists at the periphery of His world as an
all-seeing presence.

The maintenance of the dream depends on visualization, and, if a philosophy can be called a language of experience, then the Cartesian idiom is vision: "My ideas are in
me like pictures," remarked Descartes (Maritain, 1944, p.
108). His essay on human physiology, the *Treatise of Man*,
is occupied mainly with the anatomy of the eye (Descartes,
1972b, p. xxix), and the body image which emerges from
this text is one of a tangle of nerves which ends in the eyes
and is connected in the brain by a series of "coctions" to
the abdominal cavity. The eyes perceive while the gut feels;
the former transmits its information to the pineal gland
(the seat of "the reasonable soul") via the optic nerve,
while the latter makes itself felt throughout the body with
biles and "animal spirits" which rise to the cerebrum as
emotions.

The Cartesian idiom is filled with visual oppositions,
the most famous being the "clear and distinct" against the

"dark and obscure." Similar expressions suggest that, for Descartes, discourse, thinking, and even existence were essentially visual in nature. And like his well-known aphorism, "I think, therefore I am," an accurate paraphrase of the Cartesian idiom might be "seeing is being." In his "Replies" to contemporary critics, he states:

> He who says, "I think, hence I am, or exist," does not deduce existence from thought by a syllogism, but, by a simple act of mental vision, recognises it as if it were a thing that is known *per se*. (Descartes, 1955, II., p. 38)

The withdrawal from the world of sense phenomena is followed by visual activity, just as regression from the object world in the basic dream is followed by its illusory recreation in a series of images. One result of this kind of action in the seventeenth century is a screen effect, a two-dimensionality in which the world appears as only a facade (see Holland, 1959). Descartes writes:

> I shall here express myself more frankly and shall not conceal the fact that I am convinced that the only thing by which our senses are stimulated is that superficies which forms the boundary of the dimensions of the perceived body. For contact takes place only at the surface. (Descartes, 1955, II., p. 117)

This ocular mediation of experience can assume grotesque proportions, as when Descartes imagines an Argus-like philosopher, "the man who would like to have the whole of the human body covered with eyes, in order that it might appear more beautiful, because no bodily part is more beautiful than the eye" (Descartes, 1955, II., p. 225).

The eternal watchfulness of Io's guardian epitomizes Descartes's "reasonable soul" which "is always thinking" (Descartes, 1970, p. 125).

III

It is when Descartes extends his universal science to the treatment of the passions that his visual idiom breaks down. For the mode of the emotions is not the separate and distinct. As he recognized himself, the early language of experience lacks the fissionable quality of cogitation; it is, as Descartes put it, "a confused way of thinking." Just as the nightly activity of dreaming interrupts consciousness and forces Descartes to insist on eternal thought, so the question of human origins presents him with a dilemma which he must avoid by escaping from "the prison of the body" (Descartes, 1970, p. 111.) In his correspondence, the reasons for his philosophical separatism become apparent. Just as the *cogito* must disengage itself from sense experience, so must the reasonable soul disavow its corporeal habitat.

Descartes describes the elation felt by the infant in its own body and the nutritive, maternal environment in a prose that betrays a nostalgia for the "confusion" repudiated by the adult philosopher:

> At first moment of the soul's union with the body it felt joy, and immediately after love, then perhaps also hatred, and sadness. . . . I think that the soul's first passion was joy. . . . I say that love followed because the matter of our body is in a perpetual flux like the water in a stream, and there is always need for new matter to take its place, so that it is scarcely likely that the body would have been in a good condition unless there were nearby some matter suitable for food. The soul, uniting itself in volition to that new matter, felt love for it; and later, if the food happened to be lacking, it felt sadness. And if its place were taken by some other matter unfit to nourish the body, it felt hatred. (Descartes, 1970, pp. 210–211)

Beneath the philosophic rhetoric can be detected the bliss of communion with the mother and the rage of the child at separation from the source of its joy. The passage reflects in a personal way the sense of loss and resentment Descartes must have felt at the loss of his mother during his second year of life. Shortly thereafter, Descartes began a lifelong practice of morning dozing, remaining in the warmth of his bedroom—a habit which earned him the nickname "le chambriste" from his schoolfellows (von Franz, 1968, p. 60). In the same letter, Descartes explains in terms of his own psychology of the passions the dangers which follow the end of joy and the separation from food:

> If I attend to the definition of the two passions, love and hate, I consider that love for an undeserving object can make us worse than hatred for an object we love; because there is more danger being united with, and almost transformed into, a thing which is bad than there is in being separated in volition from one which is good. (Descartes, 1970, p. 216)

One might say that the adult Descartes made a virtue of his childhood condition of abandonment by creating a philosophy of solitude. In drawing a set of rigid boundaries around the *cogito,* in withdrawing the ego from the world and the body, his sustained philosophical rejection of interaction avoided what he felt was a cosmic rage:

> Evil arising from hatred extends only to the hated object, whereas disordered love spares nothing but its object, which commonly is very small in comparison with all other things which it is ready to abandon and destroy to season its violence. (Descartes, 1969, p. 119)

In the dream—or, rather, in the process of dream formation—he found an environment which satisfied both his need for autonomy and his strong epistemological interest which the dream provided for in "the illusion of an ego and object contrast" (Roheim, 1969, p. 119).

The paradoxical nature of dreaming offered Descartes another advantage. He constantly refers to his philosophy as a second home. His system is a house rebuilt from the materials of an older one which has been demolished (Descartes, 1972a, pp. 35, 45, 50); he writes to Mersenne that he is like a man who has "acquired unexpected riches" and is "starting to build another house more suitable to his condition" (Descartes, 1970, p. 9). The school chapel Descartes visited in his first dream and the palace of wisdom he erected afterwards are standard maternal tropes in the dreambook, but they have a dual meaning in the dialectic of the dream. Descartes's new house is exactly what he said it was: a new structure built with aid of ancient materials. Roheim articulates the meaning of this dual value:

> Now our theory assumes that while sleep is perceived by man's unconscious as uterine regression, the dream is a rebuilding of the lost world on a libidinal-narcissistic basis in which phallic and uterine images (symbols) predominate. In other words, the dream room as a womb would be both an attempt to regress into the womb and to get back into this world. (Roheim, 1969, p. 132)

The second house is a "rebuilding of the lost world" on an egocentric basis. Descartes rebuilt his world free from the threats of fusion and annihilation; like the God of the Deists, he was "a Great Architect . . . a manipulator of objects in visual-tactile space" (Ong, 1970, p. 73), "dwelling in the *cogito* and manipulating the data of vision to build up a new world and to protect the ego from complete extinction (sleep, dying)" (Roheim, 1969, p. 62).

The rebuilding of a home, the discovery of the new world within, were made possible by dreaming reality. The importance of the night of November 10, 1619, for the history of philosophy was great indeed. During that night one man's fitful sleep, punctuated by troubled meditations, induced in Western thought a slumber which was to last for over two centuries. For Descartes's science proposed a set of perceptual imperatives and an anatomy of the natural world based upon the dreamlike economy of his own defenses.

However brilliant and intricate a synthesis of the knowledge of his time, Descartes's version of reality depended for its inner coherence upon the visualization and quantification of experience. This "exclusion mechanism" (Schachtel, 1954, p. 310) rested, in part, upon the selective reinforcement of the sense of sight. The consequences of this perceptual reapportionment have been the subject of prolonged analysis by Marshall McLuhan in his history of modern perception, *The Gutenberg Galaxy.* He notes:

> Any sense when stepped up to high intensity can act as an anesthetic for other senses. . . . Hypnosis depends on the same principle of isolating one sense in order to anesthetize the others. The result is a break in the ratio among the senses, a kind of loss of identity. (McLuhan, 1969, p. 35)

Descartes's language of experience depended on just such an anesthesia. The Cartesian system succeeded, McLuhan points out, because "if we can devise a consistent means of translating *all* aspects of our world into the language of *one* sense only, we shall then have a distortion that is scientific because consistent and coherent" (McLuhan, 1969, p. 93).

Our awakening from Descartes's dream has proved to be a long and arduous process. But, in one of the ironies of history, René Descartes's denial of the unconscious served to facilitate its discovery. In *The Unconscious Before Freud,* Lancelot Law Whyte concludes:

> Prior to Descartes and his sharp definition of . . . dualism, there was no cause to contemplate the possible existence of unconscious mentality. . . . Descartes's dogmatism regarding a split in the nature of things provoked other thinkers, who lacked his personal dissociation, to repudiate his way of thinking. (Whyte, 1960, pp. 27; 90)

The protracted unraveling of Cartesian dualism required numerous revisions of the conceptions of natural
process, scientific investigation, and philosophic inquiry.
This process was initiated and continued throughout the
eighteenth and nineteenth centuries by a host of thinkers,
their contributions as diffuse as they were important. But
the repudiation of Descartes found its most forceful expression in another man's Olympica, Sigmund Freud's *The
Interpretation of Dreams.* With Freud's work, the science of
mental life was redreamed, and Descartes's thought
became yet another dream of reason laid to rest.

Chapter 8

NARCISSISM AND THE DEFIANCE OF TIME

E. Mark Stern

"Time," lamented Hamlet, "is out of joint," and it remained for him alone to "set it right" (Act I, Scene 5). It was an immense task for the young prince. Indeed, to take revenge on the monarch who defied the established order became a mission of superhuman defiance. Hamlet strove to restore his father's prerogative to the throne by claiming it for himself, and in so doing father and son became inextricably bound up in each other. Which one was alive, and which was dead? The ghost-father strode the ramparts of the castle while the son sulked in corners. Past and present converged. Time stopped. Hamlet, in his need for superhuman defiance, bent time to his own image and made it part of himself.

In Hamlet's case causality became supplemented by this new factor until the shaping of time was taken for granted as an existential given. Object-libido was replaced by ego-libido. Even his own death could not sever the father-son relationship for Hamlet, who looked upon his vengeance as a kind of private, even immoral, scenario: "Report me and my cause aright" (Act V, Scene 2). For a person such as Hamlet, who has totally identified himself with chance events, life is not an unfolding of coincidences but a preordained omnipotence, an overdimensionality, tinged with mania. Mania is a mission wherein object and ego remain undifferentiated.

As a mission wherein object and ego remain undifferentiated, mania appears to be what the depressive condition strives to achieve. "Primary narcissistic omnipotence," says Fenichel (1945), "is more or less regained and life is felt to be incredibly intensified" (p. 407). In this narcissistic victory boundaries disappear, and the time factor is now no longer part and parcel of obsessive striving. The time and the "I" are one.

Melanie Klein (1956, p. 323) observes that depression and feelings of worthlessness give additional impetus to the need to escape from the self. Similarly, "heightened greed and denial which characterize manic defenses against depression are, together with envy, also an important factor in projective identifications." Envy, when dynamically grouped with denial, cannot help but become identification. The time model is shaped in the image and likeness of the creator.

To transcend time is one way of forsaking a journey. The rapid move from one topic to another is parareactive and, although seemingly corrective from an emotional vantage point, is essentially short-circuited reasoning, amounting to delusion (Meyer, 1939). Nevertheless, such delusion is twisted into the appearance of a larger whole and becomes a statement of personal existence. Time is thus arrogated by the ego to itself, forestalling progression and ego-separation. Father and son are no longer separate entities, but neither is the self. Sartre (1963) cites Genet for whom "the other is conjured up only to be conjured away, together with himself, in his act of masturbation. [And it is in this act] . . . that Genet himself exists. "I exist only through those who are nothing apart from the being they have through me.' " (p. 41). Beyond reinforcing self-worth, the narcissistic leap becomes an act of affirmation by reordering all essential priorities, the self included. Galaxies of emotionally charged antitime, like antimatter, are indistinguishable parareactive forces which lend power and might to a quest. The forsaken journey, however, obviates the possibility that others may react. If I and you are the same as me, then the only contact between us will be based on the persuasiveness with which I order my universe. To masturbate is to invest the cycle with source, direction, and eternal return.

Such total control over temporal representations (time) blocks the possibility of immersion in the instant, or being receptive to meanings available when I am not simply reincorporating expectations but am vitally aware of separation. Narcissistic preoccupation specifically defends against surprise with a sense of forced (and forceful) certitude. For within the fullness of narcissistic reactions, surprise is impossible. My father and I are one just as I and myself are one; through my command time bends and holds expectancy at bay. I am in full command of my non-life. I do not rise to an occasion since I cannot, despite all protestations, achieve the mobility which enlists responsiveness. Even the negative elements in my self-appraisal have been usurped by my presumption of their right to goad me to participation. Nietsche's Zarathustra rhapsodizes on "the hour of great contempt . . . in which your happiness becomes loathsome to you, and also your reason and virtue." Such moments are not, in fact, found within the narcissistic orientation. Object-cathexis would assign all contempt to an arena outside of one's orbit, thus relieving the ego of any personal responsibility.

For one allied solely with himself, time plays an enormous role in helping the narcissist to relate:

> Time is the central category of man's finitude, for he is always under its threat; and complementary to this, it is within time that the affirming answer to its threat is found. In his estrangement man experiences a diminishing tolerance for his temporality; in guilt he remembers his past, in his transitoriness he knows his present, and in his apprehension he looks towards his future. (Macnab, 1966, p.157)

Defying time as he does, a person locked into libidinous self-directed preoccupations offers less than effective resistance to the admonitions of time. Sullivan (1940) briefly describes his patient who had been a shepherd in the Ozarks:

> One day, God spoke to him, told him of the war, directed him to enlist, and gave him assurances of his safety in this connection. . . . The grandeur seemed to be complete, without evidences of his suffering persecutions. His end suggests . . . that he had achieved omnipotence. . . . One day while walking—in sublime detachment and completeness—with a party of patients, he leapt under a moving street car and was killed instantly. I believe that this impulse arose from a sudden defect of security, that he "expected" to demonstrate his power to remain unscathed, and that there was no suicidal intention. (p. 63)

Although Sullivan acknowledged that Freud's conception of the term narcissism had been several times modified since 1914, he nevertheless seems to indicate that a full-scale paranoid development takes place in patients as a result of sublimatory failure. Perhaps theirs is not so much failure as an attempt to restructure the object-libidinous potential into boundless processes. Failing this, they surrender freedom for convenience by making "reality" conform to their exaggerated schedule. Time thus becomes characterized by hyperbolic excitement; gesture is obsessed with its own magic. To be involved in a narcissistic orientation does not so much signify grandiosity as it does a persistent need to reorder time. This recurring revision of duration leads to an excited tempo and ultimately encages itself. The narcissist becomes the prisoner of his own punctuation. The reordering of time becomes an attempt at self-rescue; it expresses fear of an incomplete journey and protests that all must be well. "My pulse, as yours," cried Hamlet

> doth temperamentally keep time, And makes as healthful
>   music; it is not madness
> That I have uttered; bring me to the test,
> And I the matter will re-word; which madness
> Would gambol from. (Act III, Scene 4)

The narcissistic answer is not wholly a pathologic response. Indeed, Hamlet's notion of reworking time is actually a matter of maintaining control. Nor is narcissism necessarily an escape. In point of fact, time is a challenge, and only when it seems to humble a person's plight does it become a point of control. Jack, a patient known to the writer, spent day after day half-heartedly involved in a supervisory position in a large engineering firm. Various elements in his life, including the death of his mother, conspired to bring him close to a severe depressive reaction. As a supervisor engaged in reviewing blueprints, he had to make accurate calculations. Jack's complaint that he could no longer stand the excruciatingly painful demands of this work and was seriously considering asking for a temporary demotion came as some surprise to his closest associates, who tended to see him as a self-confident man.

Try as he might, Jack was unable to persuade his superior that he needed a respite in order to regain his strength. He had not counted on his reputation of competence established over a long period of time. As in many such situations where the appearance of stability has been cultivated, Jack's depressive behavior was disregarded as if it were no more than a temporary reaction.

THE CASE OF JACK

Jack's biography was that of many overachievers. He was hell-bent on establishing an image which could be relied upon to save him if pressure ever threatened to sink his boat. Jack's performances were geared to accenting his popularity; what he lacked in intimacy was compensated by his illustrious reputation.

Thus, the groundwork was established for an ex post facto personality reaction. By the time his superiors decided to take his emotional disability seriously, Jack retrenched into a furor to get his work done. This obsessive stance became a personal mandate, and was soon accompanied by expressions of florid loyalty to the company. Despite the fact that his calculations began to play havoc with the structural designs he worked on, no task seemed too much. Jack began to attempt a new synchronization with his own mathematical formulas. In social relationships his fast tempo began to alarm his friends. Nevertheless, the patient sought to reassure them saying: "I've discovered that three hours of sleep is quite enough," and "I've decided that mimicking sad people in the subways ultimately cheers them up." His pace and newfound "freedom" were, of course, desperate echos of what he had always done, gross exaggerations the more apparent for their inappropriateness and lack of social sensibility.

Beneath his manic behavior, Jack's main goal was to re-establish time. The demands being made on him at his job actually were unreasonable, and he did, in fact, have sufficient power to insist that his load be lightened. But Jack unconsciously feared that agreement would induce a loss of control. When his emotions could no longer stand it, he enacted a caricature of his earlier self "in better times."

The narcissistic dimension of Jack's life confirmed the idea that in order to preserve control, time must provide the individual with "limitless extension and oneness with the universe" (Freud, 1949, p. 14). As with Hamlet, the extension of the primary ego placed him in a time-controlling destiny pattern. Defeat had to be met with the solid assumption that his power lay in not capitulating to consensual time. Just as Triton raises and calms the waves to his own delight, so too does a person's omnipotent fantasy life link him with all processes. Jack programmed himself into a can't-fail position. His precarious plight was constructed to enhance his sense of pride. And "pride," according to Calvin Hall (1954), "is a form of secondary narcissism" (p. 44). Within the spiritual traditions, there is a definite distinction between being authentically illuminated and being subject to self-glorification and pride. Meister Eckhart's meaning of being truly extensive required the notion of *inne sein, inne bleiben* which he used to indicate transcendence. In contrast to this state he preaches of "people who imagine that they have been transmuted into the Holy Trinity, who have never really got beyond self because they are loath to deny themselves."

Exacting revenge on the defeating powers nevertheless seeks reappropriation of consensual reality. No less than Hamlet, Jack needed revenge as a way of rescuing the mask of sanity. (See Reich, 1950, p. 158, "Character is essentially a narcissistic protection mechanism.") Thus, the popular notion that narcissism signifies exaggerated love of oneself is perhaps better explained as the ego's attempt to unite its every function with a personal time sequence. In this scheme, the narcissistic impulse to be and to become are one and the same. What had been termed megalomania is certainly not mere grandiosity. (*Megalo,* as used in medicine, indicates an abnormal enlargement. From a psychological vantage point it may be argued that megalomania rushes time beyond madness, so that distortion becomes so expansive as to become super-reality, "larger than life.") It is, rather, that factor which unites all hidden elements, unconscious as well as conscious, with an omnipotence that stresses a continual return to a source.

When Hamlet avenges his father's murder he becomes, in effect, his own father. He fails to become a father to anyone else, since he is preoccupied with personal immortalization and perfectibility. Hamlet's engagement of the actors to play out his high comedy commemorates his wish to speak through the notion of time passed—an appeal to a sense of nostalgia. However, a certain suspicion of his own motivation appears to win out. In a searching discourse Hamlet, the self-proclaimed "rogue . . . peasant slave . . . [and] ass" obliges himself as simply "the son of a dear father murdered, Prompted to my revenge by heaven and hell." (Act II, Scene 2). "The play's the thing," and Hamlet is determined to stop time in his effort to call attention to his plight. There is no answer beside the play. It is his only announcement. His attempts at some design of revenge and fulfillment are simple caricatures. The height of narcissism is reached when the reflection becomes the reality. Watching the performance, Hamlet confiscates himself and consequently halts time.

As becomes clear, Hamlet is a man of one cause: he needs to recapitulate his childhood. He is amoral to the core except in his own pursuit. "There is nothing either good or bad, but thinking makes it so" (Act II, Scene 2). And with this epitaph he cries out, "Oh God, I could be bounded in a nutshell and count myself a king of infinite space, were it not that I have bad dreams" (ibid.).

For the narcissist, being bound by reality is certainly not his notion of a reality principle. It is a terror which must be masked. If time were an accepted mean, then so would be attachments to a world of living flesh and blood. Hamlet does not have these. He feigns madness and love for Ophelia, but in both attempts he remains singularly unsuccessful. Neither situation provides the necessary tools to loosen his grip on time and tides. Everything must happen at his own command. Madness and love, oftentimes resembling each other in passion, are not vaunted by narcissists. One is not estranged, since the purpose of narcissistic preoccupation is the relief of excessive pressures to facilitate drawing into one's own self-made world. Small latitude was left to consider other needs or plans or to distinguish between fatigue and vitality. All had to be consumed under a plan of his own authorship.

The fusion of time and personality is not limited to narcissism. Authentic experience belongs to the whole person, and a system attains validity through personal experience. Time is no exception to this rule. Man apportions pleasure and pain in the amounts most tolerable to him. Time factors are based on personal inference; we assume a particular attitude toward time by moving from the general to the particular. After all, we are dealing with people and not with things. However, beyond self-absorption there is an ontology which stresses that our being symbolizes time, whereas our becoming carries unique distinctions which place us in opposition to a oneness with past history. The process of individuation does not make time simply an alien force; rather time must be experienced as a familiar, essentially neutral containment embodying a spectrum of options and potentials. Thus, to "waste time" is to declare a norm, a set of priorities. To try to "stop time" is a desperate undertaking which may best be described as a depressive position. And to "weigh time" is to regard ourselves as subject to a situation we must adapt to, like a person who makes decisions on the basis of the energy required.

Yet, from the vantage point of narcissism, time is an exterior rather than a temporal. It is a mask or a thing rather than a process. According to Martin Heidegger (1962), time is necessary to understand being. This being (*Dasein*) is our "in-the-worldness." To live authentically, however, existence must be viewed as finite. Possibility exists only where one realizes that non-being is proper to an understanding of becoming. Only through this sense of finitude can the person begin to actualize himself rather than merely to align himself with outside factors. Thus in order to lay claim to authentic experience, it is vitally necessary to recognize that there exists a significant set of appointed circumstances and that these circumstances, while necessary, are not unlimited. Strictly speaking, we ratify our existence as we are one with our being and separate in our choices. Resolution, a focal Heideggerian notion, is intended to make the concept of aliveness more central. The fact that a person is one with himself—with his present moment—allows him to face his temporality with courage.

Narcissism lacks courage in the face of advancing time. Ella Freeman Sharpe (1950) states that Hamlet's hold on reality denotes a narcissistic withdrawal of libido from external objects. Thus, Hamlet's "hold on reality remains in his narcissistic interests and affections" (p. 204.) Hamlet hoped that by reversing gears and avenging his father's death the proper line of succession would be reinstated. In a similar manner, Jack's personality concealment was meant to ward off enemy encroachments. In neither case was time seen as an opportunity to begin new lines of action.

Hamlet's inability to transcend his father's fate limited his activity to a kind of reclamation of his father's immortality. He had a narrow historical consciousness. Each act was calculated to have its effect outside of intervening time. Paul Tillich's (1963) notion of *kairos,* or that right time in which something is to be done, the "fulfillment in time" (p. 369) is obviously truer for a venture that enlists extrinsic events than one pursued in isolation. When others are involved, opportunity reigns for the individual to develop his own unique style rather than impose his private representation of what has been. Since time begins beyond one's control one must correspond to its demands. One has the opportunity to become a unique entity, free of parental restraint although not removed from history. The delicate balance is the acknowledgment of indebtedness to one's heritage without masquerading in the mournful costumes of a would-be play merely to enlist sympathy. Courage is the antithesis of narcissism.

The Narcissus myth is a primordial model of an inverted world view. But it also exemplifies the defiance of a sense of universal center around which any time-space notion is knit. Centrality requires dynamic movement, since order is never fixed. The fixation into which the narcissist becomes locked allows for rumination yet little self-evaluation. Narcissism confounds itself by its seeming ties to the past. For Hamlet, the past is inseparable from revenge. Narcissus returns to the past through living death. Authentic life, the opposite of narcissism, requires dexterity and flexibility. Jack and Hamlet appear to be locked into a predictable cycle in which the only chance for "recovery" is to take time into one's own hands. In a similar vein it is interesting to note that the unified field theory of modern physics carries with it enough flexibility to incorporate uniqueness. Heisenberg's indeterminacy principle stresses that momentary velocity of a subatomic particle makes its positioning impossible to know.

Nietzsche's (1967) notion of being as an end in itself is one view of an antidote to narcissism. Even though his notion of "eternal return" stands out as a central theme in his thinking, what he means is not a return to some previous status, but a re-creation of the lustfulness of life. Erich Neumann (1952) allies a person's apparent regression in behavior to renewal. "Psyche," he says, "reunites herself . . . with the feminine in her nature . . . (and) enters a new phase. It no longer consists in the self-contained beauty of a young girl who sees nothing beside herself. [It is rather] the beauty of a woman in love" (p. 123). Neumann disengages himself from the Freudian position and views narcissism as a more progressive phenomenon. At its best it implies an increased emphasis on a person's own beauty and wholeness. Neumann's concept must be distinguished from the Freudian notion which states that narcissistic fixation is an obsession "on a time before the conception of reality" (Fenichel, 1945, p. 442).

Sartre (1948) suggests that "just as consciousness sees the magical world into which it has cast itself, it tends to perpetuate this world in which it holds itself captive" (p. 79). Margaret Mahler (1968) observes that one line of development which makes for individuation "is brought about by the evolution and expansion of the autonomous ego functions [which] center around the child's developing self-concept" (p. 220–221). She goes on to say that "the culmination of the separation-individuation phase is the establishment of object constancy" (pp. 222–223). The stage of object constancy is attained when "a firmly established object image is available, the cathexis of which persists regardless of the stage of instinctual need" (p. 223).

The clinical picture of the patient whose narcissism has curtailed the process of individuation points up a shallowness in communication owing to his need to memorialize those objects which he has considered lost. In particular, the loss of the mother leaves in its wake the spectre of an idealized presence. Joyce Carol Oates (1973) describes a preadolescent boy who had "survived" an earthquake as well as his father's leave-taking when his parents divorced. During the quake, the boy was struck on the back of his head by an urn which his father, an anthropologist, had given to his mother. Doubly traumatized, the boy now refused to acknowledge his mother, convinced that his "real" mother had departed at the time of the earthquake and that the "other" woman struck him with the urn. In effect, of course, he was stopping time. Like Hamlet, he was pledging his loyalties to the lost mother from whom he would never again become separated. His overt emotions assumed a kind of denseness, but his relationship to the past locked itself tighter to counterfeit gratifications, such as prevailing upon his father to leave an extremely important assignment in order to talk with him.

The narcissistic personality often compensates for genuine emotional contact by making exploitative demands on the "outside" world. This oral orientation, while giving the illusion of reciprocation, compounds the oppressiveness of feeling regardless of maniclike episodes when the narcissist appears to be reaching out and extending himself. In fact, there can be no authentic extension without centrality. Nor can time move without springing from a nucleus of lifegiving core experiences. Discomposure of the time sequence intrudes when core relationships are absent. Time is the denominator which links significant early relationships with future endeavors in dynamic renewal. Letting go of the past consists in accepting a cosmology of "return."

Narcissistic preoccupation reverts the time span so that the return moves toward one's own image. This form of monomania does not always take the form of exhibitionism. It will be recalled that the narcissistic persona serves to deny a basic depressive state. Depression in this sense implies an unswerving alliance to those parts of life which, although filled with despair, are nevertheless familiar and predictable.

This early failure of trust in one's significant relationships—which Erik Erikson (1963) considers the battleground for the first nuclear conflict in the developing personality—diminishes the wholeness of personality. What miscarries is the authentic autobiography, especially those autonomous aspects of ego functioning which testify to individuation. Narcissism has long been associated with the artistic personality. But creativity requires transcendence of the time-self, not denial of it. To attempt to build a bridge to the far side of the abyss is hardly an act of mere self-absorption. The artist, performer, or creator who displays genuine talent is not involved in a synthetic version of design. He is trying to rework object relationships to a point where new possibilities begin to emerge. He is willing to bargain with the changeability of the unchangeable. For example, Copernicus advanced aesthetics by positing that what had been thought to be at rest was actually in dynamic motion. His placement of the sun was true for its time, yet subject to a more expansive time-space-self view in which even the sun was a revolving force. Patterns of relationship are discovered by being able to reach beyond any one given. True artistic virtue, like scientific veracity, is predicated on a willingness to move from one center to a new centrality, gather power, and then rework the patterns again.

   This is what Octavio Paz (1973) means when he speaks of the rebel prolonging "the fascination of myth" (p. 144). The rebel, the creative soul, is destined to be the precursor of actual revolution. In this new rectilinear time of history, "the past will not return, and the archetype of events is not what has been but what will be" (ibid.). Paz concerns himself with politics and ethics in his treatment of time, but the implications are far-reaching: history is conceived as "an onward march." Often the poet, obsessed as he must be with the circular time of myth, stands ready to make way for that "gravitational field," which Paz sees as shifting "from the yesterday that is known to the tomorrow that is yet to be discovered" (ibid.). Static fears of the mysterious future have been stimulated by the terror of not having had a cyclical, or predictive field in early life. Thus the reversion to primary omnipotence is a means of achieving location.

   For the narcissist whose primary objects were neither stable nor intact, temporal and spatial location is exceptionally important. The chaotic mess which frequently typifies an emotionally insecure childhood becomes malignant and yet incapable of enduring. As the time-bound life span extends, so too does the quest for certitude within various rigid stances. Embattled chaos can be warded off only when and if enough immunologic responses, based on early object certitude, are available. Such responses, like other protective phenomena, are similar to a biological phylum, a meaningful distinction between the self and the non-self. Antibodies ward off the invasion of any force which seeks to destroy the integrity of the organism. But the system itself can be self-defeating, especially if the self defies the archetypes so as to threaten the possibility of a mutation. At such times the immunologic system self-destructs.

From the nexus of developmental phenomena, chaos can be met with perceptual antibodies which insist on the primitive order of the species. This sets up a classic battle in which complex mechanisms which work toward regulation are obstructed by diseased formations. Chaos reigns, but within a tempest various antigens are often introduced by the very forces which threaten the organism. This is the reasoning behind the concept that even an inept natural mother is better than the most capable of institutions. The young organism receives from the mother patterns of pandemonium, creating the climate for purposeful regulatory patterns. This, of course, acknowledges the existence of an initial center.

For Hamlet there could be no time since there was no real differentiation from his father. Aristotle noted that in the natural order of happenings time is indebted to position. Without a proper sense of succession, no human organism can properly recognize its own sense of personal history. Dorian Gray was enclosed by a picture frame from which he only appeared to escape and which made his human struggles seem grotesque. Hamlet was similarly lost to a sense of what Aristotle termed "prior and posterior," since his avenging narcissism blurred his sense of authentic succession from father to son, thus engulfing Hamlet in an eternal nightmare:

> *Hamlet.* Methinks I see my father.
> *Horatio.* Where, my lord?
> *Hamlet.* In my mind's eye, Horatio.
> *Horatio.* I saw him once; he was a goodly king.
> *Hamlet.* He was a man, take him for all in all,
> I shall not look upon his like again. (Act I, Sc. 2)

The youngster in the Joyce Carol Oates story noted earlier was victim to an irretrievable set of parents. And my patient's, Jack's, quickened tempo made him alien to the levels of corporate succession—thus finally defeating him through his failure to recognize authentic accountability. For all of these people, time inhibited a proper sense of motion. Again, Aristotle concedes that time is a property of motion. However there can be no appreciation of chronological motion or age until both prior and posterior are given full recognition; until proper succession lays claim to the process. There must be a dynamic order of the parts of any organismic view of life. To go it alone in typical narcissistic fashion is to yearn for a distorted fantasy of what went before, with an eye on repeating it all again, thus denying any dynamic order. Historically, the narcissist is not lacking past or future, for without the dynamic actuality of both forces in his life he would be subject to delusional discontinuity. Like a frame of motion picture film, objectives would seem to remain static, without connection in either direction. Repeated internal tunes are a well-known source of annoyance, yet the "haunting melody" remains in order to stay the moment in an inexorably fluid time span. Likewise, an attempt to repeat and repeat the same experience is a narcissistic means of keeping control. If time can stop, so can the threats to omnipotence.

THE CASE OF MOSES

The symptom of stuttering can be traced to a form of narcissism. The stutterer speaks with halting articulations, repetitions and prolongations of sound and syllable. Speech impediment is reaction to threat. Moses, while hardly thought of as a narcissist, certainly needed to avenge his father's banishment in much the same way that Hamlet needed to punish Claudius and his mother for the murder of the king. (In the Bible, no mention is made of Moses' real father. However, tradition would have us believe that he came from the tribal house of Amram, a Levite family. See Exodus 6:18, 20.) It will be recalled that Moses was incapable of speaking directly to his adoptive surrogate father, the ruling Pharaoh of Egypt. Instead, he had to enlist his brother Aaron to be his spokesman. In point of fact, Moses was the chosen of the Lord, his God, but remained a stranger to his Pharaoh. His "slowness of speech" (Exodus 4:10) has been theorized as a stammer, due perhaps to an inability to stand directly against the line of succession. Thus Moses' effectiveness was aided by a strong ally, Aaron. And it may be noted that in his service to the God of his people he was eventually able to locate his source—that is, his sense of succession. But for the time being he was rendered personally impotent by an authority who seemed to offer him a father's acceptance. From a psychodynamic view one may deduce that while Moses was a person in his own right, he felt crushed between the dual aspect of his lost father— his visible patriarch, Pharaoh, and the tribal father of his lost infancy. Prenarcissistic fantasies in children often take the form of the child feeling that he has had other parents who are now purposely concealed from him. These adoption fantasies are expressed as power plays and often result in the entire family being drawn into the child's strategy. See the Oates (1973) story cited above.

These dualities may lead to intense ambivalence in

which one's own words take on magical significance capable of creating a mixed image of extreme potency and total impotence. Thus Moses' homosexual use of Aaron was a way of assigning his power elsewhere while leaving his infantile self in a protective matrix. Essentially time could stand still leaving him undisturbed while his alter ego wielded a powerful club. Nevertheless, Moses moved away from his princely narcissism.

Unlike Hamlet, Moses did not stop at avenging his father's dissolution. His larger task was to clarify the oneness of his father and thus perhaps repair the wicked impulses he was forced to internalize. Thus what might have resulted in the narcissistic arrest became a mission of stabilizing the father's function. This he was professed to have done despite his inability to report the character of this Father=God (Exodus 3:13) and his own fear that he lacked the credibility necessary for the task (Exodus 4:1). Nevertheless, Moses proceeded on his journey, and in the course of the pilgrimage found communion with the father. This encounter became manifest as he removed the veil from his eyes and spoke to his Lord face to face (Exodus 34:34, 35). The splendor of the vision allowed Moses to integrate the unity of God the father through the establishment of monotheism. His people, who seemed to play out the role of the disparate impulses within his own soul, were still at bay. However this father gave Moses signs and commandments which were meant to provide a framework of control for all of the many impulses. Only through these controls was the journey possible. The Father was now in the position of mature and meaningful superego. (David Freedman, 1971, p. 369, notes that the premise of a defined relation between the superego and the impulses has been a cornerstone of psychoanalytic structural theory since Freud's publication of *The Ego and the Id:* "It would seem to follow from this direct relation that the superego cannot 'mature' more rapidly than the drives.")

Perhaps the most significant command the Lord gave Moses is found in Chapter 24 of the Book of Deuteronomy: "The fathers shall not be put to death for the children, neither shall the children be put to death for the fathers: every man shall be put to death for his own sin" (Verse 16). It is here that individuation takes place in biblical history. Ultimately this must be seen as the resolution of narcissism, enabling each person to live in his own time. In the course of history Moses had to pay heavily for his transgressions, but even here there would be organic wholeness. In the end Moses had to stand aside as Joshua received his charge (Deuteronomy 3:26–28). So it is that history commences. Moses moves away from the narcissism and learns to restrain and repress his impulses in the presence of a torn father while still executing a trying mission; and thus he ultimately bows to a father of mixed impulses, takes his own reins for a time, and finally allows the mantle to be placed on the shoulders of Joshua, his spiritual son.

Frederick Perls (1969) deals with the way many gods became one father for Moses. According to Perls, this happened as Moses retroflected the aggression of the people (in my sense, his own hidden drives) by placing the blame squarely in their hands. Perls sees "retroflection" as a property of secondary narcissism in which everything gets turned back to oneself. Perls is wrong in this case, since it was not Moses' intention to eliminate aggression. Quite the contrary: Moses helped direct aggression into a time-dimension where the individual and the tribe were freed from the melancholy of reflecting on a father who needed avenging. His goal was to free himself—and his "people" —from submissiveness so that generations could be seen in perspective. Moses is a mythic figure who moves from a fear of the split-apart father and the rejecting/accepting mother to an incorporation of these impulses in time, thus freeing himself to become a unique part of history—a function of history, not its stalemate. His own paternity is the answer to the narcissism of pure revenge.

Moses produces purpose. His incorporation of history allowed him to be meaningful among his people. Compare this with Hamlet, who could not make way for his own ascendance to the throne, thus making impossible any succession or paternity. Moses, for his part, saved his people from his Father's wrath at their construction of a molten calf (Exodus 32:1–14). This calf would have given the idolatrous inclinations their tribute, but in so doing would have put an end to the dynamic mystery of Yahweh, the Father. Had Moses not contained his people's need to curtail the process of time, they would have ceased to exist. The golden calf represented a frozen narcissistic relationship with a dead father. God, the invisible force, wished to lead them onward toward fulfilling the purpose of life; to never reach a stalemate or to stand still. For Hamlet, the father was a compelling idol who needed to stop time. For Moses, Yahweh became the principle through which succession and movement might take place. The golden calf was merely a defensive veneration defying the father. It thus became an encrustation of time. Narcissism as a character defense plays the role of golden calf in relation to developmental tasks.

From the theses of this chapter, it may be deduced that the narcissistic orientation is one in which the golden calf is used as an immediate nonconsequence. In other words, if time itself has no eschatology, then why not fill it with an impression of what the self ought to resemble? Golden calves are fusions of instant gratification and a fear that time plays an annihilating game. In the cases of Hamlet and Jack, the creation of "heroic" personalities was meant to deflect from the basic theme of continuity and appropriate aliveness. Hamlet stated through his self-proclaimed "antic disposition" that "the time is out of joint [and] . . . I was born to set it right" (Act I, Scene 5). And Jack said in a clinical interview: "I think I'll rearrange the whole mess by my smile. You know I've taken to smiling lately." But beyond both "antic disposition" and "smile" there is no direct, honest acceptance of a variety of imperfect motives. In both cases there were attempts to establish an order of potential immortality. What remains lost is the symbolization and conceptualization of one's presentation.

The person is a repository of time. The unconscious, being unaware of linear progression, is certainly no reliable standard for perception. Without secondary means to symbolize time no messages can dawn on consciousness. Thus there would be no departure point for a definition of personhood. The fact that the unconscious and consciousness complement each other allows for a coextensive operation. In relatively normal transactions this reciprocity between the emotional components of personality bears a strong resemblance to an evolutionary process. The unconscious, with its storms of impulse, does not so defeat the conscious measures of life as to turn them into chaos. Disorientation in time, a familiar psychiatric category, is often due to neurologic dysfunction or severe psychic trauma. Nevertheless, it is difficult to locate a person whose time and space orientation has been so submerged that he has no self-aware individuality. Even the most regressed schizophrenic is not beyond some sense of continuity in the scale of history. However, disorganized time/space orientation frequently causes schizophrenics and others to freeze into a particular personality stance. The most defended schizophrenics—those for whom time is an enemy—often assume repetitive patterns and gestures. Narcissists are often persons whose character defenses just about ward off a complete regression into schizophrenia. What differentiates schizophrenics from narcissists is not so much their tendency to deny time, but rather the ways in which each appeals to the "forces" of submergence. For the narcissist this submergence takes the form of play-acting, time-defying roles. For the schizophrenic, denial of time occurs through an overinvestment in primary process.

Hamlet projects his narcissism onto what he considers to be his fellow beings' masquerade: "God has given you one face, and you make yourselves another: you jig, you amble, and you lisp, and nickname God's creatures, and make your wantonness your ignorance" (Act III, Scene 1). Hamlet's feigning of madness indicates more than a mere desire to disarm the suspicions of the reigning couple. As a weapon against his stepfather and mother, Hamlet dissolved his usual identity by displaying his forbidden instinctual life. This ambush of one's own primary processes typifies the kind of narcissism which constantly symbolizes all actions against time. For the narcissist, much effort is spent in pursuit of a particular point of attack in order to match forces against an unpredictable future. Narcissists try to remain young and are thus obsessed with strategy, while non-narcissists bring the interplay between the past, present, and future into some dynamic balance.

Moses ultimately achieved a synthesis between his loyalty to his father and his mission as patriarch. His vocation was sufficiently in tune with his Father without being at one with the father's heartbeat. By worship of his own childhood, Hamlet was driven to retaliate for his father's death, whereas Moses finally gained his power of speech in order to vindicate the generation which would follow him. Narcissism is regressive and does not allow for generativity whereas a time-aware life is free enough to pursue its own mission while yet nurturing its young. Narcissism ceases to make conscious use of those unconscious determinants which need fulfillment. Rather, narcissism carefully censors linear progression while striving to protect its own interests. This terror of time translates itself into a distance from others. Sartre (1963) says: "Narcissus fears men, fears their judgments and their real presence" (p. 341). In this fear there is a separation from age, since to grow older would signify some respect for otherness and for the temporal biography of the other.

The experience of age is a function of the non-narcissistic personality. On the other hand, the inability or refusal to cope with the demands of maturation indicates an arrest of personality development. In summarizing several observations on subjective time, J. Cohen (1966) notes that in paresis a patient may report that he has not grown older since his illness began. Cohen contrasts this finding to the phenomenon of depersonalization of the schizophrenic where the "immediate past may seem to the patient exceedingly remote" (p. 269). This fabric certainly helps us differentiate between the stoppage of time and the lack of recall. Narcissism, as stated earlier, being in some way a protective border between impulse control and schizophrenia, tends to incarnate the immediate and far past as mere notations for protective choreography. At the same time there is some bridging with the paretic patient in that all action ceases with the advent of a traumatic happening. Both Hamlet and Dorian Gray lived united to a point of reference analogous to an event in time, and could thus live free of both an immediate past and a far-distant history. In narcissism all time stops. That is, time is devoured in the service of filling in for a lost childhood.

THE CASE OF ANDREW

The following case is cited as a means of illustrating the denial of time. Andrew was a rising star in a well-established engineering firm. His arrival at the office every morning was met by the diffident welcome reserved for trusted typists and file clerks. He appeared to be disinterested in rank and position in a company which prized status as chief among the fringe benefits. Andrew had never outlived his reputation of being an unassuming overachiever. He looked 18 at age 26, and often concealed his prestigious vocational status from his friends.

Andrew was referred for psychotherapy by Fred, his erstwhile homosexual lover. Fred regarded Andrew as the "only solace" of his life. Nevertheless their relationship had been a stormy one, with arguments centering around Andrew's sexually promiscuous behavior.

During one of his early psychotherapy sessions, Andrew mentioned that he was often inclined to disguise his identity. For example, there were numerous times when he pretended to be a young male hustler (prostitute). During these escapades he would frequent a popular homosexual pick-up bar in the heart of New York. He boastfully spoke of his many conquests. Usually his johns were "substantial" men with "elegant" or "superb" apartments. On occasion he met businessmen from distant cities but would rarely take them up on their offers. As he stated in the session, "I somehow or other needed the luxuriousness of a substantial home." However, his meetings were largely one-night stands, since he feared the possibility of attachment. For Andrew, the fiction of the situation was sufficient. In subsequent sessions it developed that he became involved in a call-boy service. He recounted his delight at having established an alternative identity with an "eternally 19-year-old look." Meanwhile, he maintained his professional contacts and spent whatever spare time he could muster up with Fred.

Although Fred, a young physician, was supposedly a bosom buddy, he apparently could not see that Andrew was not especially homosexual. In the course of one interview Andrew admitted "fooling" Fred about being gay. Andrew was simply more at home in seducing males; he reported that he was basically uninterested in obtaining sexual gratification but delighted in counting up the many older men he could now call his johns. He secretly regarded Fred's position as that of unaware pimp and "true lover" of a harlot. It became increasingly difficult for him to distinguish his various realities, and before long he even regarded his activities in the office as grandstand plays filled with make-believe.

Psychotherapy soon revealed that the surest way Andrew could locate his place was to disregard any but the most obvious gratifications. These included "total" acceptance by others (even though he was incapable of reciprocating in kind) and the urgent desire to ward off any hints of conscious discomfort. In place of intimacy, Andrew engaged in sadomasochistic behavior with all of his johns. "It's a way of knowing where you stand," he would say.

Andrew's need to be perceived as an eternally pleasing son served to halt time. However, he never felt any closeness to his johns, saying that if he were to remain safe he would have to turn aside all emotion and keep it all on a business level. When asked whether there might not be some "return" to a lost situation, Andrew hesitated, but ultimately stressed that he could not afford to hypothesize. When further asked what he felt he might attain from psychotherapy, he replied that he sensed that he wanted something from life which he was only half getting, and that he wondered how long his fantasies could work for him, for basically, he felt lost to himself.

During his early childhood, Andrew experienced little stability. For him the truism, object loss=ego loss was most apt. As he entered adulthood, all activity remained geared to his sense of being lost. Like Hamlet, his life was defined by what he no longer had but still treasured. This reversion into self became above all a refusal to acknowledge the passage of time, grasping onto childhood to refute the vital present. The present was nonexistent except as a service area for revival of the past.

Andrew needed to be adored by others as a precocious and fascinating child in order to remind himself that childhood was not lost. This required an enactment so total that his inevitable withdrawal would generate suffering in others and thus affirm Andrew-as-child in the present.

He enjoyed toying with people. He appeared to welcome affection; yet, once achieved, he lost interest in his fascinated companion(s) and began to search for more fertile fields. He recalled that once, as a guest at a very select party, he purposely obscured himself, creating the appearance of a seductive young man out to be won by the most artful bidder. Men and women were caught up in his web, yet upon making advances each would be dropped for another guest. Quite consciously he saw each person present as a conquest and regarded his own behavior as a splendid performance. Andrew's entanglement with his incomparable exhibition became so narcissistically compelling that he carried himself through the next few days in a succession of activities which included attracting and warding off male admirers in homosexual spas, bars, and selective street haunts. The psychological game of attraction and repulsion took priority over sexuality per se.

Andrew's early life had indeed been filled with a sense of loss. His mother was raised in a Midwestern city in a family which prided itself on being socially prominent. In fact, her parents were conspicuous because of their attempts to hobnob with the town's bluebloods. According to Andrew, a disenthralled great-aunt had once set his mother in tears by accusing her parents of social-climbing. However, during Andrew's childhood his mother maintained a measured distance from all associations and foreswore any ambitions, either for herself or for her son.

His father, 20 years older than his wife, had been part of a livewire theatrical set in New York City. Andrew always wondered whether his father might not have been overtly homosexual. In several pictures he had, the father looked like an aesthete. By the time Andrew was born his father was age 58, and whatever relationship existed between father and son was untrusting and punitive. Daily beatings of Andrew were associated with the father's jealous accusations that the mother was paying entirely too much attention to the boy. He recalled having had fantasies in which he turned on his father, beat him, and urinated all over his clothes. Nevertheless, Andrew recounted how he used to love to hear his father reminisce about his days in show business.

The boy's teen years brought a temporary truce with his father. At this point his mother had almost completely withdrawn into herself and become alcoholic. The father began to make it clear that he relied upon Andrew to take major responsibility for the mother's care. Despite Andrew's best efforts at saving face for his mother, his father continued to display horror at her thinly disguised drinking. Andrew remembered being caught in macabre fights between his parents in which his own loyalty was tested. His father would resort to severe coughing spells and complain about chest pains while his mother piteously wailed about her fate. Andrew had to act rapidly to spirit his mother off to bed, away from her husband.

Eventually Andrew's father began investing his son with noble ambitions, drawing analogies with himself and his own troubled childhood. To the youth it seemed as if the father was proposing a pact of coexistence: "If you, Andrew, begin to see the light, you will relieve me of excess pressures through your realizing how deeply we are in this life together. Furthermore, you may be called upon to assume my own fate by perpetuating my care and love for your mother." When Andrew's father died at age 78, the pact was well established. Andrew, who had been primed to feel teased and unreal, could relate to men only by finding an approach which would nullify their deadly hostility. Capping his "successes," Andrew often had fantasies that this or that man might feel inclined to make him his heir or want to take him on a prolonged journey. Nothing of this sort ever happened, due as much to Andrew's withdrawal as to anything else. Nevertheless, Andrew continued in his repeated seductions. It was enough for him to imagine the bonds he had with these older men. And while they paid for sexual satisfaction, Andrew enjoyed teasing them, sometimes even to the point of inflicting mild to intense pain.

Psychotherapy was difficult for Andrew. He regarded the earliest stages of treatment as punitive. "I know that I'm probably a boring and unimaginative patient," he would say with an apologetic smile. After several broken appointments following the third month of weekly sessions, the therapist fell into an easy trap: he pleaded with Andrew not to miss appointments. Andrew saw this as his chance to please the therapist. Short of actual seduction, Andrew attempted to play up to the therapist by becoming the "ideal" patient, by learning the ropes of therapeutic strategy. Quite consciously he saw his maneuvers as ways of joining forces with a latter-day father. The therapist grew somewhat aware of the threat. (Carl Whitaker and Thomas Malone, 1953, p. 171, make the following observation: "The immature therapist may be able to tolerate certain symbolic roles, for example, the mother and the father role, and yet be panicked if he suddenly finds himself symbolized as a homosexual partner.") In his pretense at candor, the patient drew the therapist into an alliance not unlike the one into which Fred had been drawn. Andrew had finally removed all traces of anxiety from the therapeutic situation. The therapist had become for Andrew both the ghost of his father and the new father. What remained for him to deal with was much the same predicament that Hamlet found himself in: the death of the father and the new king, who was to be seduced into oblivion. The split between the father-to-be-avenged and the father-to-be-killed allowed for a stoppage of time.

In the case of Andrew, psychotherapy was unsuccessful in loosening the hands of the clock. There have been further attempts at therapy. Recently Andrew became part of an ongoing therapy group. The first few sessions were seen by him as a place in which "no one gets away with anything." It remains to be seen what future movements will follow from this form of intervention.

THE SYMBIOTIC TRANSFERENCE

What can be learned from Hamlet, Jack, and Andrew is that narcissistic time bonds are the product of two-person systems. Two parties are involved in what becomes a fear of forward movement, and both stand aside while the threat of time continues. It well may be that many psychotherapeutic arrangements become deadlocked in a nonlinear clinch because of fear of movement away from territory familiar to both patient and therapist. Transference is a reciprocal arrangement; the question of countertransference is a separate issue altogether. In an authentic transference, some willingness develops on the part of the therapist to subtly play out a portion of the patient's past. This largely unrecognized aspect of transference is basic to an understanding of narcissism, since it becomes the task of the therapist to calibrate his image of himself with the images of the past.

To be locked into the transference is to have been seduced into the patient's system. Countertransference, while often compelling, nevertheless serves as the therapist's indicator of how strong the transference might become. To see the transference as largely unconscious and the countertransference as preconscious allows for some understanding of how both work synchronistically for the therapist. Transference is real for the narcissist. It is his way of eternalizing time.

Psychotherapy with narcissistic patients becomes difficult because of what I shall term a symbiotic transference. This type of transference immobilizes time, thus making the early warning system of the countertransference a prerequisite for the therapist to provide the patient with a link to his (the therapist's) own time sequence. Although many therapists choose to veer away from asserting their own range of realities in the treatment situation, since they may fear either losing contact with the patient or being drawn into an even more involved relationship with him, it is nevertheless important that they work toward maximum separation from the patient without rejecting him. Whitaker (1967) comments that "the therapeutic process involves the overt interaction of the two individuals and the use of the experience of each of them for the patient's growth" (p. 517). Asserting the necessity of time means an affirmation of differentiation. In the case of Andrew, the transference became a fulfilled lure and not an opportunity for asserting distinctions. Not infrequently therapists, like patients, hold onto the earliest strategies which the patient and his parental antagonist held onto as their only lifeline.

Freud (1933) has revealed that "we have made far too little use in our theory of the indubitable fact that the repressed remains unaltered by the passage of time—this seems to offer us the possibility of an approach to some really profound truths. But," continues Freud, "I myself have made no further progress here" (p. 105). Perhaps progress can be made only be restructuring the therapeutic situation, by breaking the clenched fist of dormant time to encourage movement away from a prevailing narcissistic life-style. Timeworn patterns with repressed roots are reinforced by environments which the narcissist has developed great skill in recreating. Charms, threats, promises of friendship all fit into his scenario. Ernest Jones (1961) spoke of such gestures under the broad category of "God-complex" (p. 257). The patient commands the situation through his behavior and declarations which state in the broadest possible terms that his time is more valuable and correct than anyone else's, and that his feeling for future events is, in fact, prophetic. How easy it is to wangle an environment where past collusions have conspired to reaffirm such happenings. Once again Hamlet: "I essentially am not in madness, but mad in craft" (Act III, Scene 4).

Andrew's inability to sustain friendship was related to his need to control all aspects of every interpersonal situation; from our point of view, to silence freedom and halt time. Indeed what other way could there be for him? Alluring and entrapping all signs of childhood terror and transforming them into contemporary objects who could be manipulated into being unhurtful became Andrew's mode of existence. For Hamlet, time was rendered tedious by his sense of apprehension and dread. For Jack, there was the repeated effort to reconstitute himself "in better times." In each instance, others were enlisted in the service of dammed-up time, creating the *illusion* of life space. Time is locked into the baseline of exteriority; as such it becomes a thing to be manipulated. The notion of temporality requires a constantly renewing sense of individuation and separation, making living space a coordinate of authentic time.

The Therapeutic Function

In his quest for individuation the patient must be helped to see what actual distances separate him from his therapist. This goal is achieved through determined focus on the here and now of a situation, regardless of the memories and images which are continuously recalled. Narcissism is a rupture of genuine movement from past to present. If the therapeutic enterprise is to make any headway at all it must reaffirm the vitality of the present moment. The direction, therefore, must be toward the patient's firm recognition of the person's present. This necessary dimension introduces a new criteria for what has been called insight.

Insights are those moments which focus on actual responses to present reality. The therapist's duty is to announce an ultimate division between a distant past and a set of present realities. An example from another field of treatment—that of the autistic child—illustrates how the objective of anchoring in the present may work: "George had in his impulsive way thrown a rock and hit one of the children shortly before group time. When the group started, Jane [another patient] lectured him this: 'Now you better stop throwing stones. If you killed somebody you'd be sorry all the rest of your life. You've got a right to live. Everybody's got a right to live. So you stop throwing stones.' George looked up into her face with concentrated attention during this tirade, then turned to the therapist and said, 'Some day grow up, have control like Jane.' Jane's reply, backed by the therapist, was, 'Not some day—now' " (Coffee and Wiener, p. 63).

Present realities can divest the patient of his present terrors and give him enough room to try out a totally new set of responses. Narcissism invokes repression since it inveighs against anything but a predictable set of strategies. In order to work toward a freer expression of feeling, the therapist does well to announce who he is and where the ego boundaries may be shifting. His interpretation of the transference must not bind either participant to representational imagery. In other words, the aim is not merely to reconstruct the past, but to face the now courageously.

Recalling Whitaker's (1953) comment about what a therapist may fear, it is vital to allow these expectations to play a role in what patient and therapist talk about. To the narcissist: "I can go along with your tugging me in directions that suit only you, but have the appearance of pleasing me. I think you may be surprised to discover how little you can truly know me by simply trying to accommodate your wishes to what you think I might want. I would like you to know me somewhat better than you seem to." Following this there may be an open exchange of experiences in the present moment such as:

Patient.   But I really do like you and want to please you.

Therapist.   It may be rough on you for the time being, but I have to like you on my own terms.

Patient.   I want to explore my creativity, my paintings, which I've been told have great promise.

Therapist.   If you want to risk showing me what you've done, that's just fine. But I intend to take my own time in judging how they suit *my own* taste.

Patient.   I feel lost among all of those strangers. I just have to cater to all of their ugly demands while preserving my own sense of purity.

Therapist.   I understand and I'd like to have a chance at letting you know how compatible and/or how estranged I feel from them. I'll need to know much more, and in descriptive terms which I can grasp.

While the nature and quality of interaction between therapist and patient is filled with paradox, it should not indicate that one party is right and the other wrong. What it does assume is a focus on micro-identity in the present, as opposed to the too easy tendency to lump all associations together in one grand macro-statement of past-present-future. If the latter, the patient simply assumes he "knows" the therapist; he engineers all movement and writes all prescriptions. His activity is so practiced that his skill hardly goes unrecognized until the exclusionary tactics of the past demand expression. There is, of course, no victory. Anxiety is barely visible; in its place lurks a vast sense of emptiness and terror. Time is stilled, and if any telltale signs of aging emerge, they are skillfully denied.

The possibilities for narcissistic patients to be enabled to live in the present depends on expansion of their capacity for spontaneity and expectation. This requires moving aside from easy assumptions. *Hamlet* is structured on the notion that the earth is subject to orderly control. God becomes the ghost of a father who needs to be avenged. In other stories this need for closure may be amended to include the unexpected. For the patient with a narcissistic life-plan, the amendment can gradually begin to include happenings which transcend expectation.

Here the therapist plays a vital role. He is in a position to reawaken the preconflicted fantasies which form a major part of the patient's potential. Similarly, the therapeutic relationship nurtures fantasies which patients often report as brand new. This implies that there is something to be gained in taking risks in the consensual present, beyond those afforded by the overconflicted childhood. To open the patient's life up to himself requires steps outside the history of parental guidelines. The therapist who refuses to reward repetitive past behavior patterns can begin to point the way beyond himself into a vast world of unpredictable experiences and uncontrolling relationships. Then time becomes possible again since its framework demands pro-active as opposed to re-active responses. A patient gradually moves into his own orbit, which while it cannot outwit the cruel historical forces of the past, nevertheless embarks him on a course which begins to yield new time options, unique designs, and the bittersweet sadness of an anticipated end.

> Rather at once our time devour
> Than languish in his slow-chapped power.
> Let us roll all our strength and all
> Our sweetness up into one ball,
> And tear our pleasures with rough strife
> Through the iron gates of life;
> Thus, though we cannot make our sun
> Stand still, yet we will make him run.
> (Andrew Marvel, "To his Coy Mistress")

Chapter 9

THE MATHEMATICIAN AS A HEALTHY NARCISSIST

**Reuben Fine, Ph.D. and
Benjamin Fine, Ph.D.**

With very few exceptions—Paul Federn is particularly notable in this regard—analytic authors, including Freud himself, Kernberg (1975), Kohut (1971), and others less
celebrated, have neglected to consider the connection between narcissism and intellectual achievement. In the main,
they have approached the subject from the point of view of
pathology. A widespread misunderstanding of the gifted
individual has been the result. The present essay will center
on one class of such misunderstood personalities: the
gifted mathematician.

There is a vast difference between the schizoid mathematician who pours his life into his work, even at the expense of much personal suffering, and the adolescent who
breaks down, stays home, and never leaves his mother.
Otto Rank (1932) made this point with regard to the artist,
but the eccentric quality of his therapeutic views have de-
tracted from the valuable contributions he made in other
areas. In recent times one finds a growing tendency to

evaluate psychosis from the interpersonal point of view rather than from the medical-psychiatric standpoint. It is in the understanding of the relation between achievement and pathology that the weakness of the traditional psychiatric approach, with its diagnostic categories, makes itself felt most keenly (Fine, 1970). The many ego-psychological profiles currently being offered (for the best of these see Bellak, 1975) emphasize the inadequacy of the single-shot diagnosis.

The youth who is mathematically gifted has objective reasons during his adolescence to know that in this area he is well ahead of most of his classmates. The interpretation of this fact depends on his ego structure.

In the emotionally adequate youth it results in an enhancement of self-esteem, a decision to adopt mathematics as a major or a total element in his life's work; he enjoys an increase in healthy narcissism and a great devotion to his chosen field. The true mathematician loves mathematics in the same way that the artist loves painting and the musician, music. Again, in this sense he is a healthy narcissist who derives justified gratification from the exercise of his abilities.

THESES

This paper will discuss eleven major theses related to the above observations:

1.   Inherently, mathematics is part of the autonomous ego. Its development can be traced in considerable detail, and has been so traced by experimental-observational methods. It matures in adolescence.

2.   The understanding of behavior in the mathematician therefore requires a careful consideration of the mutual influences of ego and id. This does not lend itself to any clear-cut simplification.

3.   Because of the late maturation of mathematical ability it is difficult to point to clear antecedents in earliest childhood. It may be hypothesized that a good relationship to one's mother is a prerequisite to the formation of the strong ego that the mathematician demonstrates.

4.   From his mother the youth then turns to his father. Mathematics is part of this turn, and the dynamics center particularly about the relationship with the father. Both rivalry and identification occur. In the physical scientist the father-figure is projected to the real world, in the chess master the father is seen as the hated rival, in the mathematician he is projected to the eternal verities, the abstract world of mathematics. Because of the nature of the material the conflict and identification are more concealed in mathematics than anywhere else.

5.   Mathematics is an achievement. It becomes manifest some time in adolescence, occasionally sooner. As an achievement, it must be handled differently from a pathological manifestation. The psychology of the mathematician centers around this achievement: how it is reached, what it means, and how he reacts to it.

6.   In the route to the achievement two broad ideal types are described: the schizoid and the type we have come to know as the "renaissance man." The schizoid man strengthens his tie to mathematics by using it as a compensation for a series of disappointments. The renaissance man is competent at many fields, but chooses mathematics because of the growth of his personality. In practice some mixture is found, but statistically the schizoid type seems to predominate.

7.   Particularly important in the route to the achievement are (a) abstraction; (b) aggression; (c) certainty, with its concomitant difficulty.

8.   The psychopathology seen can best be understood as an exaggeration of or a decompensation from the above traits. Thus abstraction deteriorates into isolation and

withdrawal, aggression becomes rivalry, hostility, and a chase for superiority, while certainty may again uncover the anxieties which it formerly covered up, leading to a hunt for power and paranoid mechanisms. Depression, anxiety, paranoid ideation, and schizoid mechanisms are frequently seen in varying degrees.

9.   The narcissism of the mathematician derives, to begin with, from pride in his achievement; it is thus a form of healthy narcissism. Many mathematicians, like scientists in general, make a satisfactory adjustment on the basis of healthy narcissistic gratification in their work, and a mother-marriage which gives them enough sexual and emotional gratification to keep going.

10.   These observations force a reconsideration of the concept of narcissism, one of the most confused concepts in the whole area of psychoanalytic theory. It is suggested in particular that the relationship between narcissism and achievement must be systematically conceptualized; hitherto it has been totally ignored.

11.   The concept of "psychosis," so often applied to withdrawn scientists, also requires a total reconsideration in the light of the existence of healthy narcissism. The moribund diagnostic systems in existence create sheer confusion in the field. They must be replaced by ego-psychological profiles, of which a number can be found. In these profiles the achievement must be given high priority.

In the light of the central significance of the achievement in mathematics, the psychological investigation can profitably use that achievement as a central focus; that is the proposal of this paper. Three questions then arise:

1.   By what route is the achievement reached?
2.   What does the achievement mean to the individual?
3.   How does he react to the achievement once he recognizes what he has done?

The achievement of the mathematician can also be compared with that of the physical scientist on the one hand and the chess master on the other; relevant data will be cited below.

PSYCHOLOGICAL PERSPECTIVES

The first question which arises with regard to any unusual achievement is that of native endowment. Psychologists have studied both the eminently successful (the "genius") and those who excel in only one area (the "idiot savant"). It is noteworthy that since the advent of intelligence tests the concept of "idiot savant" has disappeared from the literature, on the assumption, often unstated, that the extraordinary ability has been developed at the expense of the rest of the personality.

Guilford (1967) summarizes some of the findings with regard to unevenness of abilities within intelligence as follows (pp. 27–28): "Unevenness in profiles is found throughout the range of general intellectual level, from the mentally deficient to the near-genius." There are notable examples of unevenness among the highly gifted, as seen in the one-sided geniuses of historical importance. Sandor (1932) studied the Polish calculation prodigy, a Dr. Finkelstein, who exhibited unusual feats in numerical memory and computation. He could memorize a matrix of numbers 5X5 in very short order, and a list of 35 digits in one minute, and yet he was only average in his ability to memorize visual figures. Among four such individuals there was a difference in preferred mode of presentation of numbers for memorizing; some preferred visual presentation, and some auditory.

In an ordinary kind of population, Bloom (1963) found that if we were to define as "gifted" a child who is in the highest 10 percent on any of Thurstone's primary mental abilities tests (PMA), as many as 60 percent could be regarded as gifted. If the number of tests were increased to extend the range of intellectual factors involved, the percentage might approach 100, reminding us that where abilities differ in kind and the number is large, almost any child can be "gifted" in something.

Other dramatic instances of uneven abilities can be cited. Scheerer, Rothmann, and Goldstein (1945) cite an 11-year-old boy who stood very high in certain respects and very low in others. He had good musical aptitude, played by ear, and had absolute pitch. He had remarkable memory for words and unusual numerical skills. On the other hand, he had little general information, was lacking in social awareness, and was generally low in verbal tests, with an IQ of 50. Anastasi and Levee (1959) cite the case of a young man with an IQ of about 70 on either the Stanford-Binet or the Wechsler-Bellevue. He became an accomplished pianist and composer and was a good sight reader of music. He could recite two and one half pages of prose after reading it once, but he could not report ideas from the passage. He did well in reciting lists of digits backward and remembered dates very well. He was especially poor in visual memory and in tests of induction and made a zero score on the Picture Arrangement Test. His verbal IQ was 92, but his performance IQ was 52 on the Wechsler scale. Rimland (1964) reported some unusual abilities within an autistic group. One child could reproduce an aria sung in a foreign language on hearing it once.

The factorial structure of intelligence depends on the methods of computation used. Nevertheless, it is widely agreed that numerical or mathematical skills can be separated from verbal or linguistic ones and that on the whole boys do better in numerical skills, girls in linguistic (Guilford, 1967; Thurstone, 1955; Maccoby and Jacklin, 1974).

It may thus be assumed that the ability to achieve at mathematics is to some extent a native one, and that it appears more often in males than in females in all cultures studied. Nevertheless, as numerous studies also show, mere native ability does not explain the empirical ascertainable attainments. Translating these observations into analytic language, it can be stated that mathematical ability is an aspect of the autonomous ego, but the degree to which it is fostered and developed depends on id factors and the total ego structure.

Other work in intelligence and the IQ bears out and supplements the above conclusion. Broman, Nichols, and Kennedy (1975), in the largest study of the preschool IQ ever undertaken, found that the level of maternal education and the socioeconomic status of the family were the prime determinants of IQ at age 4. Terman (1959) in his well-known studies of genius IQ showed that the great majority of gifted children do indeed live up to their abilities (Oden, 1968). One of Terman's significant findings was that gifted children are broadly superior in all areas, differentiation only occurring in adolescence or shortly before.

For the mathematician as such, the broadest statistical survey available is the recently published book *Mathematical Talent*, by Stanley, Keating, and Fox (1974), all of Johns Hopkins; this work will be referred to here as the Johns Hopkins study. These investigators had a grant to study mathematically and scientifically precocious youth. They attempted to identify, study, and educationally facilitate those youngsters who are especially adept at mathematical reasoning while still in the first two years of junior high school—that is, grades seven and eight and ages 12 to 14. Among their findings was that a number of accelerated ninth- and tenth-graders handled twelfth-grade honors advanced placement calculus well at age 13 in competition with the mathematically ablest twelfth graders. Two 10-year-olds had no difficulty with college algebra and trigonometry. One boy completed 23 college credits in computer science, mathematics, and chemistry shortly after his fourteenth birthday, being the best student in the calculus class I at a selective college, and went on to calculus II and III. One boy earned his master's degree in computer science and, while still 17 years old, began work for the doctorate at a major university. The authors state:

> It seems uncomfortably probable that much of the intellectual alienation of brilliant high school graduates is due to their having been educated at a snail's pace too many years. (p. 19)

With regard to personality characteristics, the study confirmed previous ones which had shown that gifted children have fewer, not more, personality problems than non-gifted ones (correlation rather than compensation). The mathematically gifted were found to be independent, quick, sharp-witted, foresighted, versatile, and intelligent. Their personality seems to have facilitated their achievement. What uniquely characterized them was a blend of independent achievement and even-tempered but malleable disposition.

Marked sex differences were found, as in other studies. Boys scored significantly higher than girls on tests of mathematical and scientific aptitude, and the discrepancies between boys and girls increased with age.

Precocious sixth-grade children tend to come from typical middle-class families in which the mother tends to be more ambitious and achievement-oriented than the father. The boys are described as having shown interest and precocity in math and/or science at a much earlier age than the girls. The parents encouraged them by giving them science kits, telescopes, microscopes, and other science-related gifts. Parents describe both boys and girls as very likable children, indicating a minimum of parent-child friction in these families.

Psychoanalytic Studies

The psychoanalytic literature on mathematics is singularly sparse and not especially illuminating. The two available studies will be considered in some detail.

On the basis of the analysis of a mathematician, Victor Rosen (1953) attempted an interpretation of mathematical illumination and the mathematical thought process. By "mathematical illumination" is meant the frequently reported self-observation of mathematicians (cf. Poincaré, 1952, and Hadamard, 1945) that they "suddenly" see the solution to a problem, even though they have not been working at it.

Rosen's patient was a 21-year-old graduate student about to enter graduate school for his doctorate. He was the youngest of three siblings coming from an old American family of wealth and respected standing in the community in which he was born. For two generations before the patient's birth, the men on the paternal side of the family had been able to follow rather specialized and narrow fields of scientific endeavor without any concern for the practical problems of earning a living, thanks to the wealth handed down by the paternal grandfather. Several members of the family, including the father, had high academic rank in leading universities. The tradition among them was to return their salaries as donations to the university.

The patient grew up with the feeling that the opportunity to pursue scholarly research is sufficient compensation in itself and that the possession of wealth places a great burden of social responsibility for the contribution of creative or original work. At the age of 21 he had come into an income which made him financially secure for the rest of his life.

From early infancy he is said to have been a very sensitive child. At an early age he had shown extreme intolerance of loud noises. There had been a lifelong interest in music and the building of high-fidelity record players of ever increasing refinement. At the age of three he was subjected to a flashbulb exposure during the taking of an indoor family photograph. It is said that his eyes teared and appeared reddened for several days thereafter. One of his presenting symptoms (on starting treatment) was a marked photophobia, especially on awakening in the morning.

He first became aware of psychological difficulties at age 18 when he was rejected by the draftboard as too "neurotic." When he came to analysis, complaining of strephosymbolia (specific reading disability) and various life problems, he declared:

> I seem to get periods of panic. I have a confusion about life values. I am particularly concerned about my failure to talk to girls on an ordinary human level. I seem to keep a great distance from them. It gives me a sense of social isolation. I seem to want to idealize women and get to know them better, but if a girl begins to like me I seem to do everything possible to make her feel I am detached and uninterested. At other times I get all mixed up with women I don't really care for.

The mother appeared as a good woman without strong intellectual interests, interested in poetry, gardening, and literature, a bustling inefficient creature who expended her energy on too many tasks and who, in attempting to organize the lives of her relatives, produced great disorganization in her own life. The patient felt her as neglectful of him, and it always angered him to have to remind his mother to do something for him.

The father was seen as a cold, detached scientist, closeted in his study with little time for his children. His vocational field dealt with inanimate objects, for which he was said to have had a greater affection than for his children. The patient said of him: "I am certain that he neither knew how, nor had time, to beget children—we were probably conceived by artificial insemination." He accused his father of paying too little attention to his (the patient's) mathematical attainments, which first became apparent when he was in the eighth grade. He saw his father as an envious man who would not countenance an intellectual rival in the home. He complained frequently of his father's inability to listen to him because of preoccupation with his own thoughts. "We only speak to each other in terse phrases about immediate everyday matters." Later in the analysis it was revealed that the father also had frequent violent outbursts, which were very frightening.

The comments about the patient's study habits are revealing. He had a marked preference for doing his mathematical work during the hours of darkness. On many occasions he began to work in the early evening and had the experience of suddenly noticing that it was morning. It was not unusual for him to have intense periods of concentration on mathematical work, lasting as long as 14 hours, during which he was unaware of hunger, fatigue, or the stimuli arising from a full bladder. He was unaware of any desire to sleep during such periods; he experienced instead a mild elation.

The analysis worked out quite successfully. The patient developed a greater capacity for spontaneity in personal relationships. He was able to engage in active, though disturbed, heterosexual relationships. There was definite improvement in his reading and writing ability, especially in the speed of reading and the accuracy of spelling, which were his most burdensome academic handicaps.

One interesting dream he had is the following:

> I see a small e^x in an equation. I realize that I should factor it out and that e^x is a psychoanalyst which should be taken into account in each factor.

As far as the general psychology of mathematics and the problem of mathematical illumination go, Rosen comments as follows: The concept of number arises normally in connection with certain stages of the maturation of the perception apparatus during the Oedipal period. In those with a special mathematical "gift," it is probable that this maturational sequence takes place at an earlier period in ego development; so that along with the precocious concepts of number and quantity there remain certain archaic ego defense mechanisms which are later utilized in the creative aspect of the process. A large part of the ordinary process of mathematical thought in these gifted individuals is preconscious and utilizes a capacity for decathexis of the conscious perceptual system. The "illumination" experience is a creative act, as is inspiration in other fields, and utilizes the ego's capacity for controlled regression to unformalized, infantile modes of perceiving space and number.

These considerations of Rosen's seem to fall wide of the mark, based as they are more on an older id psychology than on an understanding of the range of the ego's autonomy. What he presents about his patient fits in with the basic theses, confirmed from many sources, that mathematical ability is inherently part of ego autonomy, but how it is molded depends on personal and socioeconomic circumstances. Typical is his patient's discovery of his mathematical ability in the eighth grade (cf. the Johns Hopkins study) and his further exploitation of that ability to handle his conflicts, especially with his father.

As far as illumination is concerned, it will be argued later that this results from a scanning process in which the individual tries out a large number of different possibilities and then finds that one embodies the solution. But the scanning must be based on a heavy background of mathematical knowledge, especially in the area under investigation; otherwise it will be a waste of time. "Illumination" is not specific to the mathematical process. It is found in all thought and is similar to or identical with the "aha" experience emphasized by the Gestalt psychologists. The roles of the preconscious, and of the primary and secondary processes stressed by Rosen, are of no real importance here— except as interferences from the id, in which respect they are of major consequence.

The second analytic reference to mathematics is the discussion of the famous dream by Descartes on Nov. 10, 1619, which he claimed changed his entire life. It has been subjected to exhaustive scrutiny by Lewin in his book *Dreams and the Uses of Regression* (1958); Freud also commented on it briefly, and Wisdom wrote a paper about it (1947). Dr. Samuel Moskowitz informs me that he is also preparing an essay on Descartes's dreams. The text of the dream appears in Chapter 7 of this volume.

Lewin's interpretation of the dream is essentially that it was an escape from unpleasant bodily feelings. Further, he hypothesizes that the Cartesian view of the world, in which body and mind are sharply separated, arose from his personal experience, which was delineated in this dream. For this Lewin presents very little evidence. Freud had earlier been made aware of the dream, saw it as a "dream from above," not very different from conscious thought, and refused to speculate further about it.

Bell (1937, pp. 39–40) sees the dream as heralding the discovery of analytic geometry, Descartes's great mathematical triumph, even though 18 years passed before he announced it to the world. Bell describes the circumstances under which the dream occurred. Descartes, whose life motto was "I desire only tranquillity and repose," was 22 at the time. After various uncoordinated efforts he had joined the army, which was then lying inactive in its winter quarters near the little village of Neuburg on the banks of the Danube. The dream occurred on St. Martin's Eve, which elicited considerable drinking. Descartes asserts that he was not drunk, and that he had not had anything to drink for three months before the dream. Although Lewin and

Baillet (his biographer) both accept this assertion, it is plainly a strange one to be made by a 22-year-old with an inactive army; besides, the exact figure of three months makes one suspicious. If he had been drinking with his army companions, Bell's explanation that the dream represents the unconscious resolution of a conflict between his desire to lead an intellectual life and his realization of the futility of a soldier's life makes good sense. For the rest of his days, Descartes remained a pure intellectual.

In the absence of associations from Descartes, one can only guess at the meaning of the dream. A patient of the writer's, also a mathematician, had a series of somewhat similar dreams, in which he was continually threatened by tornadoes; in analysis these turned out to be symbolic of his mother's rages and the terrible anxiety aroused by them.

It would seem likely that Descartes was suffering from similar panic states, and that he was looking for a way of life which would rescue him from these panicky feelings ("I desire only tranquillity and repose"). The famous *"cogito ergo sum"* may be the expression of a last hold on reality; almost swept away by the winds, he can still hold onto a thought, which thus reminds him that he is still alive.

However, whichever way one turns it, the dream and the whole experience tell us nothing about his relationship to mathematics. Even if the night marked the birth of analytic geometry, as Bell asserts, the dream per se would have no connection with it. Again, what is presented here is id interference with an autonomous ego function.

CLINICAL DATA

Apart from statistical studies, source material for the dynamic interpretation of mathematics is available from a host of biographies (Bell: *Men of Mathematics* is the best), autobiographies (Wiener, Russell, etc.), personal contacts, and analyses of mathematicians conducted by the senior author and/or students in supervision. Although it is scarcely possible to present the evidence in any systematic way, considerable empirical support for our conclusions is available.

With regard to the analysis of mathematicians, here are three clinical vignettes from the senior writer's own practice which highlight some common personality constellations. (The names are fictitious and some identifying material has been altered, but the essential relationships remain).

1. John

John, a 17-year-old college freshman, asked for analysis because he was "dissatisfied" with his personality. "I want a new personality." On investigation this turned out to relate quite specifically to girls. Since the age of six he had had a crush on one girl or another, averaging about one a year, none of whom had ever reciprocated his interest. The call for analysis came right after his latest rejection.

He was the older of two boys. His mother, a clerical worker, stated that for the first four months of his life she did not know what mother love was, since she felt nothing for him. When he was one and one half years old she had a "nervous breakdown" for which a local GP prescribed "rest in the country." When she returned she made her adjustment by withdrawing from John and, later, his younger brother. She described herself as tense and nervous. When John entered analysis she agreed to go into group psychotherapy, which eventually benefited her considerably.

The father was an engineer, a more stable personality than the mother. He remained close to the boys until they reached high school. In fact, John used to share his mathematical work with him until high school, when it became too difficult for the father to follow.

John felt rejected by his mother from the earliest years, a feeling which, in the light of what came out, seemed justified but was later corrected. However, even during the analysis John made a quasi-suicidal attempt by taking 40 libriums which had been prescribed by his college psychiatrist (who later committed suicide himself). As a consequence he slept for some 40 hours, the parents being totally oblivious to his dilemma.

Mathematics was always an easy subject for John, and as time went on it became more and more the center of his life, though he did retain some other interests. Many dreams of greatness occurred throughout his analysis, a number directly related to famous mathematical problems; for example, he once dreamt that he had solved Goldbach's conjecture (that every even number is uniquely the sum of two primes).

The analysis was a highly successful experience. Positive transference emerged early and remained throughout. He related to girls, improved his work, and expanded in many different directions.

2. Stewart

Stewart, an 18-year-old college student, came to a therapist after he had read Camus's book, *The Stranger;* he identified strongly with the hero, recognizing his alienation from the world. Stewart was the younger of two brothers. His mother had died at birth, and he was taken care of for the first three years by a nurse, who then married his father— in order to make sure that he got proper care, she said. Father was a cameraman who developed a crippling muscle disease later in life, which Stewart feared was hereditary.

Stewart had a variety of somatic difficulties, particularly in visual-motor coordination. In ball playing he was always hopeless because he simply could not see the ball when it was up in the air. Later it was discovered that he had been wearing the wrong glasses. Motor coordination was poor, and some arthritis emerged prematurely. His stepmother was overprotective—warning him particularly against designing women who would try to trap him into marriage, on the one hand, and loose women who would give him VD, on the other. She was particularly graphic in her descriptions of the horrors of VD, which naturally frightened the boy away from girls. Prior to therapy he was a virgin without even minimal social contacts with girls.

Mathematics always intrigued Stewart, but he was overshadowed by his older brother, who was regarded as a "genius" in math and the sciences. Nevertheless, he persisted, reaching a considerable degree of success. The analysis was also quite effective with him; his self-esteem was raised, he learned to relate to girls, and he went quite far professionally. Negative transference was worked out early as he feared the analyst would "ensnare" him into something disastrous (the bad women who give VD).

3. Allen

Allen, now a 27-year-old college professor, was in treatment as a child for uncontrollable temper tantrums. He was the son of divorced parents, and his mother maintained a bitter hatred of his father, who was extremely devoted to him. Torn between the two parents, he could no longer restrain his aggression in the latency years. Relatively brief therapy was sufficient to solve this problem.

Thereafter he moved from one success to another. He showed competence in all academic fields, securing an "A" grade in every course taken after the freshman year at college. In addition, he maintained a keen interest in sports, achieving some competence at several. In high school he played football, even though he was too small, sustaining injury week after week, yet enduring. In college he made the track team. Early marriage to a childhood sweetheart was one mark of his continued success. There was no indication of any undue sexual difficulties. After the second year in college, Allen concentrated more and more on mathematics, publishing half a dozen papers shortly after he received his Ph.D.

SPECIAL PROBLEMS OF ACHIEVEMENT

These brief examples represent the twin sides of the route to achievement in mathematics: the schizoid route and the route of the "renaissance man." The schizoid man finds himself increasingly inadequate in relation to other men. Once the mathematical ability—which is inherently an endowment, an aspect of the autonomous ego—is discovered, he concentrates on that more and more. Gradually the mathematics may displace all other activities, as in the case of Stewart, or may leave him with a feeling of being one-sided but not too isolated, as with John. Sexual difficulties are prominent. Further developments depend on the total ego structure, which cannot easily be generalized (some aspects will be considered below). By contrast, the renaissance man finds himself succeeding at everything—school, sex, sports, self-esteem. Gradually he is forced to choose some specialty, and is drawn more to mathematics than to other fields. Personality difficulties rarely emerge.

Among the great figures of history Newton is perhaps the prototype of the schizoid man, while Bertrand Russell would be a model of the renaissance development.

The extraordinary esteem in which most people hold mathematicians can be attributed to two major factors: their great mental power, on the positive side, and their distance from the body, on the other. Whether mathematics requires greater intellectual power than, say, physics is hard to judge. There can, however, be no doubt that of all the sciences none is as remote from the body as mathematics. Perhaps this is one reason why the term "pure" arose in connection with it. In the first two cases above, bodily and sexual difficulties were prominent, as is the case with many mathematicians of the schizoid type. A kind of circular conflict then ensues: mathematics is pursued as an escape from the somatic conflict, which then becomes worse because of the escape. For a while an equilibrium can be reached, in which the rewards from mathematics are sufficient to counterbalance the bodily deprivation; but eventually, in many people, this equilibrium breaks down, and serious psychological conflicts ensue.

However, a note about "serious conflicts" is relevant here. The mathematical achievement, reached at some time in adolescence, requires a fairly strong ego structure. At some point this ego structure begins to decompensate. But severe decompensation to the point of a total psychotic regression is very rare. The senior writer has inquired of a number of clinical psychiatrists whether they have ever seen a completely regressed mathematician, and only one case has been reported. In the literature the only eminent mathematician who had a severe regression was Cantor, the discoverer of transfinite numbers. (Cantor died in a mental hospital, but the details are not available). It would appear that the ego strength which leads to mathematical achievement is sufficient to ward off the worst kinds of regression. A similar observation was made by the senior writer about chess masters (Fine, 1967).

Many writers, following the popular example, tend to look upon the mathematician as "crazy" or "psychotic." Even Rosen, in the case described above, debated in the beginning whether his patient suffered from a "latent psychosis," and the psychological report done by Molly Harrower and reported in his paper erred in the same way. The confusion arises from a unitary concept of psychosis as a "disease" rather than a way of living. There is a vast difference between a Newton who developed a paranoid depression at age 50, when he could no longer tolerate his isolation, and a regressed boy who never develops beyond the infantile fixation to his mother. Neither psychosis nor narcissism can be properly understood without reference to achievement.

On the more positive side, certain aspects of mathematics stand out as psychologically significant. We can enumerate: (1) abstraction; (2) aggression; and (3) certainty and difficulty.

Abstraction

The mathematician must possess the ability to abstract himself from the real world. "Mathematics," Bertrand Russell once quipped, "is the field where you never know what you are talking about nor whether what you are saying is true." It has already been remarked that this capacity to distance oneself from ordinary human concerns, especially the body, is the most awe-inspiring aspect of mathematics to the average person.

In the schizoid man this capacity would arise as an answer to the feeling of inadequacy about the body. In the renaissance man it would primarily be an outgrowth of healthy ego development: with adequate libidinal gratification from his mother and father he can then move on to the outside world.

Whatever the basis in infantile terms, later this capacity for abstraction becomes one of the chief hallmarks of the mathematician. Of Gauss, Bell writes:

> Part of the riddle of Gauss is answered by his involuntary preoccupation with mathematical ideas—which itself of course demands explanation. As a young man Gauss would be "seized" by mathematics. Conversing with friends he would suddenly go silent, overwhelmed by thoughts beyond

his control, and stand staring rigidly oblivious of his surroundings. Later he controlled his thoughts—or they lost
their control over him—and he consciously directed all his
energies to the solution of a difficulty till he succeeded. A
problem once grasped was never released till he had con-
quered it, although several might be in the foreground of his
attention simultaneously.

In one such instance [referring to the *Disquisitiones,* page
636] he relates how for four years scarcely a week passed
that he did not spend some time trying to settle whether a
certain sign should be plus or minus. The solution finally
came of itself in a flash. But to imagine that it would have
blazed out of itself like a new star without the "wasted"
hours is to miss the point entirely. Often after spending days
or weeks fruitlessly over some research Gauss would find on
resuming work after a sleepless night that the obscurity had
vanished and the whole solution shone clear in his mind. (p.
254)

Regardless of the route by which it is reached, the
mathematician's capacity to abstract requires some analytic
explanation. Apart from normal cognitive development,
which will be discussed below, three factors seem opera-
tive: libidinization, displacement of aggression, and sense
of mastery.

Inherently mathematical symbols come to have a
libidinal meaning in the course of his life, which is expressed in various ways. Mathematicians themselves speak
of an "elegant" solution; they also speak of theorems and
proofs that are "beautiful," "exciting," "lovely," and the
like, all connoting some libidinal involvement. Perhaps this
has been overlooked because mathematics appears late in
the life of the individual, and the roots of libidinization are
always sought in earliest infancy.

The term "symbol" is part of mathematics; it embodies, of course, a different meaning from the analytic usage.
Sometimes the mathematical symbols come to hold some
unconscious meaning for the person; however an abundance of or preoccupation with such meanings would mili-

tate against successful work. Some studies indicate that both chess masters and physical scientists use visualization more than mathematicians (Fine, 1967), who thus are able to employ the symbol in its purest form. The libidinization would thus arise primarily from the mastery associated with it and the gratification of aggressive aims, rather than as a sublimation or translation of some more basic libidinal concepts. The latter, however, may also occur.

> One mathematician in analysis related that when he was first shown the existence of positive and negative numbers in junior high school, at the age of 11, he experienced a sexual thrill. Now, was his association, he could really move out into the outside world. For years thereafter mathematics became his ruling passion. "Plus" and "minus" did have various unconscious meanings for him but they did not affect his work.
>
> Another mathematician displayed a direct connection between sexual intercourse and mathematical work. He acquired girl friends primarily for sexual contacts. With one such girl friend he would spend his time first working at a problem. When he was "stuck" he would have intercourse with her; directly thereafter he would get up, discovering that he had found a new approach to what had baffled him before. In this case it was clear that the tension of mathematical work was unconsciously equated with sexual tension. When the sexuality reached a certain point it took over from the mathematics. It was only after this sexual tension had been discharged that he was able to go back to his mathematics. It was not without significance that this man came from another country, where he had left his wife and children; mathematics was associated with the taboo on extramarital sex, which he could gratify here but not in his home country.

Aggression

Equally significant is the gratification of aggressive aims through mathematics. The mathematician "proves" a theorem once and for all, thereby demonstrating his superiority to his competitors. Indeed, mathematics, as ordinarily taught, involves intense competition with others, including contests in which superior students have to solve problems more quickly and more correctly than others.

In the childhood of many mathematicians, serious conflicts about aggression abound. One man, later a professor of mathematics, was so unruly as a child that a conference was held when he was about 12 as to whether to send him to a reformatory. This frightened him so that an abrupt change in his personality took place.

This man presented a good example of the sublimation of libidinal, aggressive, and mastery aims in his mathematics. He would describe himself as prancing about in front of his class, demonstrating first this, then that, and deriving great pleasure from his performance. Both father and mother had been stage performers in the days of vaudeville, and he had actually been taken on the stage with them at the age of five. He was also an excellent piano player and loved to entertain groups of friends with his piano.

As with artists, the lives of most mathematicians are described more from a mythological than from a psychological perspective. Here and there, however, glimpses of the truth break through. Thus More, in his *Life of Newton* (1934), quotes from the notes of John Conduitt, who married Newton's niece and lived with Newton for the last ten years of the latter's life:

> When he was last in the lowermost class but one, the boy next above him, as they were going to school, gave him a kick in his belly which put him to a great deal of pain. When school was over Newton challenged him to fight, and they went into the churchyard. When they were fighting the Master's son came out, and encouraged them by clapping one on the back, and winking at the other. Isaac Newton had the more spirit and resolution, and beat him till he would fight no more. Young Stokes told Isaac Newton to treat him like a coward and rub his nose against the wall, and accordingly

> Isaac Newton pulled him along by the ears and thrust his
> face against the side of the church. Determined to beat him
> also at his books, by hard work he finally succeeded, and
> then gradually rose to be the first in the school. (p. 11)

Actually, Newton remained an exceedingly argumen-
tative and quarrelsome person all his life. For example, the
famous controversy with Leibniz over priority in the discovery of the calculus was carried on with much more
acrimony and bitterness by Newton than by Leibniz (Manuel, 1963). Nor is it too surprising to learn that when he was
warden of the mint in later years he personally took some
role in the torture of prisoners who had counterfeited
money. Even when he was writing the *Principia,* one of his
extraordinary contributions, he took time out to pen a long
letter to his tenants, going into minute details about repair-
ing a house and barn and threatening them with a lawsuit
if they did not mend their ways (More, p. 460).

Naturally, as in the case of chess masters and natural
scientists, the aggressive element has to be denied. Still, we
find, even superficially, that Descartes's dream came while
he was soldiering—that is, preparing to kill or to be killed
—and that the life of scholarship took him away from that.
Bertrand Russell first defied the violence of the British in
World War I, choosing to go to prison rather than be si-
lenced, even though his grandfather had been a prime min-
ister. After World War II he at first advocated an atomic
war on Russia, before that country had the atomic bomb,
then suddenly switched, setting himself up in a grandilo-
quent gesture to "try" the United States for its crimes in
Vietnam; it looks as though he fantasized himself ruler of
the world. Norbert Wiener, in his autobiography, relates
how he "inadvertently" volunteered for the police force in
Boston during the strike that Coolidge put down, not realizing that he was serving as a scab. In his autobiography he
comments on this incident: "For myself I was left with
nothing but the shame of having acted as the Governor's
dupe and strikebreaker" (p. 276).

In the first volume of his autobiography, *Ex-Prodigy* (1953), Wiener reveals much of the aggression and consequent anxiety that haunted him all through childhood, later to be transformed into mathematical channels. From his early years he recalls a lively terror of injury and mutilation, as well as a fear of death. Pictures of suffering and mutilation remained prominent among his early memories. He was pleased when playmates showed him how an earthworm could be cut in two. At age five he found a little nest with blue eggs, which he touched. His cousin Olga told him that because he had touched them the mother bird would leave them alone and never come again, that the eggs would not hatch and the nestlings would die. That made him as good as a murderer in his own mind, and for years afterward the consequent sense of guilt troubled him sorely.

Muscular incoordination in childhood he attributed to poor eyesight rather than to conflicts about aggression, which a psychoanalyst would look into. Wiener admits freely that he was a very disturbed child, and that nowadays such a child might well be taken to a psychoanalyst.

At age eight he and some friends decided to run away to the wars and block the cruelty of the Turks against the Armenians. Much fighting occurred among his childhood companions. In one snowball fight a friend lost an eye. Thereafter, he says, his parents punished him for fighting, and otherwise discouraged fighting at all costs. Still this of course did not end the aggression. Even as he relates it, many surprising incidents occurred. At nine he "accidentally" burned the skin off the back of a playmate's hand. At thirteen he began to fool around with biological experimentation. He ligated one of the femoral arteries of a guinea pig; the surgery was botched and the animal died. The professor in charge, he says, was rightfully indignant, since the vivisection, unsupervised, was actually a criminal act. Later, in histology, even when supervised, Wiener broke glass, bungled section-cutting, and could not follow the meticulous order of killing and fixing, staining, soaking, and sectioning.

Most striking is his recital of the violence that came out when he joined the Harvard Regiment prior to World War I. One day, while walking across the company street, he "accidentally" crushed a man's glasses; frightened, he hit and ran. Then he relates the following:

> [My tentmates] had already learned how easily they could make me squirm by their obscenity, and I was completely miserable. I was so angry that I laid my hand on one of the rifles stacked in the tent, with no intent whatever to use it as a rifle and very little intention of using it as a club, but more as a gesture of anger and despair than anything else. Of course, they disarmed me without any trouble, but I was unspeakably shocked when I saw clearly for the first time the murderous construction that could be put on my actions. (p. 239)

In later years Wiener was notorious for the childish way in which he would try to prove his superiority to anyone who came along. Before faculty meetings he would use his encyclopedic memory to inform himself on some abstruse subject, such as the pottery of Ming China, then steer the conversation around to that topic. It was difficult for him to accept a loss at chess, even though he was only a mediocre player; sometimes when he lost he would say, "Anyhow, I'm a better mathematician than you." In his autobiography he makes the revealing comment (p. 21) that in mathematics it is only a man's best moments that count, while in chess his worst are brought out; one mistake costs him the game.

Related to aggression is the experience of mastery. From a very early age the mathematician feels that he can master problems which his contemporaries find difficult or impossible. This self-observation can then be exploited in a variety of different ways. It tends to reinforce his interest in mathematics, discouraging him from areas in which he does not have the same mastery. With the schizoid man, these areas would refer particularly to human relationships, but also to other intellectual subjects. Depending on the amount of skew in the personality, varying degrees of one-sidedness can then develop, from the extreme of the "grind" who does not exist outside mathematics to the relatively diversified individual who can function well in many areas.

From an early stage the mutual influences in the development of the ego and the id (Hartmann, 1952) come into play, contributing to the complexities of development. In this connection information from experimental and clinical psychology about the average data on intelligence and special ability growth must be incorporated into psychoanalytic thinking. It is readily demonstrable that the vast majority of people have considerable ability in various areas which they do not use; this is particularly true of mathematics. The capacity to remember digits (digit span), arithmetic, digit symbol (transformations), spatial and perceptual reasoning, logical thinking, all seem to follow clear-cut lines of growth which vary within relatively circumscribed limits.

This growth is continuous from birth to maturity, which is reached somewhere in the period of adolescence. But it differs with different abilities. Thurstone (1955) gives the following approximate ages for reaching 80 percent of maturity for each of his seven primary mental abilities:

P–perceptual speed	12
S–space	14
R–reasoning	14
M–memory	16
N–numerical facility	16
V–verbal comprehension	18
W–word fluency	later than 20

Piaget (various) dates the period of formal operations, when mathematics proper begins, from about the age of 11, which would fit in with other material. One of his most striking findings is that the growth of logical abilities in the child corresponds to the complexities of the propositional calculus (1957). Guilford (1967) in his structure of intellect (SI) theory factors out five categories of operation: cognition, memory, divergent production, convergent production and evaluation, and states:

> As for the categories of operation, the brain is apparently predesigned to perform in the five major ways, and it may also be predesigned to handle information in the form of the different kinds of products. But the child's environment is probably mostly responsible for the kinds of products as well as for the kinds of content, for . . . the contents-times-products interaction represents an epistemology, a set of systematic, natural classifications of information . . . Intelligence develops by virtue of interactions between these categories as they impinge upon the child and the five hereditarily determined operations. (p. 417)

Certainty

Certainty is the third characteristic of mathematics, which distinguishes it particularly from physical science and chess. For mathematics is proved, and once established, never disproved. What seems to the layman to be disproof, such as the replacement of Euclidean by non-Euclidean geometry, is merely a way of generalizing the data; thus Euclidean geometry merely becomes a special case of a broader theory. This process of increasing generalization is typical of mathematics, especially in modern times, when the more elementary propositions have all been well established.

This element of certainty serves to enhance the self-esteem of the mathematician more than that of any other scientist. As Descartes's dream indicates, in childhood the mathematician is frequently ridden with anxieties; Wiener makes the point quite explicitly. The certainty of mathematics serves to overcome these anxieties; here at least is one area where nothing is in doubt.

Allied with and added to the element of certainty is the factor of *difficulty*. Not only does the mathematician prove something which stands for all time, but what he proves is never a trivial matter. Again the secondary effect on his narcissism is great. The obverse of this point, that his failure to prove a theorem rearouses all the old anxieties, becomes crucial in the development of his psychopathology.

Summary

The psychological concomitants of mathematical achievement are: It becomes apparent to the outside world in adolescence, at a time when the requisite faculties mature. Mathematics requires a high degree of abstraction, frequently facilitated by an unconscious libidinization of the material. It forms an outlet for aggression. The aspects of certainty and difficulty serve to enhance narcissistic gratification and professional self-esteem. All through the mathematician's development, accruals from the autonomous ego, (increase in performance capacity and in grasp of mathematics) interact with the id and the remainder of the ego structure to yield the final personality result. On the surface, at least, mathematicians are often forthright, aggressive individuals who know their place and know how to make a mark for themselves. Two extreme types can be distinguished: the schizoid, who confines himself exclusively to mathematics, and the renaissance, who is competent over a wide range.

The development of the mathematician can then be conceptualized in this way. At an early age, usually in the latency period, though often before, competence in various school subjects leads to a sense of mastery which serves to control the strong aggressive drives, bind them, and steer them into channels in which social recognition is obtained. At each step from then on, mastery brings additional rewards. While mathematics may begin with symbolic meanings, the mathematics itself soon acquires secondary autonomy, reinforced by the success experiences that it engenders. Much of it may be libidinized, yet in a manner that still keeps it clear of superego reproaches. The varying degrees of success in other areas will determine how exclusively the youngster will devote himself to mathematics.

Much more social recognition is available for boys than for girls, hence boys exploit their perhaps inherent advantage to a far greater extent than girls; the result is an overwhelming preponderance of men among professional mathematicians, out of all proportion to their innate superiority. (The same observation holds for physical scientists and chess masters).

The narcissism of the mathematician is attached to his mathematical exploits; like the artist he shifts his self-involvement to an external object of his own creation or choice—since he does not create much new mathematics, if any at all. He shows a cross between the aesthetic and the artistic attitudes (Fine, 1975). In this sense the narcissism is essentially of the healthy variety, since it is based on real achievement, not on fantasy. Naturally, in many cases it can extend to fantasy, when it suffers a fate similar to that of more pathological narcissism. However, since a secure ego base was needed to reach the achievement, the mathematician almost never displays the depths of regression seen in other narcissistic personalities.

Nevertheless, while the above analysis may be theoretically correct, empirical studies of mathematicians and other scientists repeatedly show that the modal personality is that of the schizoid, not that of the so-called renaissance man.

PATHOLOGY

The psychopathology found in mathematicians can best be understood in the light of the exaggeration of the traits that lead to success in mathematics in the first place. Thus abstraction deteriorates into isolation and withdrawal, aggression becomes constant quarreling, and certainty leads to paranoia, grandiosity and a search for power.

The most common symptoms found among mathematicians are depression, anxiety, paranoia, and schizoid behavior. Newton, who displayed all of these in marked degree, is perhaps the outstanding historical example. Even his biographer, More, describes him as "often silent and abstracted in general society." He never married and had few friends. Flamsteed, the royal astronomer who was of inestimable value to Newton in confirming his predictions yet with whom Newton maintained a lifelong battle, described him as insidious, ambitious, excessively covetous of praise, and impatient of contradiction. In his famous self-evaluation towards the end of his life Newton wrote:

> I do not know what I may appear to the world; but to myself I seem to have been only like a boy, playing on the sea-shore, and diverting myself, in now and then finding a smoother pebble or a prettier shell than ordinary, whilst the great ocean of truth lay all undiscovered before me.

This statement should be taken more literally than it has been. Newton did regard himself as a little boy playing on the seashore. In fact, he made his remarkable discoveries between ages 22 and 25, and thereafter did very little work. Yet it was easy to see that his abilities remained undiminished. When Bernoulli in 1696 challenged the mathematicians of the world to solve two problems connected with the brachistochrone (the curve connecting two points along which a body acted upon by gravity will fall in the shortest possible time), allowing one and one half years for the solution, Newton, who happened on the problem by chance, solved it in one day. When Leibniz in 1716 sent a problem as a challenge to English mathematicians, Newton received it at five o'clock and had it solved before he went to bed the same day (More, pp. 474–75).

Most of Newton's life was spent in religious speculation, especially on the Asian heresy (denying the Trinity). John Maynard Keynes, who saw his manuscripts, reports that they run to more than a million words and prove nothing (*Essays in Biography,* 1951). In other words, after the initial accomplishments he really retreated from the world of science into one of theological speculation, intrigue, and schizoid isolation. All agreed that he had a serious depression in 1690, when he was just short of fifty. At that time he became suspicious of John Locke, whom he accused of trying to embroil him with a woman!

Episodes of depression have been reported by many mathematicians, especially in the critical years of middle age (Einstein, Born, Wiener, Russell). Shortly before his death Einstein came out with the enigmatic statement that he wished he had been a plumber, suggesting his despair at the lack of physical gratification in his life.

Most episodes of depression, as is usually the case, are accompanied by varying degrees of paranoia. One mathematician was observed running away from things with the pitiful complaint, "Don't hit me, don't hit me." In spite of this paranoia he was able to function as a college professor. Norbert Wiener is reported to have had numerous depressive episodes throughout his life, but the paranoid component came out more in his grandiosity.

The difficulty of doing any new work in mathematics, which grows with the years, produces depressive reactions in many mathematicians. Some studies indicate that more than half of those who get their doctorates in mathematics never publish anything else in the course of their lives.

Even those who publish suffer from the problem of new publications. One eminent mathematician who had solved a difficult problem in his younger years could never do anything else, reacting with increasing depression. He had mastered a trick which he displayed to his college classes: at the beginning of the semester he would have them line up against the wall, calling off their names. Then they would sit down alphabetically and he would repeat the names of each member in correct alphabetical order.

Schizoid behavior, with the absence of human relations, excessive devotion to work, and blockage of feelings —especially sex and anger—is no doubt the most common profile of pathology seen, as the above studies indicate. Yet, as has been noted, total regression almost never seems to develop. It would seem that once the ego strength required to achieve success in mathematics is attained it is never completely lost, thereby avoiding the most malignant kind of regression.

Sibling rivalry and unresolved oedipal conflicts may also impede the talented individual's ability to evaluate himself realistically, or to recognize the meaning of what he has done. Some competitor may have done better; one child with a genius IQ whose case history has been published as "The Uncommunicative Genius" (Fine, 1976) had an average of 94.317 in high school; but his focus was on another boy whose average was 94.319, ahead of him by .002 points. Or the pathology may virtually obliterate the meaning of what he had done; in Newton's case, with his self-evaluation as a little boy playing, it led to a 20-year postponement of publication of an epoch-making piece of work. Then again, Norbert Wiener, in the shadow of a father whom he idealized, could not see himself as a mathematician until he was well past his doctorate. He continued to believe that his father was a capable mathematician, even though the father's abilities lay in languages and mathematics was a sore point. Possibly his father had a fantasy about his potentially great mathematics ability (he was a queer duck in many ways), which Norbert then unconsciously came to share.

In one case, not atypical, the boy attributed his success to a teacher who had sponsored him all through school; in analysis it took him years to realize that the achievement was his, not his teacher's. But to dismiss the teacher in his mind meant an increase in isolation which he could not tolerate, so he clung to his masochistic self-distortion, much as Wiener did.

What happens to the individual afterwards depends on his original interpretation of the achievement. If it is within relatively normal bounds, he goes on to pursue mathematics as his life's work, with all its attendant rewards and frustrations. Many times there are alternating moods of depression and elation, as with Rosen's patient described above. Not infrequently the excessive devotion to work leads to a further withdrawal from human relations which at some point becomes too hard to take. The result is a work block and a return to some more direct form of libidinal gratification.

Perhaps the outstanding success story in this genre is the Harvard professor who left mathematics to become a songwriter and became a great hit. Others are less fortunate, and quite often the inability to work and the search for more direct libidinal gratification eventuate in some form of pathology. Nowadays the pathology usually leads them to treatment, which as a rule is quite successful, as with Rosen's patient and the other patients cited above. Again, inherent ego strength carries the day.

The reaction to the achievement may also lead to an increase in aggression which makes those around the achiever miserable but leaves him unscathed. One patient, the son of a mathematics professor, had the most painful memories of his father's sadism; he was always telling the boy that he did not have a head on his shoulders. Another professor, who had made a most original contribution to the field, was notoriously critical of students. One of his favorite classroom demands was, "Prove any theorem that I have proven."

SUMMARY

This paper examines the relationship between achievement and narcissism, a topic otherwise virtually neglected in the literature. It focuses upon the mathematician, but the same or similar methodology applies to other gifted individuals.

Inherently unusual achievement is part of the autonomous ego. Full understanding requires a careful consideration of the mutual influences of ego and id.

The psychology of the gifted narcissist should be approached via his achievement: how it is reached, what it means, and how he reacts to it. Two broad ideal types are described: the renaissance man and the schizoid. In many cases narcissistic concentration on any field, particularly one as difficult as mathematics, is a manifestation of a strong and healthy ego.

Chapter 10

THE EGO IDEAL: AN ASPECT OF NARCISSISM

Esther Menaker, Ph.D.

The concept of narcissism in psychoanalysis is an energic one and, true to its mythological origins, refers to the concentration of libidinal energy on the ego. (Freud, 1914) As our knowledge of the ego, of the processes of introjection and identification upon which much of it is built, and of its various substructures has grown, so our understanding of the role of the investment of narcissistic energy has deepened. It is with this energy that the ego nourishes itself and those of its component parts whose successful and integrated functioning maintain that inner psychic balance which normally guarantees the individual a goodly measure of self-esteem. The distribution of narcissistic energy—whether it is vested in intrapsychic structures, in internalized representations of the self and of others or projected onto others in the outer world—is often an important indicator of the nature and extent of the psychic balance or imbalance of the individual.

The ego-ideal, of all the substructures of ego, is perhaps most heavily invested with narcissistic energy, and that from a very early point in development. An exploration, therefore, of the role of the ego-ideal in relation to individual issues of emotional health, and of its significance as the vehicle for social cohesion as well as for change and progress, points to the vital importance of normal narcissism in human development.

The fact that the study of human personality involves an attempt at understanding individual intrapsychic dynamics, the relationship of the individual to his outer environment and to other individuals in the areas of his most significant involvements, and that these factors impinge on social and philosophical issues, is never more clearly exemplified than in the study of the ego-ideal. In the early psychoanalytic literature there was but minimal concern with the ego-ideal, which was often not clearly differentiated from the superego. Within the last 10 to 15 years, however, this has changed. Perhaps greater concern with a refinement of concepts of ego structure and dynamics has brought this about. But growing interest in the role of values in human psychology, resulting from social, cultural, and moral changes that are worldwide, has also played a large role in a concern with the ego-ideal.

If we forget for a moment the issues of the derivation, development, and maturation of the ego-ideal in the course of an individual's life and shelve momentarily the issues of its content and the sources of its energy to formulate a common-sense definition of the ego-ideal, we would say that it is the experience, generally perceived in some verbal form, of the individual's aspirations, of the broadest framework that gives meaning to his life and from which he derives self-esteem and a sense of worth relative to his capacity to fulfill these aspirations. Such a definition refers to the maturing or mature ego-ideal, since the idea of aspiration does not belong to early childhood years. Yet it is the very factor of the motivation toward aspiration, toward striving, which remains insufficiently accounted for in the psychoanalytic literature on the ego-ideal. However, in a recent article on the "Genealogy of the Ego-Ideal," Blos (1974) has expressed a keen awareness of the scope and significance of the ego-ideal for human life beyond its onto-genetic development. He says:

> The ego-ideal spans an orbit that extends from primary narcissism to the "categorical imperative," from the most primitive form of psychic life to the highest level of man's achievements. Whatever these achievements might be, they emerge from the paradox of never attaining the sought-after fulfillment or satiation, on the one hand, and of their never ceasing pursuit, on the other. This search extends into the limitless future that blends into eternity. Thus, the fright of the finity of time, of death itself, is rendered non-existent, as it once had been in the state of primary narcissism.
>
> Potentially, the ego-ideal transcends castration anxiety, thus propelling man toward the incredible feats of creativity, heroism, sacrifice, and selflessness. One dies for one's ego-ideal rather than let it die. It is the most uncompromising influence on the conduct of the mature individual: its position always remains unequivocal.

The question then arises: are these feats, these creative achievements arising out of ego-ideal motivation, an expression of man's need to master the anxiety which the giving up of his position of primary narcissism—oneness with the mother—has induced, or are they in fact manifestations of a kind of immortality? I am aware that to formulate the question in this way is to lay one's self open to the criticism that the issue transcends the field of psychological concern and enters the realm of philosophy and religion. Yet is this really the case? In biological terms, we have become accustomed to regard the genetic material and its reproduction as an expression of species, if not individual, immortality. Would it be so farfetched to regard the transmission and perpetuation of psychological traits through the vehicle of internalized dynamic structures such as the ego-ideal as serving psychosocial immortality?

This would then be a phylogenetic understanding of the ego-ideal, its origins lying in man's potentiality for psychological internalization; its function, the psychological survival, continuity, and advance of human society; its meaning, to provide the individual in the course of the ontogenetic development of his ego-ideal, with a future-directed meaningfulness for his life through participation in the ego-ideals—either through acceptance or rejection —of the ideals of the society with which he is identified.

Before we explore the deeper meaning of this dimension of the ego-ideal, let us review the psychoanalytic view of its development in the life history of the individual. Lampl-de-Groot (1962) has given us an excellent exposition of the Freudian view. The so-called hallucinations of early infancy, which are attempts to deal with the inevitable frustrations and deprivations of the child's life situation (hunger, cold) by reducing tension and restoring equilibrium, are described as forerunners of the ego-ideal. They take place in a narcissistic phase when self and object are not yet differentiated and are thus entirely self-centered. In the course of development, as self and object become more differentiated but the problem of maintaining a narcissistic balance, of retaining self-esteem, is not solved in the face of frustration and deprivation, the child tries to accomplish this through fantasies of omnipotence and self-idealization.

But these fantasies have little effect on reality and the child then projects the omnipotent expectation upon his parents, who in fact have the greater mastery of the actuality of his world; and secondarily, he introjects this idealization of them so that his own self–ideal partakes of their omnipotence. Finally, with the passing of the oedipus complex, the attachment to parents becomes desexualized and the ego-ideal, which is one legacy of this attachment, is also desexualized. In Freudian terms, this means that the goals and aspirations of the growing child shift from unrealistic, sexual goals to neutralized and attainable ones in the realm of learning, in the development of skills, and in the acceptance of norms and ethical standards.

To the extent that the individual lives up to these goals, his narcissistic balance, his self-esteem, is maintained. Thus the forerunners as well as the finally structured ego-ideal serve wish-fulfilling functions in Freud's sense of tension reduction. The ego-ideal supports the ego in its attempt to deal with the inevitable disappointments and frustrations of life; it is a need-satisfying agency.

The superego, by contrast, is a restricting, prohibiting, sometimes commanding agency, which can interact with the ego-ideal in an attempt to force the carrying out of its goals.

Jacobson (1964), too, sees idealization processes of parents and self as enabling the child to master sexual and aggressive tendencies. The ego-ideal is eventually molded from idealized object and self-images which are ultimately combined with more realistic self and other representations. It is this duality in the ego-ideal which reflects a split between the individual's acceptance of reality and his belief in magic.

There may be variations in emphasis in the writings of authors with a Freudian orientation regarding the genesis of the ego-ideal. But all are in agreement that the function of idealization is defensive, that it is the human organism's attempt to deal with the frustration of instinct, be it sexual or aggressive. The instinctual drives of the individual are thus the nodal point of psychic development. The motivation for inner growth—even of the highest and most human of structures, the ego-ideal, as well as the motivation for action in the outer world of reality—originates in the need for the reduction of tension.

When we consider that all the achievements of mankind—in art, literature, religion, philosophy, social structure, ethics—derive ultimately from the striving to fulfill ego-ideal goals, it hardly seems plausible to attribute the genesis of this unique capacity for culture to a defensive response to the frustration of instinctual drives. Surely there is more here than the purely biological life history of the individual, or perhaps it would be more accurate to say that the concept of the biological must be broadened to include the social nature of man as well as the larger phylogenetic, evolutionary perspective.

In the psychoanalytic literature all the authors concerned with understanding ego-ideal formation speak of two processes which are crucial for its development: idealization and internalization. Of the latter we know a good deal from clinical observation and experience and from the theoretical formulations of many workers in the field; and I propose later in this discussion to bring some clinical examples which shall illustrate the wide spectral range of such internalizations from seemingly simple suggestions to the intricate and complex relationships of identifications to other aspects of the personality as well as to outer reality.

But what of idealization? The term is used with such ease as if its meaning were self-evident. Do we really understand what happens in idealization, and how it happens?

When a child idealizes a parent he is in the grip of a creative ego process, for he is taking the reality of his experience—as it exists in his memory imagery, both conscious and unconscious—and embroidering, embellishing, altering it to create illusion. But to create illusion he must have experienced reality, and he did so in the emotions of childhood, of love and hate, of dependency and anxiety, of the wish to be autonomous and the fear of separation. While the human capacity to create illusion through idealization of a love-object or of oneself (narcissism) may be placed in the service of tension reduction, its main function, to my mind, is ego-building.

In the course of individuation and differentiation the ego depends for its development on the experience of the outer world of reality, on its encounter with this world, and on the internalization of significant love-objects. Were this internalization merely a duplication within the psyche of outer reality—were the parents mirrored within as they actually exist in external reality, without idealization—then the element of aspiration, of progress toward higher goals, would disappear from human experience.

The history of man's cultural development contradicts such a possibility. Mankind has always been characterized by striving; the human being in his struggle to become individuated is always future-directed. It is because the child *believes* his idealization to be real that in the course of the growth of his ego he has the potentiality for exceeding his predecessors. Thus the capacity for idealization through the use of creative imagination is a major factor in man's sociocultural evolution as well as in the psychological evolution of ego. Obviously not all idealizations are used constructively in individual development, nor is the course of cultural history a consistently progressive one. Nevertheless, it is the ability to idealize that makes for change in the direction of higher levels of organization, both in individual and social history.

In psychoanalytic practice we are accustomed more frequently to distortions of a negative nature. It is the image of the bad parent that is often magnified and made the cause and justification for neurotic conflict. Just as ego-ideal formation is viewed, for example, by Jacobson, as serving the mastery of sexual and aggressive impulses, so Fairbairn (1954) views the internalization of the bad object as the child's attempt to master the inevitable frustrations of his life by placing the source of control within himself, taking the burden of badness upon himself, and maintaining the environment—that is, the love object—as good.

In either view, the ability to deal with reality by playing with its internalized reflection is seen as a defensive operation. I think it is because we deal with the pathology of internalized images and with negative distortions that idealization has been regarded too exclusively in its defensive capacity. Defense, in itself, while understood as an essential aspect of the life process, has nevertheless acquired an aura of disapproving condescension, and with this attitude, idealization, the creation of illusion, has come to be viewed pejoratively as an aspect of outmoded romanticism, as an escape from reality.

Let me propose that ego-ideal formation, through the ceaseless creation of illusion and the attempts at its actualization are man's reality. In discussing the relationship between truth and reality, Otto Rank (1936) has said:

> To be able to live one needs illusions, not only outer illusions such as art, religion, philosophy, science and love afford, but inner illusions which first condition the outer. The more a man can take reality as truth, appearance as essence, the sounder, the better adjusted, the happier will he be.

By "reality" Rank means the actuality of feeling and its transformation into the creative products of his imagination, as opposed to "truth," which he equates with intellectual knowledge and understanding.

I spoke earlier of the wide range of ego-ideal phenomena from simple suggestion to complex fragmentation of ego structure. The power of the internalization of words spoken by a much loved person in a highly charged emotional situation came home to me on a European trip some years ago when I met a survivor of the Holocaust. She was a middle-aged woman at the time, living in a central European country behind the Iron Curtain and, because of special circumstances, was able to take a short vacation in one of the neutral, more or less affluent, countries of Europe. Perhaps it was the contrast with her current, rather difficult life-style that brought to her mind the days of the Second World War when her family was caught between two invading armies.

She recounted the story of her anguished escape. In the hope that some members of the family would survive, they split up, each going to a separate hiding place. At the moment of parting from her father he had said to her, "Be brave." The words sustained her through countless trials and difficulties, through terror and despair. They were spoken by a deeply loved person whose image she internalized and whose words became in content, her ego-ideal, in their imperative form, her superego. Their impact was probably reinforced by the fact that she never saw her father again, and the idealization could be maintained. Thus the idealized internalization nourished her ego and made possible her actual physical survival as well as her psychological survival.

Since this was for me but a passing encounter with a tragic life story, I had no opportunity to learn more of the dynamic structure of her personality. However, within the framework of my knowledge of these events of her life, I would say that the words "be brave," as they became part of her ego-ideal, functioned as a hypnotic suggestion. Perhaps the effectiveness of suggestion in general as it is a part of therapy rests on how closely, both in its form and content, it approximates an already internalized ego-ideal.

As we know from clinical experience, the internalized parental images are not always idealized to healthy proportions. The actual parents in their relationship to the child may be either so overwhelmingly critical or so narcissistic that the incorporation of their images becomes a source of profound conflict and of character disturbance. It has been my impression from recent work with patients that the fragmentation of the ego due to the pathological character of the ego-ideal and superego and the conflict between them, is as responsible for much of the inhibition which we en-counter in the area of sex and work as is conflict surround-ing the gratification of instinctual drives.

Let me bring a case in point. A young, attractive, and highly intelligent girl of about 21, whom we shall call Lisa, came to me for analysis (which she recently completed) about seven years ago. She had just graduated from college and had returned to New York to live again in the home of her parents. She was depressed, unhappy, at sea about her vocational life, and in difficulty in her sexual and social life. I have mentioned the length of her treatment specifically because the analysis of conflicts surrounding the ego-ideal came only in the last year of her therapy—and, I believe, could only have come after the analysis of what I shall call, for the moment, the family neurosis.

This fact would seem to point to the extremely early formation of ego-ideal processes. They are therefore an-chored in an early phase of narcissistic development, and in form, process and quality, remain deeply unconscious. Their content is synthesized much later, is conscious, and is superimposed on the primitive, narcissistic, and uncon-scious form.

Lisa's analysis began with the struggle between her wish for autonomy and her extreme dependency on her parents, especially her mother, for although she had been away from home for four years she never entirely overcame her homesickness. The exposure of this infantile depen-dency and its partial resolution, in that she moved away from home, might have heralded the deeper intrapsychic dependencies of ego function on ego-ideal and superego processes, but much had to be analyzed in the realm of her instinct life before we could return to an analysis of her ego-ideal formation.

Prominent in her sexual conflict was her omnipotent wish to be both boy and girl. She grew up in a home in which her parents had ostensibly thrown convention overboard. Their goals and aspirations were expressed verbally in rebellion and criticism of existing society; much of their behavior, however, conformed to the most conventional of social values. They were aquisitive, placed great importance on material possessions and social status, and were eager for their daughter to marry and have children in the socially accepted way. As a little girl Lisa went through a long tomboy phase. She wore overalls, climbed trees, and enjoyed sporting her leather jacket and being as messy and dirty as possible. But in the afternoon of the same day in which she played like the boys, she would suddenly run home and change into her prettiest, daintiest, party dress. Clearly, her sexual identity was not consolidated, and this was in large measure due to the contradictory and confused messages which she received from her parents, especially from her mother, who herself was not secure in her role as a woman.

Her normal oedipal wishes, her rivalry with her brother (her only sibling), her competition with her mother, her rebelliousness and hostility, her fear of abandonment, her homosexual impulses, all made their appearance in her treatment. All were analyzed and worked through to a point, with good therapeutic results. Her social relationships improved; her relationships with men became more stable and long-lasting; there was less conflict with her parents and less demand upon them; she was able to focus her intellectual interests and to choose a profession, attending graduate school and working at the same time.

But these gains covered deeper levels of ego pathology which she experienced, subjectively, as hypochondriacal anxiety, a low threshold for injured self-esteem in interpersonal relations, and a troublesome, relentlessly competitive attitude toward others in almost all phases of her life. It was in the detailed analysis of her competitive stance, which was at variance with her conscious social values, that we discovered the true nature of the fragmentation of her ego based upon the character of her introjects.

Lisa had always been competitive with her women friends. Was her boyfriend as good as Marjorie's? Did he love her as much? Did he make love to her as frequently? Was her sexual experience as fulfilling as her friend's? The constant comparison disturbed her. She was never able to immerse herself in experience, to live the moment. One day, in a self-created, competitive situation with a colleague, she suddenly became aware of the depth and extent of her self-centeredness. In the school where she had been teaching, a group of teachers had gotten together to discuss some professional problems. One of the teachers happened to mention that some students had a crush on her. Lisa was disturbed by what she perceived as the other woman's bragging but was also jealous of her. In the midst of these emotions she suddenly realized that she thought of and related to others entirely in terms of herself. She was entirely focused on a comparison, to her disadvantage, of herself with the other person, struggling to retrieve her self-esteem. She lost judgment and a clear perception of reality in these situations and finally experienced a sense of loss of self.

There was something in the quality of the feeling of loss which she described that recalled to me her fear of and feeling of abandonment by her mother in childhood. Once, as a small child of almost five, her mother had gone into a store and had left her in a parked car, and she had become so certain that she had been abandoned that in panic she had left the car and was found some time later running distractedly along the highway.

She now experienced the same feeling of loss of self at the height of her hypochondriacal anxiety, when she feared imperfection in some part of her body. Or if her sexual partner did not make love to her when she wished it, she felt equally abandoned, lost, not accepted.

The mother who she feared had abandoned her in the parking lot is not only present in every competitor who might outdo her, in every lover who might reject her, indeed in her very body which might disappoint her with its illnesses and imperfections, but resides within her. It is that part of the mother which failed to accept her unless she was perfect which she has introjected, and it is this introject which constitutes a major part of her superego and her ego-ideal.

A relative of Lisa's recently told her that soon after her mother was married, she said: "If I were to have a daughter, I would make her perfect." It is relatively unimportant what the content of the ideal of perfection was for the mother— perhaps it meant being both boy and girl, being both self-sufficient yet dependent on and devoted to her, being sexually emancipated yet adhering to more traditional sexual codes—whatever the content, since an ideal of perfection is unrealizable, the child felt constantly criticized, either explicitly for overt behavior or implicitly for the very nature of her being. She was insufficiently accepted for what she was. She was the vehicle for the gratification of her mother's narcissistic needs, and the price she paid to retain her mother's love was to identify with these needs, to merge with her mother by internalizing the mother's perfection-istic demands upon the standards for her. The mother introject, because of its extreme narcissistic character, militated against differentiation of the child as a separate individual.

The mother's personality as it resided in her daughter consumed the girl's ego and rendered it powerless in the face of the relentless inner measuring of a perfectionistic superego against the realization and actualization of an ego-ideal of perfection. This continuous internal competition between discrete ego functions was projected by Lisa onto the outer world, so that her relationships with others was characterized by a constant measuring of herself against them. It would seem that the function of this projection, however ineffectual, was an attempt, as is the case in paranoia, to rescue some relatedness to the outer world, to emerge from the undifferentiated narcissistic cocoon in which her mother introject enveloped her.

We must not neglect the hostile, aggressive impulses and emotions which accompany the imposition of perfectionistic standards, first from without then from within, and which inevitably mean a failure in acceptance of self, at times even a hatred of oneself. In the course of our work on these issues, Lisa realized that her parents were frequently critical, often humiliated her in the presence of others, and were identified with her competitor. To the extent that she internalized the criticality in the nature of her superego, she failed to accept herself. She realized this and one day asked me, "How do I achieve an acceptance of myself?"

Before I go into my answer to this question, I should like to return to the issue of idealization and ego-ideal formation. Early in this discussion I emphasized the striving, creative aspects of idealization as these processes eventuate in the formation of the ego-ideal. The ego-ideal, as it represents the individual's aspirations, gives meaning and direction to his life, and because the individual is part of a larger social unit, as he interacts with others, his ego-ideal may come to influence society as a whole and may ultimately affect the evolution of culture itself.

While I am aware that this may be something of an idealization of the ego-ideal itself, the important point here is that the effectiveness of the ego-ideal as an agent of individual psychic health, and of social progress, depends on its normal development. In the case of Lisa, we witness a pathologic development of the ego-ideal. The root of the pathology lies in the developing ego's inability to become sufficiently individuated, sufficiently separate from the parental introjects to structure an independent, autonomous value system. In Lisa's case, as in a number of other cases which I have observed, the most important impediment to the development of such autonomy is the overwhelmingly narcissistic character of the mother's love.

If the mother lives through her child and the child, out of the normal dependency needs of childhood, introjects an image of the mother in which the gratification of her needs predominates, the child lives for the mother. The fulfillment of the ego-ideal is for the mother, and because of the lack of differentiation between ego and object, the child has little opportunity to form a healthy ego-ideal based on the experience of an independent outer reality which can be idealized and woven into the fabric of useful, ego-building illusions. Thus the ego is crippled, not only in its relationship to the ego-ideal and super-ego, since it is constantly concerned with the fulfillment of foreign ego-ideal requirements, but in its functioning in the outer world of reality. Lisa expressed this when she reported a loss of judgment and clear perception of reality as well as a feeling of loss of self in a competitive situation which aroused in her the fear that she could not meet the requirements of her ego-ideal and would thus be abandoned by her mother introject—an introject so closely attached to her own ego that in losing it, she would lose herself.

These considerations lead to my answer to Lisa's question, "How do I accept myself?" Since the issue of self-acceptance, of healthy self-love, hinges on being autonomous to begin with, the answer must lie primarily in becoming separate from the maternal introject. As a separately delineated personality, Lisa's ego would function not solely to fulfill the needs of an introject, which was too great a portion of her personality, but primarily in relation to the demands of reality and of her own needs as these could be adapted to reality. My answer to her, therefore, was that when she succeeded in detaching herself from her mother through insight and the experience of gratification in other relationships, the actual achievements of her ego in the fulfillment of realistic ego-ideal goals which she set up for herself would bring her the acceptance of herself which she failed to get at the hands of her mother.

What I advisedly did not say, but thought, was that the experience of my acceptance of her and of her goals and aspirations would help to liberate her from the mother introject, thus helping to consolidate her identity and to formulate an independent ego-ideal. For just as the patient's ego must make an alliance with the analyst in the therapeutic undertaking, that is, pass critical judgment on his neurosis and seek to overcome it—both superego and ego-ideal functions—so the analyst must make an alliance with the patient's realistic ego-ideal aspirations. It is this alliance which accepts and supports the ego's normal striving for growth and development, and which is the effective therapeutic agent above and beyond the use of insight, the emotional working through of conflictful experience, or the analysis of the transference.

In summary we may say that the human mind, because of the survival value of planfulness, is future-directed; because it is capable of internalizing experience through memory images, it is imaginative; because awareness and self-awareness demand meaningfulness, continuity and perpetuity, the imagination of man had to create ideal images. To maintain the meaningfulness of existence and to insure a sense of his own continuity, man sought to fulfill in reality the idealizations which he created in his mind— that is, to actualize his ego-ideal. As an individual his self-esteem depends in large measure on the extent to which he succeeds in the realization of these idealizations. For society, its cohesion and survival may depend on the commonality of its ego-ideals; its progress on a flexibility which will permit viable modifications of its ideals.

We have explored the pathology of ego-ideal formation and function in an individual case and have seen its
close relationship to the narcissistic involvement of a
mother with her child. I might add that a pathologically
narcissistic relationship of either parent with the child can
have similar effects on ego-ideal and superego formation.
Generally, however, because the process of individuation
and separation begins in the mother relationship, it is this
relationship, with its normal propensity for narcissistic involvement, which is more crucial for ego autonomy and
therefore for the healthy development of the ego-ideal.

And so we must conclude that in the final analysis the
ego-ideal, upon which man's achievements and aspirations
depend and which is at one and the same time the carrier
of tradition and the vehicle for innovation, depends for its
healthy development in the individual, on the parental capacity to love and accept the child as a discrete individual
—that is, to maintain a sound balance between narcissistic
investment in self and other.

NOTES

Chapter 1

Allen, J. R., and West, L. J. 1968. Flight from violence: hippies and the green rebellion. *American Journal of Psychiatry* 125(3): 364–370.

Anthony, E. J. 1970. Two contrasting types of adolescent depression and their treatment. *Journal of the American Psychiatric Association* 18: 841–859.

Baba, M. 1971. *Beams from Meher Baba on the spiritual panorama.* New York: Perennial Library.

Cameron, C., ed. 1973. *Who is Guru Maharaj Ji?* New York: Bantam Books.

Campbell, C. 1974. Transcendence is as American as Ralph Waldo Emerson. *Psychology Today*, 7: 37–38.

Castaneda, C. 1968. *The teachings of Don Juan: A Yaqui way of knowledge.* New York: Ballantine Books.

Erikson, E. H. 1962. *Young man Luther.* New York: W. W. Norton.

_____. 1964. *Insight and responsibility.* New York: W. W. Norton.

_____. 1970. Reflections on the dissent of contemporary youth. *International Journal of Psycho-Analysis* 51: 11–22.

Esman, A. H. 1972. Adolescence and the consolidation of values. *Moral values and the superego concept in psychoanalysis,* ed. S. C. Post. New York: International Universities Press.

Evans, C. 1974. *Cults of unreason.* New York: Farrar, Straus & Giroux.

Framo, J. L. 1972. Symptoms from a family transactional viewpoint. *Progress in group and family therapy,* ed. C. J. Sager and H. S. Kaplan. New York: Brunner/Mazel.

Freud, A. 1972. Comments on aggression. *International Journal of Psycho-Analysis* 53(2):163–171.

Freud, S. (1930). *Civilization and its discontents.* Trans. J. Strachey. New York: W. W. Norton, 1961.

Fromm, E. 1941. *Escape from freedom.* New York: Farrar & Rinehart.

Heinlein, R. A. 1961. *Stranger in a strange land.* New York: Berkeley Medallion.

Hoffer, E. 1966. *The true believer.* New York: Harper & Row.

Horton, P. C. 1973. The mystical experience as a suicide preventive. *American Journal of Psychiatry* 130(3):294–296.

Houriet, R. 1971. *Getting back together.* New York: Coward, McCann & Geoghegan.

Jacobson, E. 1964. *The self and the object world.* New York: International Universities Press.

Janus, S., and Bess, B. 1973. Drug abuse, sexual attitudes, political radicalization, and religious practices of college seniors and public school teachers. *American Journal of Psychiatry* 130(2):187–191.

Keniston, K. 1968. *Young radicals.* New York: Harcourt, Brace & World.

Levine, F. 1974. *The strange world of the Hare Krishnas.* Greenwich, Connecticut: Fawcett.

Liebert, R. 1971. *Radical and militant youth: A psychoanalytic inquiry.* New York: Praeger.

"Lord of the Universe." 1974. Television Documentary, WNET-TV.

Lukas, J. A. 1967. The two worlds of Linda Fitzpatrick. *New York Times,* October 16, p. 1.

Mitscherlich, A. 1963. *Society without the father.* Trans. E. Mosbacher. New York: Harcourt, Brace & World.

Montgomery, P. L. 1974. How a radical-left group moved toward savagery. *New York Times,* January 20, p. 1.

Needleman, J. 1970. *The new religions.* Garden City, New York: Doubleday.

Nicholi, A. M. 1970. Campus disorders: A problem of adult leadership. *American Journal of Psychiatry* 127(4): 424–429.

———. 1974. A new dimension of the youth culture. *American Journal of Psychiatry* 131(4):396–400.

Nuttall, J. 1968. *Bomb culture.* London: MacGibbon & Kee.

Nyoiti, S. 1965. *You are all sanpaku.* Trans. W. Dufty. New York: University Books.

Pittel, S. M.; Calef, V.; Gryler, R. B.; Hilles, L.; Hofer, R.; Kempner, P.; and Wallerstein, R. S. 1975. Developmental factors in adolescent drug use: A study of psychedelic drug users. Prepublication draft.

Powers, T. 1971. *Diana: The making of a terrorist.* New York: Bantam Books.

Robbins, T., and Anthony, D. 1972. Getting straight with Meher Baba: A study of mysticism, drug rehabilitation and postadolescent role conflict. *Journal for the Scientific Study of Religion* 11(2):122–140.

Rosen, B. C. 1955. Conflicting group membership: A study of parent-peer group cross-pressures. *American Sociological Review* 20:155–161.

Sanders, E. 1971. *The family.* New York: E. P. Dutton.

Speck, R. V. 1972. *The new families.* New York: Basic Books.

Speck, R. V., and Attneave, C. L. 1973. *Family networks.* New York: Pantheon.

Stickney, J. 1971. *Streets, actions, alternatives, raps.* New York: G. P. Putnam's Sons.

Wangh, M. 1972. Some unconscious factors in the psychogenesis of recent student uprisings. *Psychoanalytic Quarterly* 41(2):207–223.

Wetering, J. van de. 1974. *The empty mirror: experiences in a Japanese Zen monastery.* Boston: Houghton Mifflin.

Wilson, W. P. 1972. Mental health benefits of religious salvation. *Diseases of the Nervous System* 33:382–386.

Wolf, L. 1968. *Voices from the love generation.* Boston: Little, Brown.

Chapter 2

Freud, S. (1914). On narcissism: an introduction. *The Complete Psychological Works of Sigmund Freud* Vol. 14. London: Hogarth Press, 1957.

Spotnitz, H. 1972. *The theory of modern analytic supervision.* Unpublished lecture series given at The New York Academy of Science under the auspices of The Center for Modern Psychoanalytic Studies.

Chapter 3

Channon, 1968. G. Bulljive-language teaching in a Harlem School. *The Urban Review* 1:5–12.

———. 1970. *Homework.* New York: Dell.

Freud, S. (1915) Instincts and their vicissitudes. *Standard Edition,* Vol. 14. London: Hogarth Press.

———. (1919) A child is being beaten. *Standard Edition,* Vol. 17. London: Hogarth Press.

Jencks, C. 1969. A reappraisal of the most controversial educational document of our time. *New York Times Magazine,* August 10.

Meerloo, J., and Nelson, Marie C. 1965. *Transference and trial adaptation.* Springfield, Illinois: Charles C. Thomas.

Nagera, H. 1970. *Basic psychoanalytic concepts on a theory of instincts.* Vol. 3, New York: Basic Books.

Rochlin, G. 1973. *Man's aggression.* Boston: Gambit.

Rosenthal, R., and Jacobson, L. 1967. Self-fulfilling prophecies in the classroom: teachers' expectations as unintended determinants of pupils' intellectual competence. In *Social class, race, and psychological development,* M. Deutsch, I. Katz, and A. Jensen. New York: Holt, Rinehart and Winston.

Rubin, S., and Pisciotto, A. 1974. *Racial interaction in school and society.* New York: Vantage.

Silberman, C. 1970. *Crisis in the classroom,* New York: Random House.

Spotnitz, H. 1967. *The couch and the circle.* New York: Grune & Stratton.

Whiteman, M. and Deutsch, M. 1967. Social disadvantage as related to intellective and language development. *loc. cit.* under Rosenthal, R. and Jacobson, L.

Chapter 4

Ovid. *Metamorphoses.* Loeb Classical Library, 2nd ed., Vol. 1. Cambridge: Harvard University Press, 1951.

Pausanias. *Description of Greece.* Loeb Classical Library, 2nd ed. Vol. 4. Cambridge: Harvard University Press, 1935.

Smith, W., ed. 1904. *A classical dictionary of Greek and Roman biography, mythology, and geography.* Revised by G. E. Marindin. London: Murray.

Spotnitz, H. 1969. *Modern psychoanalysis of the schizophrenic patient.* New York: Grune & Stratton.

_____. 1975. Object-oriented approaches to severely disturbed adolescents. In *The adolescent in group and family therapy,* ed. M. Sugar. New York: Brunner/Mazel.

Spotnitz, H., and Resnikoff, P. 1954. The myths of Narcissus. *The Psychoanalytic Review* 41:173–181.

Chapter 5

Abraham, K. 1921. Contributions to the theory of the anal character. *Selected papers on psychoanalysis.* New York: Basic Books, 1953.

_____. 1924a. The influence of oral erotism on character formation. *Selected papers on psychoanalysis. Ibid.*

_____. 1924b. A short study of the development of the libido, viewed in the light of mental disorders. *Selected papers on psychoanalysis. Ibid.*

_____. 1925. Character formation on the genital level of libido development. *Selected papers on psychoanalysis. Ibid.*

Alexander, F. J. 1923. The castration complex in the formation of character. *International Journal of Psycho-Analysis.* 4:11–42.

Arlow, J., and Brenner, C. 1969. The psychopathology of the psychoses. *International Journal of Psycho-Analysis.* 50:5–14.

Balint, M. 1968. *The basic fault.* London: Tavistock Publications.

Bibring, E. 1953. The mechanism of depression. *Affective disorders,* ed. P. Greenacre. New York: International Universities Press.

Bursten, B. 1967. *Mobility in the establishment of boundary.* Unpublished thesis presented to the Western New England Institute for Psychoanalysis.

_____. 1973a. *The manipulator: a psychoanalytic view.* New Haven: Yale University Press.

_____. 1973b. Some narcissistic personality types. *International Journal of Psycho-analysis.* 54:287–300.

Ekstein, R., and Rangell, L. 1961. Reconstruction and theory formation. *Journal of the American Psychoanalytic Association.* 9:684–697.

Elkisch, P. 1957. The psychological significance of the mirror. *Journal of the American Psychoanalytic Association.* 5:235–244.

Erikson, E. H. 1950. *Childhood and society.* New York: W. W. Norton.

Freud, S. 1911a. Psycho-analytic notes on an autobiographical account of a case of paranoia. *Standard Edition.* 12. London: Hogarth Press, 1958.

———. 1911b. Formations on the two principles of mental functioning. *Standard Edition.* 12. London: Hogarth Press, 1958.

———. 1914. On narcissism: an introduction. *Standard Edition.* 14. London: Hogarth Press, 1957.

———. 1923. The ego and the id. *Standard Edition.* 19. London: Hogarth Press, 1961.

———. 1926. Inhibitions, symptoms and anxiety. *Standard Edition.* 20. London: Hogarth Press.

———. 1937. Constructions in analysis. *Standard Edition.* 23. London: Hogarth Press, 1957.

———. 1940. An outline of psychoanalysis. *Standard Edition.* 23. London: Hogarth Press.

Gunderson, J. G. 1974. The influences of the theoretical model of schizophrenia on treatment practice. *Journal of the American Psychoanalytic Association.* 22:182–199.

Hartmann, H. 1950. Comments on the psychoanalytic theory of the ego. *Psychoanalytic Study of the Child.* 5:74–96.

Hartmann, H. and Kris, E. 1945. The genetic approach in psychoanalysis. *Psychoanalytic Study of the Child.* 1:11–30.

Hoch, P., and Polatin, P. 1949. Pseudoneurotic forms of schizophrenia. *Psychiatric Quarterly.* 23:248–276.

Holt, R. B. 1967. Beyond vitalism and mechanism: Freud's concept of psychic energy. In *Science and psychoanalysis,* Vol. 11. Masserman, J., ed. New York: Grune and Stratton.

Jacobson, E. 1954. The self and the object world: vicissitudes of their infantile cathexes and their influence on ideational and affective development. *Psychoanalytic Study of the Child.* 9:75–127.

———. 1964. *The self and the object world.* New York: International Universities Press.

Joffe, W. G., and Sandler, J. 1967. Some conceptual problems involved in the consideration of disorders of narcissism. *Journal of Child Psychotherapy.* 2:56–66.

Kernberg, O. 1970. Factors in the psychoanalytic treatment of narcissistic personalities. *Journal of the American Psychoanalytic Association.* 18:51–85.

Klein, G. 1969. Freud's two theories of sexuality: perspectives to change in psychoanalytic theory. In *Clinical-cognitive psychology: models and integrations.* ed. L. Breger. Englewood Cliffs, New Jersey: Prentice-Hall.

Kohut, H. 1966. Forms and transformations of narcissism. *Journal of the American Psychoanalytic Association.* 14:243–272.

———. 1971. *The Analysis of the Self.* New York: International Universities Press.

———. 1972. Thoughts on narcissism and narcissistic rage. *Psychoanalytic Study of the Child.* 27:360–400.

Lewin, B. D. 1950. The psychoanalysis of elation. New York: W. W. Norton.

Lichtenstein, H. 1964. The role of narcissism in the emergence and maintenance of a primary identity. *International Journal of Psychoanalysis.* 45:49–56.

Loewald, H. 1971. On motivation and instinct theory. *Psychoanalytic Study of the Child.* 26:91–128.

London, N. J. 1973. An essay on psychoanalytic theory: two theories of schizophrenia. *International Journal of Psycho-analysis.* 54:169–193.

Mahler, M. 1967. On human symbiosis and the vicissitudes of individuation. *Journal of the American Psychoanalytic Association.* 15:740–763.

Novey, S. 1968. *The second look: the reconstruction of personal history in psychiatry and psychoanalysis.* Baltimore: The Johns Hopkins Press.

Pulver, S. 1970. Narcissism: the term and the concept. *Journal of the American Psychoanalytic Association.* 18:319–341.

Rado, S. 1928. The problem of melancholia. *International Journal of Psycho-analysis.* 9:420–438.

Rapaport, D. 1959a. Edward Bibring's theory of depression. In *The Collected Papers of David Rapaport.* New York: Basic Books, 1967.

———. 1959b. The structure of psychoanalytic theory: a systematizing attempt. *Psychological Issues,* Monograph 6. New York: International Universities Press.

Rapaport, D., and Gill, M. M. 1959. The points of view and assumptions of metapsychology. *International Journal of Psycho-analysis.* 40:153–162.

Reich, A. 1960. Pathological forms of self-esteem regulation. *Psychoanalytic Study of the Child.* 15:215–232.

Rose, G. 1966. Body-ego and reality. *International Journal of Psycho-analysis.* 47:501–509.

Sandler, J., and Rosenblatt, B. 1962. The concept of the representational world. *Psychoanalytic Study of the Child.* 17:128–145.

Schafer, R. 1972. Internalization: process or fantasy? *Psychoanalytic Study of the Child.* 27:411–436.

Shapiro, D. 1965. *Neurotic styles.* New York: Basic Books.

Shengold, L. 1974. The metaphor of the mirror. *Journal of the American Psychoanalytic Association.* 22:97–115.

Tolpin, M. 1971. On the beginnings of a cohesive self: an application of the concept of transmuting internalization to the study of the transitional object and signal anxiety. *Psychoanalytic Study of the Child.* 26: 316–352.

Wexler, M. 1971. Schizophrenia: conflict and deficiency. *Psychoanalytic Quarterly.* 40:83–99.

Winnicott, D. W. 1953. Transitional objects and transitional phenomena. *International Journal of Psycho-analysis.* 34:89–97.

Chapter 6

Berger, P., and Luckmann, T. 1966. *The social construction of reality.* New York: Doubleday.

Daly, R. W. 1968. Schizoid rule following. *Psychoanalytic Review* 55: 400–414.

———. 1970. The spectres of technicism. *Psychiatry* 33:417–432.

Eliot, T. S. 1934. The love song of J. Alfred Prufrock. In *Collected poems of T. S. Eliot.* New York: Harcourt.

Ellenberger, H. F. 1970. *The discovery of the unconscious.* New York: Basic Books.

Fairbairn, R. 1954. *An object-relations theory of the personality.* New York: Basic Books.

Freud, S. 1924. *Collected papers,* Vol. 2. London: The Institute of Psychoanalysis.

Fromm, E. 1961. *Marx's concept of man.* New York: Ungar.

Glover, E. 1958. *The technique of psychoanalysis.* New York: International Universities Press.

Guntrip, H. 1961. *Personality structure and human interaction.* New York: International Universities Press.

———. 1969. *Schizoid phenomena, object-relations and the self.* New York: International Universities Press.

———. 1971. *Psychoanalytic theory, therapy, and the self.* New York: Basic Books.

Havens, L. L. 1972. The development of existential psychiatry. *Journal of Nervous and Mental Diseases* 154:309–331.

———. 1974. The existential use of the self. *American Journal of Psychiatry* 131:1–10.

Israel, J. 1971. *Alienation: From Marx to modern sociology.* Boston: Allyn & Bacon.

272 THE NARCISSISTIC CONDITION

Jaspers, K. 1963. *General psychopathology*. Chicago: University of Chicago Press.

Johnson, F. A. 1973. Alienation: Overview and introduction. In *Alienation: concept, term, and meanings*, ed. F. A. Johnson. New York: Seminar Press.

_____. 1974. Some problems of reification in existential psychiatry. (Working paper). Eighth World Congress of Sociology, Toronto, Ontario, August 1974.

Jourard, S. M. 1964. *The transparent self*. New York: Van Nostrand & Reinhold.

Keniston, K. 1960. Alienation and the decline of the utopia. *American Scholar* 29:182–186.

Kernberg, O. F. 1972. Early ego integration and object relations. *Annals of New York Academy of Science* 193: 223–247.

_____. 1974. Contrasting viewpoints regarding the nature and psychoanalytic treatment of narcissistic personalities. *Journal of American Psychoanalytic Association* 22:255–267.

Knoff, W. F. 1969. A psychiatrist reads Camus' 'The stranger'. *Psychiatric Opinion* 6:19–25.

Kohut, H. 1971. *The analysis of the self*. New York: International Universities Press.

Laing, R. D. 1965. *The divided self*. London: Tavistock Publications.

_____. 1967. *The politics of experience*. New York: Pantheon Books.

Lifton, R. J. 1971. Protean man. *Archives of General Psychiatry* 24:298–304.

May, R. A.; Angel, E.; and Ellenberger, H. F. 1958. *Existence: A new dimension in psychiatry and psychology*. New York: Basic Books.

May, R. A. 1959. The existential approach. Chapter 66 in *Handbook of American psychiatry*, ed. S. Arieti. New York: Basic Books.

Minkowski, E. 1969. Existence and psychology. Trans. D. Duclow. *Existential Psychiatry* 7:8–17.

Needleman, J. 1963. Critical introduction to Ludwig Binswanger's existential psychoanalysis. In *Being-in-the-world*, L. Binswanger, ed. New York: Basic Books.

Nelson, B. 1961–62. Phenomenological psychiatry, *Daseinsanalyse* and American existential analysis: a progress report. *Psychoanalysis and the Psychoanalytic Review*, 48:4, 3–23.

_____. 1965a. The psychoanalyst as mediator and double agent. *Psychoanalytic Review* 52:3, 375–389.

_____. 1965b. Self-images and systems of spiritual direction in the history of European civilization. In *The quest for self-control: classical philosophies and scientific research*, ed. S. L. Klausner. New York: Free Press, pp. 49–103.

Riesman, D. 1961. *The lonely crowd.* New Haven: Yale University Press.

Rosenfeld, H. 1964. On the psychopathology of narcissism. *International Journal of Psycho-analysis* 45:332–337.

Sarte, J. P. 1956. Existential analysis. Chapter 2 in *Being and nothingness.* Trans. H. E. Barnes. New York: Philosophical Library.

Schacht, R. *Alienation.* 1970. Garden City, New York: Doubleday.

Stein, H. 1967. Reflections on schizoid phenomena. *Psychiatry and Social Science Review* 3:23–28.

Strachey, J. 1934. The nature of the therapeutic action of psycho-analysis. *International Journal of Psycho-analysis,* 15:127–159.

Vespe, R. 1969. Ontological analysis and synthesis in existential psychotherapy. *Existential Psychiatry* 7:83–92.

Wyss, D. 1966. *Depth psychology: a critical history.* New York: W. W. Norton.

Chapter 7

Beguin, A. 1946. *L'Ame romantique et le rêve.* Paris: Jose Corti.

Brown, N. O. 1968. *Love's body.* New York: Vintage.

Descartes, R. 1633. *Treatise of man.* Trans. T. S. Hall. Cambridge: Harvard University Press, 1972b.

———. 1637. *Discourse on method and the meditations.* Trans. F. E. Sutcliffe. Baltimore: Penguin, 1972a.

———. 1637. *Discourse on method, optics, geometry, and meteorology.* Trans. Paul J. Olscamp. New York: Bobbs-Merrill, 1965.

———. 1657. *Philosophical letters.* Trans. and ed. Anthony Kenny. Oxford: Clarendon Press, 1970.

———. 1835. *Oeuvres philosophiques,* Vol. I. Ferdinand Alquie, ed. Paris: Garnier, 1963.

———. 1955. *The philosophical works of Descartes.* 2 vols. Trans. L. S. Haldane and G. R. T. Ross. New York: Dover.

Erikson, E. H. 1962. Reality and actuality: an address. *Journal of the American Psychoanalytic Association.* 10:451–474.

Feuer, L. S. 1963. The dreams of Descartes. *American Imago.* 20:3–26.

Freud, S. 1911. Psychoanalytic notes upon an autobiographical account of a case of paranoia (dementia paranoides). *Collected Papers,* Vol. 3. Trans. and ed. Alix Strachey and James Strachey. New York: Basic Books, 1959, 387–470.

Holland, N. N. 1959. *The first modern comedies.* Bloomington: Indiana University Press.

Lewin, B. 1958. *Dreams and the uses of regression.* New York: International Universities Press.

————. 1968. *The image and the past.* New York: International Universities Press.

Maritain, J. 1944. *The dream of Descartes.* Trans. M. L. Andison. New York: Philosophical Library.

McLuhan, M. 1962. *The Gutenberg galaxy.* New York: The New American Library, 1969.

Ong, W. J. 1967. *The presence of the word.* New York: Simon and Schuster, 1970.

Roheim, G. 1969. *The gates of the dream.* New York: International Universities Press.

Schachtel, E. G. 1954. The developement of focal attention and the emergence of reality. *Psychiatry* 17:309–324.

Schönberger, S. 1939. A dream of Descartes: reflections on the unconscious determinants of the sciences. *International Journal of Psychoanalysis* 20:43–57

Spengler, O. 1965. *The decline of the West.* Arthur Helps, ed. New York: Modern Library.

Thass-Thienemann, T. 1967. *The subconscious language.* New York: Washington Square Press.

Van Den Berg, J. H. 1962. The human body and the significance of human movement. In *Psychoanalysis and existential philosophy,* ed. H. Ruitenbeek. New York: Dutton, 90–129.

Von Franz, M. L. 1952. The dream of Descartes. Trans. Andrea Dykes and Elizabeth Welsh. In *Timeless Documents of The Soul.* Evanston: Northwestern University Press, 1968, 55–147.

Vrooman, J. R. 1970. *René Descartes: a biography.* New York: G. P. Putnam.

Whitehead, A. N. 1925. *Science and the modern world.* New York: Mentor, 1956.

Whyte, L. L. 1960. *The unconscious before Freud.* New York: Basic Books.

Wisdom, J. O. 1947. Three dreams of Descartes. *International Journal of Psycho-analysis* 28:11–18.

Chapter 8

Albee, E. 1967. *Who's afraid of Virginia Woolf?* New York: Athenium Press.

Aristotle. 1967. *Categories.* Cambridge: Harvard University Press.

Arnheim, R. 1971. *Entropy and art.* Berkeley: University of California Press.

Blakney, R. 1957. *Meister Eckhart: A modern translation.* New York: Harper Torchbooks.

Coffee, H. S., and Wiener, L. L. 1967. *Group treatment of autistic children.* Englewood Cliffs: Prentice Hall.

Cohen, J. 1966. Subjective time. *The voices of time*, ed. J. T. Fraser. New York: George Braziller, 1966.

Erikson, E. 1963. *Childhood and society*, 2nd ed. New York: W. W. Norton, 1963.

Fenichel, O. 1945. *The psychoanalytic theory of the neurosis*. New York: W. W. Norton.

Freedman, D. 1971. The genesis of obsessional group phenomena. *The Psychoanalytic Review*, 58:367–384.

Freud, S. 1933. *New introductory lectures on psychoanalysis*. New York: W. W. Norton.

_____. 1949. *Civilization and its discontents*. London: Hogarth Press.

_____. 1950. *An autobiographical study*. London: Hogarth Press.

Hare, R. D. 1966. Psychotherapy and the choice of immediate vs. delayed punishment. *Journal of Abnormal Psychology* 71:25–29.

Heidegger, M. 1962. *Being and time*. New York: Harper & Row.

Jones, E. 1951. *Essays in applied psychoanalysis*. London: Hogarth Press.

Jung, C. 1955. *Synchronicity: An acausal connecting principle*. New York: Pantheon.

Klein, M. 1956. In M. Klein, P. Heimann, and R. E. Money-Kyrle, *New directions in psychoanalysis*. New York: Basic Books.

Laing, R. D. 1969. *The Self and Others*. New York: Pantheon.

Macnab, F. A. 1966. *Estrangement and relationship*. Bloomington: Indiana University.

Mahler, M. 1968. *On human symbiosis and the vicissitudes of individuation*, Vol. 1. New York: International Universities Press.

Meyer, A. 1939. In *Psychobiology and psychiatry*. ed. W. Muncie. St. Louis: C. V. Mosby.

Neumann, E. 1952. *Amor and Psyche: the psychic development of the feminine*. London: Routledge & Kegan.

Nietzsche, F. 1885. *Thus spoke Zarathustra*. New York: Heritage, 1967.

Oates, J. C. 1973. Problems of adjustment in survivors of natural/unnatural disasters. In *Marriages and other infidelities*. Greenwich: Fawcett.

Orme, J. E. 1969. *Time, experience and behaviour*. London: Iliffe Books.

Paz, O. 1973. *Alternating current*. New York: Viking Press.

Perls, F. 1969. *Ego, hunger and aggression*. New York: Random House.

Reich, W. 1950. *Character analysis*. London: Vision Press.

Sartre, J. P. 1948. *The emotions: outline of a theory*. New York: Philosophical Library.

_____. 1963. *Saint Genet: actor and martyr*. New York: George Braziller.

Shakespeare, W. 1942. Hamlet. In W. A. Nielson, *Complete plays and poems of William Shakespeare*. Cambridge: Harvard University Press.

Sharpe, E. F. 1950. *Collected papers on psychoanalysis.* London: The Hogarth Press.

Sullivan, H. S. 1940. *Conceptions of modern psychiatry.* Washington: William Alanson White Foundation.

Tillich, P. 1967. *Systematic theology,* Vol. 3. Chicago: University of Chicago Press.

Whitaker, C., and Malone, T. 1953. *The roots of psychotherapy.* New York: Blakiston.

Whitaker, C. 1967. Discussion between commentators. In *The therapeutic relationship and its impact.* ed. C. Rogers. Madison: University of Wisconsin Press.

Chapter 9

Anastasi, A., and Levee, R. F. 1959. Intellectual deficit and musical talent. A case report. *American Journal of Mental Deficiency* 64:695–703.

Bell, E. T. 1937. *Men of mathematics.* New York: Simon and Schuster.

Bellak, L.; Hurvich, M.; and Gediman, H. K. 1973. *Ego functions in schizophrenics, neurotics and normals.* New York: John Wiley.

Bing, F.; McLaughlin, F.; and Marburg, R. 1959. The metapsychology of narcissism. *Psychoanalytic Study of the Child* 7:9–28.

Bloom, R. S. 1963. Testing cognitive ability and achievement. In *Handbook of Research on Teaching.* ed. N. L. Gage. Chicago: Rand McNally.

Born, M. 1968. *My life and my views.* New York: Scribner's.

Broman, S. H., Nichols, P. L.; and Kennedy, W. A. 1975. *Preschool IQ.* New York: John Wiley.

Clark, R. W. 1971. *Einstein: The life and times.* New York: World.

Danieli, Y. 1963. Narcissism and the need for infinity. Unpub. Dissertation. Tel-Aviv University.

De Groot, A. 1946. *Het Denken van den Schaker.* Amsterdam: Noord-Holland Maatschappij.

Federn, P. 1929. On the distinction between healthy and pathological narcissism. In *Ego psychology and the psychoses.* New York: Basic Books.

Fine, R. 1967. *The psychology of the chess player.* New York: Dover.

———. 1970. Therapeutic accessibility as a basis for diagnosis. In *New approaches to personality classification,* ed. A. Mahrer. New York: Columbia University Press.

———. 1975. *Psychoanalytic psychology.* New York: Jason Aronson.

———. 1976. The uncommunicative genius. *Psychoanalytic Review.* In press.

Freud, S. 1914. On narcissism: an introduction. *Standard Edition*, 14: 67–102.

_____. 1929. Letter to Maxim Leroy on a dream of Descartes. *Standard Edition*, 21:203–204.

Gruber, H. F.; Terrell, G.; and Wertheimer, M., eds. 1962. *Contemporary approaches to creative thinking.* Chicago: Atherton.

Guilford, J. P. 1967. *The nature of human intelligence.* New York: McGraw-Hill.

Hadamard, J. 1945. *The psychology of invention in the mathematical field.* Princeton: Princeton University Press.

Hartmann, H. 1952. The mutual influences in the development of ego and id. *Psychoanalytic Study of the Child* 7:9–30.

Kernberg, O. 1975. *Borderline conditions and pathological narcissism.* New York: Jason Aronson.

Keynes, J. M. 1951. *Essays in Biography.* New York: Norton.

Kline, M. 1972. *Mathematical Thought from Ancient to Modern Times.* New York: Oxford University Press.

Knapp, R. H., and Goodrich, H. B. 1952. *Origins of American Scientists.* Chicago: University of Chicago Press.

Kohut, H. 1971. *The analysis of the self.* New York: International Universities Press.

_____. 1972. Thoughts on narcissism and narcissistic rage. *Psychoanalytic Study of the Child,* 27:360–400.

Lewin, B. D. 1958. *Dreams and the Uses of Regression.* New York: International Universities Press.

Maccoby, E. E., and Jacklin, C. N. 1974. *The psychology of sex differences.* Stanford: Stanford University Press.

Manuel, F. 1963. *Isaac Newton: historian.* Cambridge: Harvard University Press.

McClelland, D. C. 1955. Some social consequences of achievement motivation. *Nebraska Symposium on Motivation.* Lincoln: University of Nebraska Press.

_____. 1964. *The roots of consciousness.* New York: Van Nostrand.

More, L. T. 1934. *Isaac Newton: a biography.* New York: Dover.

Oden, M. H. 1968. The fulfillment of promise: 40-year follow-up of the Terman gifted group. *Genetic Psychology Monographs,* 77:3–93.

Piaget, J. 1954. *The construction of reality in the child.* New York: Basic Books.

_____. 1957. *Logic and psychology.* New York: Basic Books.

Poincaré, H. 1952. *Science and method.* New York: Dover.

Rank, O. 1932. *Art and the artist.* New York: Tudor.

Reich, A. 1953. Narcissistic object choice in women. *Journal of the American Psychoanalytic Association* 1:22–44.

Rimland, B. 1964. *Infantile Autism.* New York: Appleton-Century-Crofts.

Roe, A. A. 1951. A psychological study of physical scientists. *Genetic Psychology Monographs* 43:121–239.

———. 1953. *The Making of a Scientist.* New York: Dodd, Mead.

———. 1956. *The Psychology of Occupations.* New York: John Wiley.

Rosen, V. H. 1953. On mathematical "illumination" and the mathematical thought process. *Psychoanalytic Study of the Child* 8:127–154.

Russell, B. 1967–1970. *Autobiography.* New York: Norton.

Sandor, B. 1932. The functioning of memory and the methods of mathematical prodigies. *Character and Personality,* 1, 70–74.

Scheerer, M.; Rothmann, E.; and Goldstein, K. 1945. A case of idiot savant. *Psychological Monographs* 58, No. 4 (Whole No. 269).

Smith, D. E. 1951. *A history of mathematics.* New York: Dover.

Smith, N. K. 1952. *New studies in the philosophy of Descartes.* London: MacMillan.

Stanley, J. C.; Keating, D. P.; and Fox, L. H. 1974. *Mathematical talent.* Baltimore: Johns Hopkins.

Stein, M. I. 1956. A transactional approach to creativity. In *Research conference on the identification of creative scientific talent,* ed. C. W. Taylor. Salt Lake City: University of Utah Press, 171–181.

Terman, L. M. 1954. Scientists and nonscientists in a group of 800 gifted men. *Psychological Monographs* 68: No. 7.

———. 1959. The gifted group at mid-life. *Genetic studies of genius,* vol. 5. Stanford: Stanford University Press.

Thurstone, L. L. 1955. *The differential growth of mental abilities.* Chapel Hill. University of North Carolina.

Van der Waals, H. G. 1965. Problems of narcissism. *Bulletin of the Menninger Clinic* 29:293–311.

Wiener, N. 1953. *Ex-prodigy.* New York: Simon and Schuster.

Wisdom, J. O. 1947. Three dreams of Descartes. *International Journal of Psycho-analysis* 28:11.

Chapter 10

Blos, P. 1974. The genealogy of the ego ideal. *Psychoanalytic Study of the Child* 29:85. New Haven: Yale University Press.

Fairbairn, W. Ronald D. 1954. Chapter 7 in *An object-relations theory of personality.* New York: Basic Books.

Freud, S. 1914. On narcissism: an introduction. *Standard Edition,* 14:69. London: Hogarth Press.

Jacobson, E. 1964. *The self and the object world.* New York: International Universities Press, 109–118.

Lampl-de-Groot, J. 1962. Ego ideal and superego. *Psychoanalytic Study of the Child* 17:94–106. New York, International Universities Press.

Rank, O. 1936. *Truth and reality.* New York: Knopf.

CONTRIBUTORS

BEN BURSTEN, M. D.   Chief of psychiatry, U.S. Veterans Administration Center, Hampton, Virginia. Professor of psychiatry, Eastern Virginia Medical School. Psychoanalyst in private practice. Author of *The Manipulator: A Psychoanalytic View* (Yale University Press, 1973) and numerous essays emphasizing the problems of narcissism.

JOEL EMANUEL, M. S.   New York State certified guidance counselor. Taught for eight years in New York City public school system. Student analyst, Center for Modern Psychoanalytic Studies, New York, and doctoral candidate, California Graduate Institute, Los Angeles.

BENJAMIN FINE, PH.D.   Assistant professor of mathematics, Fairfield University and son of Reuben Fine, a former mathematician. Their collaborative essay in this volume affords unique access to the psychological dimensions of that profession.

REUBEN FINE, PH.D.   Director, Metropolitan Training Center for Psychoanalytic Studies. Past faculty member of University of Southern California, Brooklyn College, Adelphi University and other centers of higher learning. Former mathematician and International Chess Master. Author of *The Healing of the Mind* (David McKay, 1971) and numerous psychoanalytic essays. Psychoanalyst in private practice.

JOHN H. HANSON, PH.D.   Doctorate in literature and psychology from the State University of New York at Buffalo. Supervisor of welfare policy study for the city of Buffalo. Dr. Hanson's interests include the Enlightenment, modern literature, art and social history.

ANN BRADEN JOHNSON, M.S.W.   Psychiatric social worker at Heights Hill Day Hospital of South Beach Psychiatric Center, Brooklyn, New York. "My education," says the author, "was notable only for its haphazard and chaotic nature, involving several academic fields and six different institutions of higher learning, a pattern not unfamiliar to those who grew up in the 1960s." Mrs. Johnson also wrote "Drifting on the God Circuit," in *Psychology of Adolescence,* ed. Aaron H. Esman, M.D. (International Universities Press, 1975).

FRANK A. JOHNSON, M.D.   Professor of psychiatry, Upstate Medical Center, State University of New York at Syracuse. Dr. Johnson's research interests lie in the area of alienation phenomena. His writings are principally concerned with theoretical and practical intersections between psychiatry and the social sciences. He is also engaged in private practice.

ESTHER MENAKER, PH.D.   Faculty member, Training Institute of the National Psychological Association for Psychoanalysis, New York, and adjunct professor of psychology, New York University Postdoctoral Program, Graduate School. Dr. Menaker, who received her doctorate from the University of Vienna in 1934, is noted for her pioneer studies in psychoanalytic ego psychology. With her late husband, William Menaker, she is co-author of *Ego in Evolution* (Grove Press, 1965).

BENJAMIN NELSON, PH.D.   Professor of sociology and history, Graduate Faculty of the New School for Social Research, New York, and president of the International Society for the Comparative Study of Civilizations (U.S.). In addition to several books and edited anthologies, Professor Nelson has published more than 50 scholarly essays on central social and cultural structures and transformations, illustrating his interest in comparative historical and civilizational perspectives. His writings include: *Freud and the Twentieth Century*, "Self-Images and Systems of Spiritual Directions in the History of European Civilization," "Sartre, Genet and Freud," "Max Weber as a Pioneer of Civilizational Analyses," and "The Omnipresence of the Grotesque." He has also edited 6 special issues of the *Psychoanalytic Review* on the relations of psychoanalysis to the humanities and social sciences.

MARIE COLEMAN NELSON   Editor of the Self-in-Process Series, of which this work is Volume I. Editor of *The Psychoanalytic Review*, official publication of the National Psychological Association for Psychoanalysis. Certified psychologist and psychoanalyst in private practice. Faculty, Manhattan Center for Advanced Psychoanalytic Studies, New York, and Advanced Institute for Analytic Psychotherapy, Queens, Fellow, American Academy of Psychotherapists. Editor and author, *Roles and Paradigms in Psychotherapy* (Grune & Stratton, 1968) and other psychoanalytic writings.

SAMUEL S. RUBIN, PH. D.   Supervision psychologist and faculty member, advanced Institute for Analytic Psychotherapy, Queens, New York. Author (with A. Pisciotto) of *Racial Interaction in School and Society* (Vantage, 1974) and numerous professional articles. Psychoanalyst in private practice.

HYMAN SPOTNITZ, M. D., MED. SC. D.   Research psychiatrist engaged in the private practice of psychoanalytic psychiatry in New York City. His books include *Modern Psychoanalysis of the Schizophrenic Patient* (Grune & Stratton, 1969) and *The Couch and the Circle* (Knopf, 1961). Author of more than 80 papers on analytic psychotherapy in the severe psychiatric disorders, analytic group therapy and neurophysiology. He is a life fellow of the American Psychiatric Association and other professional organizations and honorary president of the Manhattan Center for Advanced Psychoanalytic Studies.

E. MARK STERN, PH. D.   Editor, *Journal of Pastoral Counseling.* Associate professor in pastoral counseling, Graduate Division, Iona College, New Rochelle, New York. Adjunct professor, Seton Hall University, South Orange, New Jersey. Dr. Stern has authored papers on various aspects of psychotherapy and counseling and also engages in private practice.

The Study of Narcissism:
Selected Recommended Readings

Theoretical and Clinical Perspectives

ABRAHAM, K. 1927. A particular form of neurotic resistance against the psycho-analytic method. *Selected Papers of Karl Abraham.* London: Hogarth Press.

AICHHORN, A. 1964. The narcissistic transference of the 'juvenile imposter.' *Delinquency and child guidance: selected papers by August Aichhorn.* Eds. O. Fleischmann, P. Kramer, and H. Ross, N.Y.: International Universities Press.

ANDREAS–SALOMÉ, L. 1962. The duel orientation of narcissism. Tr. Stanley H. Leavy, M.D. *Psychoanalytic Quarterly,* 31:1–30.

———. 1964. *The Freud journal of Lou Andreas-Salomé.* New York: Basic Books.

BALINT, M. 1953. *Primary love and psychoanalytic technique.* New York: Liveright.

BATESON, G. D. JACKSON, J. HALEY and J. WEAKLAND. 1956. Toward a theory of schizophrenia. *Behavioral Sciences,* V. 1.

BING, J., and MARBURG, R. O. 1962. Panel Report: Narcissism. *Journal of the American Psychoanalytic Association,* 10:593–605.

BION, W. R. 1962. *Learning from experience.* New York: Basic Books.

———. 1965. *Transformations.* New York: Basic Books.

BOWLBY, JOHN. 1960. Ethology and the development of object relations. Symposium on psycho-analysis and ethology. *International Journal of Psychoanalysis,* 41:313 (July–October).

———. 1969. *Attachment.* New York: Basic Books.

BRESSLER, B. 1965. The concept of the self. *Psychoanalytic Review,* 52:425–445.

BRODEY, W. M. 1965. On the dynamics of narcissism. *The Psychoanalytic Study of the Child,* 20:165–193.

BYCHOWSKI, G. 1958. Struggle against the introjects. *International Journal of Psychoanalysis,* V. 39.

——— and J. L. DESPERT, eds. 1952. *Specialized techniques in psychotherapy.* New York: Basic Books.

CLARK, L. PIERCE. 1925. The phantasy method of analyzing narcissistic neuroses. *The Psychoanalytic Review,* V. 13.

EIDELBERG, L. 1959. The concept of narcissistic mortification. *International Journal of Psychoanalysis,* 40:163–168.

EISNITZ, A. J. 1969. Narcissistic object choices, self–representation. *International Journal of Psychoanalysis,* 50:15–25.

EISSLER, K. R. 1958. Remarks on some variations in psycho–analytic Technique. *International Journal of Psychoanalysis,* V.39.

ELLIS, H. 1927. The conception of narcissism. *Psychoanalytic Review,* 14:129–153. Reprinted in *Psychoanalysis in America,* ed. M. Sherman. 403–430.

EPHRON, L. R. 1967. Narcissism and the sense of self. *Psychoanalytic Review,* 54:499–509.

ERIKSON, E. H. 1950. *Childhood and society.* New York: Norton and Company.

———. 1959. *Identity and the life cycle.* New York: International Universities Press. (Psychological Issues).

FAIRBAIRN, W. R. D. 1954. *An object relations theory of the personality.* New York: Basic Books.

———. 1963. Synopsis of an object relations theory of the personality. *International Journal of Psychoanalysis,* V. 44.

FEDERN, P. 1952. *Ego psychology and the psychoses,* ed. E. Weiss. New York: Basic Books. (Esp. Chaps. 2, 15, 16).

FERENCZI, S. 1950. Confusion of tongues between adults and the child. *Further contributions to psychoanalysis.* New York: Basic Books.

FINE, R. 1975. *Psychoanalytic psychology.* New York: Aronson.

FREEMAN, T. 1963. The concept of narcissism in schizophrenic states. *International Journal of Psychoanalysis,* 44:293–303.

———. 1964. Some aspects of pathological narcissism. *International Journal of Psychoanalysis,* 12:540–561.

FREUD, A. 1946. *The ego and the mechanisms of defense.* New York: International Universities Press.

FREUD, S. 1955. A difficulty in the path of psycho-analysis (1917b). *Standard Edition of the Complete Psychological Works of Sigmund Freud.* Ed. James Strachey. 17:137 *ff.* London: Hogarth Press.

———. 1955. Beyond the pleasure principle (1920). *New introductory lectures on psycho-analysis, SE.* 18:3 *ff.*

———. 1953. Constructions in analysis (1937). *SE* 23:256 *ff.*

———. 1957. Instincts and their vicissitudes (1915a). *SE* 14:117 *ff.*

———. 1955. Lines of advance in psychoanalytic therapy (1919). *SE* 17:158 *ff.*

———. 1957. On narcissism (1914). *SE* 14:69 *ff.*

———. 1961. On the economic problems of masochism (1924). *SE* 19:165 *ff.*

———. 1957. On the history of the psychoanalytic movement (1914). *SE* 14:3 *ff.*

———. 1958. Psycho-analytic notes on an autobiographical account of a case of paranoia (1911). *SE* 12:52 *ff.*

———. 1964. Splitting of the ego in the process of defence (1940). *SE* 23:271 *ff.*

———. 1964. The anatomy of the mental personality (1932). *SE* V. 22:3 *ff.*

———. 1961. The ego and the id (1923). *SE* 19:3 *ff.*

———. 1963. The libido theory and narcissism (1916). *SE* 16:415 *ff.*

GIOVACCHINI, P., ed. 1972. *Tactics and techniques of psychoanalytic therapy.* New York: Science House.

GITELSON, M. 1962. Narcissism. Scientific proceedings, *Journal of the American Psychoanalytic Association,* 10:593–605.

GLOVER, E. 1956. *On the early development of mind.* New York: International Universities Press.

GREENSON, R. 1958. Variations in Classical Psychoanalytic Technique: An Introduction. *International Journal of Psychoanalysis,* V.39.

GUNTRIP, H. 1961. Personality structure and human interaction. New York: International Universities Press.

———. 1971. *Schizoid phenomena, object relations and the self.* New York: International Universities Press.

———. 1971. *Psychoanalytic theory, therapy, and the self.* New York: Basic Books.

———. 1971. *The analysis of the self.* New York: International Universities Press.

HALEY, J. 1963. *Strategies of psychotherapy.* New York: Grune and Stratton.

HART, H. H. 1947. Narcissistic Equilibrium. *International Journal of Psychoanalysis,* 28:106–114.

HARTMANN, H. 1956b. The development of the ego concept in Freud's work. *International Journal of Psychoanalysis,* V.37.

———. 1964. *Essays in psychology.* New York: International Universities Press. Ch. 3.

——— and LOWENSTEIN, R. M. 1946. Comments on the formation of psychic structure. *Psychoanalytic Study of the Child,* V.2. New York: International Universities Press.

HENDRICK, I. 1964. Narcissism and the pre-puberty ego ideal. *Journal of the American Psychoanalytic Association,* 12:522–528.

JACOBSON, E. 1964. *The self and the object world.* New York: International Universities Press.

JOFFE, W. G. and SANDLER, J. 1967. Some conceptual problems involved in the consideration of disorders of narcissism. *Journal of Child Psychotherapy,* 2:56–66.

KANNER, L. 1943. Autistic disturbances of affective contact. *Nervous Child,* V.2.

KANZER, M. 1964. Freud's uses of the terms 'autoerotism' and 'narcissism.' *Journal of the American Psychoanalytic Association*, 12:529–539.

KERNBERG, O. 1966. Structural derivatives of object relationships. *International Journal of Psychoanalysis*, 47:236–253.

———. 1970. Factors in the psychoanalytic treatment of narcissistic personalities. *Journal of the American Psychoanalytic Association*, 18:51–85.

———. 1975. *Borderline conditions and pathological narcissism.* New York: Aronson.

———. 1975. *Object relations theory and its applications.* New York: Aronson.

KHAN, M. R. 1974. *The privacy of the self.* London: Hogarth Press.

KLEIN, M. 1963. *Our adult world.* New York: Basic Books.

KOHUT, H., 1966. Forms and transformations of narcissism. *Journal of the American Psychoanalytic Association*, 14:243–272.

———. 1968. The psychoanalytic treatment of narcissistic personality disorders. *Psychoanalytic Study of the Child*, 23:86–113.

———. 1971. *The analysis of the self.* New York: International Universities Press.

KRIS, E. 1956. On some vicissitudes of insight in psycho-analysis. *International Journal of Psychoanalysis*, 37:445–455.

LAMPL-DE GROOT, J. 1965. Superego, ego ideal, and masochistic fantasies. *The development of mind.* New York: International Universities Press.

LANGS, R., ed. 1975. *The frontiers of psychoanalytic technique.* New York: Aronson.

LEWIN, B. D. 1954. Sleep, narcissistic neurosis and the analytic situation. *Psychoanalytic Quarterly*, 23:487–510.

LICHTENSTEIN, H. 1964. The role of narcissism in the emergence and maintenance of a primary identity. *International Journal of Psychoanalysis*, 45:49–56.

LILLY, J. C. 1958. Some considerations regarding basic mechanisms of positive and negative types of motivations. *American Journal of Psychiatry*, V.115.

LOEWALD, H. W. 1960. On the therapeutic action of psycho-analysis. *International Journal of Psychoanalysis*, V.41.

LOEWENSTEIN, R. M. 1954. Some remarks of defenses, autonomous ego and psycho-analytic technique. *International Journal of Psychoanalysis*, V.25.

MAHLER, M. S. 1968. *On human symbiosis and the vicissitudes of individuation.* New York: International Universities Press.

———. 1963. Thoughts about development and individuation. *Psychoanalytic Study of the Child.* V. 18.

MEERLOO, J. and MARIE C. NELSON. 1965. *Transference and trial adaptation.* Springfield, Ill.: Charles C. Thomas.

MODELL, A. 1968. *Object love and reality. An introduction to a psychoanalytic theory of object relations.* New York: International Universities Press.

MURPHY, L. 1960. Pride and its relation to narcissism, autonomy and identity. *Bull. Menninger Clinic,* 24:136–143.

MURRAY, J. M. 1964. Narcissism and the ego ideal. *Journal of the American Psychoanalytic Association,* 12:477–511.

NAGELBERG, L. 1958. Strengthening the ego through the release of frustration-aggression. *The American Journal of Orthopsychiatry,* 28:794–801.

NEIDERLAND, W. G. 1965. Narcissistic ego impairment in patients with early physical malformations. *The Psychoanalytic Study of the Child,* 20:518–534.

NELSON, B. 1964. Actors, directors, roles, cues, meanings, identities: further thoughts on anomie. *The Psychoanalytic Review,* 51:135–159.

_____. 1962. Faces of 20th century analysis: psycho, linguistic, phenomenological, *Daseins,* existential (onto-), etc. *American Behavioral Scientist* (February): 16–18.

_____. 1965. Self-images and systems of spiritual direction in the history of European civilization. *The Quest for Self Control.* Ed. S. Z. Klausner, ed. New York: The Free Press.

_____. 1965. The psychoanalyst as mediator and double agent. *The Psychoanalytic Review,* 52:45–60.

NELSON, M. C. 1962. *Paradigmatic approaches to psychoanalysis: four papers.* Eds. Arnold Bernstein, Benjamin Nelson, Marie Coleman Nelson. New York: Department of Psychology, Stuyvesant Polyclinic.

_____, B. NELSON, M. SHERMAN, and H. STREAN. 1968. *Roles and paradigms in psychotherapy.* New York: Grune and Stratton. Esp. Ch. 8.

OSTOW, M. 1967. The syndrome of narcissistic tranquillity. *International Journal of Psychoanalysis,* 48:573–583.

SCHAFER, R. 1968. *Aspects of internationalization.* New York: International University Press.

SEARLES, H. F. 1960. *The non–human environment in normal development and in Schizophrenia.* New York: International Universities Press.

_____. 1965. *Collected papers on schizophrenia and related subjects.* New York: International Universities Press.

SECHEHAYE, M. 1951. *Symbolic Realization.* New York: International Universities Press.

SEGEL, N. P. 1969. Panel report: narcissistic resistance. *Journal of the American Psychoanalytic Association,* 17:941–954.

SHERMAN, M. H. 1959. Clues to the third ear. *Psychoanalysis and Psychoanalytic Review*, 46:43–50.

SPIEGEL, L. 1959. The self, the sense of self and perception. *Psychoanalytic Study of the Child*, v. 14. New York: International Universities Press.

SPOTNITZ, H. 1961. The narcissistic defenses in schizophrenia. *Psychoanalysis and the Psychoanalytic Review*, 48:24–42.

———. 1976. *Psychotherapy of preoedipal conditions.* New York: Aronson.

STIERLIN, H. 1969. *Conflict and reconciliation.* Garden City, New York: Anchor Books (Doubleday).

STOLOROW, R. D. 1975. Toward a functional definition of narcissism. *International Journal of Psychoanalysis*, 56:179.

SULLIVAN, H. S. 1953. *The interpersonal theory of psychiatry.* Eds. S. W. Perry and M. L. Gawel. New York: Norton Company.

TURNER, R. H. 1962. Role-taking: process versus conformity. *Human Behavior and Social Process.* Ed. A. Rose. Boston: Houghton Mifflin.

WEIL, A. P. 1953. Certain severe disturbances of ego development in childhood. *The Psychoanalytic Study of the Child*, V. 8.

WEXLER, M. 1952. The structural problem in schizophrenia: the role of the internal object. *Psychotherapy with schizophrenics.* New York: International Universities Press.

WHITMAN, R. M. and KAPLAN, S. M. 1968. Clinical, cultural, and literary elaborations of the negative ego-ideal. *Comprehensive Psychiatry*, 9:358–371.

WINNICOTT, D. 1958. *Collected papers.* New York: Basic Books.

Social, Cultural, and Historical Perspectives

ADLER, NATHAN. 1972. *The underground stream: new life styles and the antinomian personality.* New York: Harper Torchbooks.

BAUMGOLD, JULIE. 1975. Hollywood narcissus: why the movies are in love with themselves. *New York* Magazine, Dec. 15:45–53.

BLACK, DAVID. 1975. Totalitarian therapy on the upper West Side. *New York* Magazine, Dec. 15:54–67.

BOYERS, R. and ORRILL, R. (eds.). 1971. *R. D. Laing and anti-psychiatry.* New York: Harper & Row.

BROWN, NORMAN O. 1966. *Love's body.* New York: Random House.

FEUER, LEWIS S. 1968. *The conflict of the generations.* New York: Basic Books.

ISAACS, HAROLD R. 1975. *Idols of the tribe: group identity and political change.* New York: Harper & Row.

KECSKEMETI, PAUL. 1956. The all-powerful 'I'. *Commentary Magazine* (February).

KING, RICHARD. 1972. *The party of eros: radical social thought and the realm of freedom.* Chapel Hill, N.C.: University of North Carolina Press.

KRACAUER, S. 1947. *From Caligari to Hitler: a psychological history of the German film.* Princeton, N.J.: Princeton University Press. PB. ed. 1966.

LAING, R. D. 1967. *The politics of experience.* New York: Pantheon Books.

MARCUSE, HERBERT. 1955. *Eros and civilization: a philosophical inquiry into Freud.* Boston: Beacon. (PB ed.) 1966. Esp. ch. 8, The images of Orpheus and Narcissus.

NELSON, BENJAMIN. 1962. Sociology and psychoanalysis on trial. *Psychoanalytic Review,* 49:144–160.

———. 1970. The ominpresence of the grotesque. *Psychoanalytic Review,* 57:505–518.

———. 1973. The games of life and the dances of death. *The phenomenon of death.* E. Wyschogrod, ed. New York: Harper & Row.

POOLE, ROGER. 1972. *Toward deep subjectivity.* New York: Harper Torchbooks.

ROSEN, GEORGE 1969. *Madness in society: chapters in the historical sociology of mental illness.* New York: Harper Torchbooks. Preface by Benjamin Nelson.

TOFFLER, A. 1970. *Future shock.* New York: Bantam Books.

ZARETSKY, IRVING and LEONE, MARK (eds.). 1974. *Religious movements in contemporary America.* Princeton: Princeton University Press.

EDITOR'S NOTE: These recommended readings were compiled in consultation with Benjamin Nelson. The Editor also expresses appreciation to Professor Nelson for valuable suggestions regarding the assemblage of essays in this volume. M.C.N.

NAME INDEX

SUBJECT INDEX